16

CLAMP

TRANSLATED AND ADAPTED BY
William Flanagan

LETTERED BY
North Market Street Graphics

BALLANTINE BOOKS · NEW YORK

xxxHOLiC, volume 16 is a work of fiction. Names, characters, places, and incidents are the products of the author's imagination or are used fictitiously. Any resemblance to actual events, locales, or persons, living or dead, is entirely coincidental.

A Del Rey Manga/Kodansha Trade Paperback Original

Published in the United States by Del Rey, an imprint of The Random House Publishing Group, a division of Random House, Inc., New York.

Publication rights arranged through Kodansha Ltd.

First published in Japan in 2009 by Kodansha Ltd., Tokyo

ISBN 978-0-345-52412-6

Printed in the United States of America

www.delreymanga.com

9 8 7 6 5 4 3 2 1

Translator and Adapter—William Flanagan
Lettering—North Market Street Graphics

xxxHOLiC crosses over with *Tsubasa*. Although it isn't necessary to read *Tsubasa* to understand the events in *xxxHOLiC*, you'll get to see the same events from different perspectives if you read both series!

Contents

Honorifics Explained

Throughout the Del Rey Manga books, you will find Japanese honorifics left intact in the translations. For those not familiar with how the Japanese use honorifics and, more important, how they differ from American honorifics, we present this brief overview.

Politeness has always been a critical facet of Japanese culture. Ever since the feudal era, when Japan was a highly stratified society, use of honorifics—which can be defined as polite speech that indicates relationship or status—has played an essential role in the Japanese language. When you address someone in Japanese, an honorific usually takes the form of a suffix attached to one's name (example: "Asuna-san"), is used as a title at the end of one's name, or appears in place of the name itself (example: "Negi-sensei," or simply "Sensei!").

Honorifics can be expressions of respect or endearment. In the context of manga and anime, honorifics give insight into the nature of the relationship between characters. Many English translations leave out these important honorifics and therefore distort the feel of the original Japanese. Because Japanese honorifics contain nuances that English honorifics lack, it is our policy at Del Rey not to translate them. Here, instead, is a guide to some of the honorifics you may encounter in Del Rey Manga.

-san: This is the most common honorific and is equivalent to Mr., Miss, Ms., or Mrs. It is the all-purpose honorific and can be used in any situation where politeness is required.

-sama: This is one level higher than "-san" and is used to confer great respect.

-dono: This comes from the word "tono," which means "lord." It is an even higher level than "-sama" and confers utmost respect.

-kun: This suffix is used at the end of boys' names to express familiarity or endearment. It is also sometimes used by men among friends, or when addressing someone younger or of a lower station.

-chan: This is used to express endearment, mostly toward girls. It is also used for little boys, pets, and even among lovers. It gives a sense of childish cuteness.

Bozu: This is an informal way to refer to a boy, similar to the English terms "kid" and "squirt."

Sempai/Senpai: This title suggests that the addressee is one's senior in a group or organization. It is most often used in a school setting, where underclassmen refer to their upperclassmen as "sempai." It can also be used in the workplace, such as when a newer employee addresses an employee who has seniority in the company.

Kohai: This is the opposite of "sempai" and is used toward underclassmen in school or newcomers in the workplace. It connotes that the addressee is of a lower station.

Sensei: Literally meaning "one who has come before," this title is used for teachers, doctors, or masters of any profession or art.

-[blank]: This is usually forgotten in these lists, but it is perhaps the most significant difference between Japanese and English. The lack of honorific means that the speaker has permission to address the person in a very intimate way. Usually, only family, spouses, or very close friends have this kind of permission. Known as *yobisute*, it can be gratifying when someone who has earned the intimacy starts to call one by one's name without an honorific. But when that intimacy hasn't been earned, it can be very insulting.

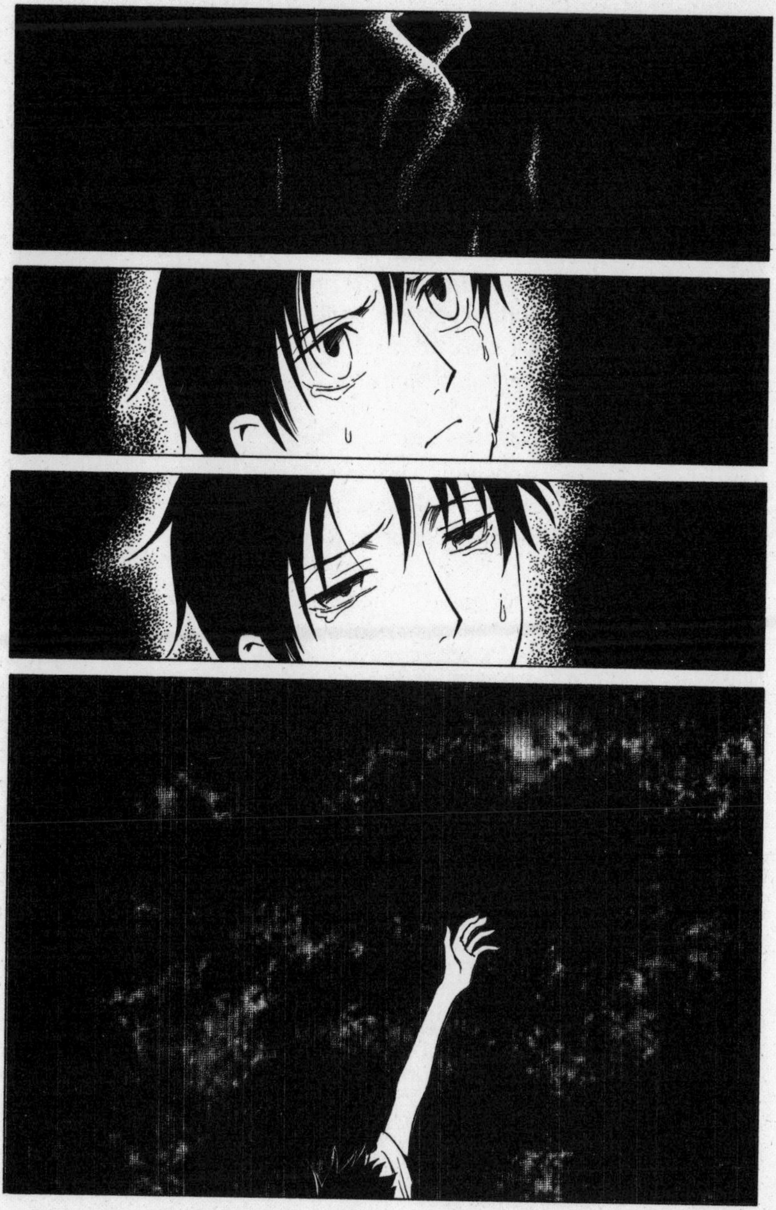

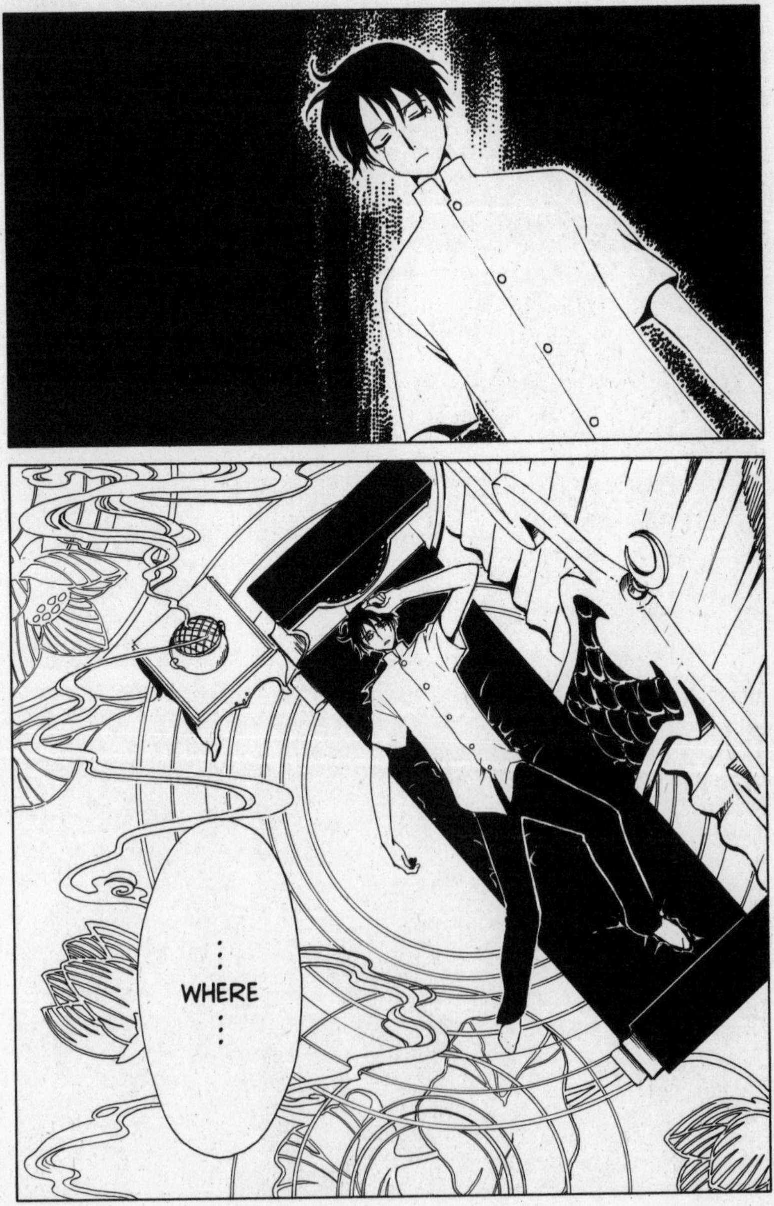
... WHERE ...

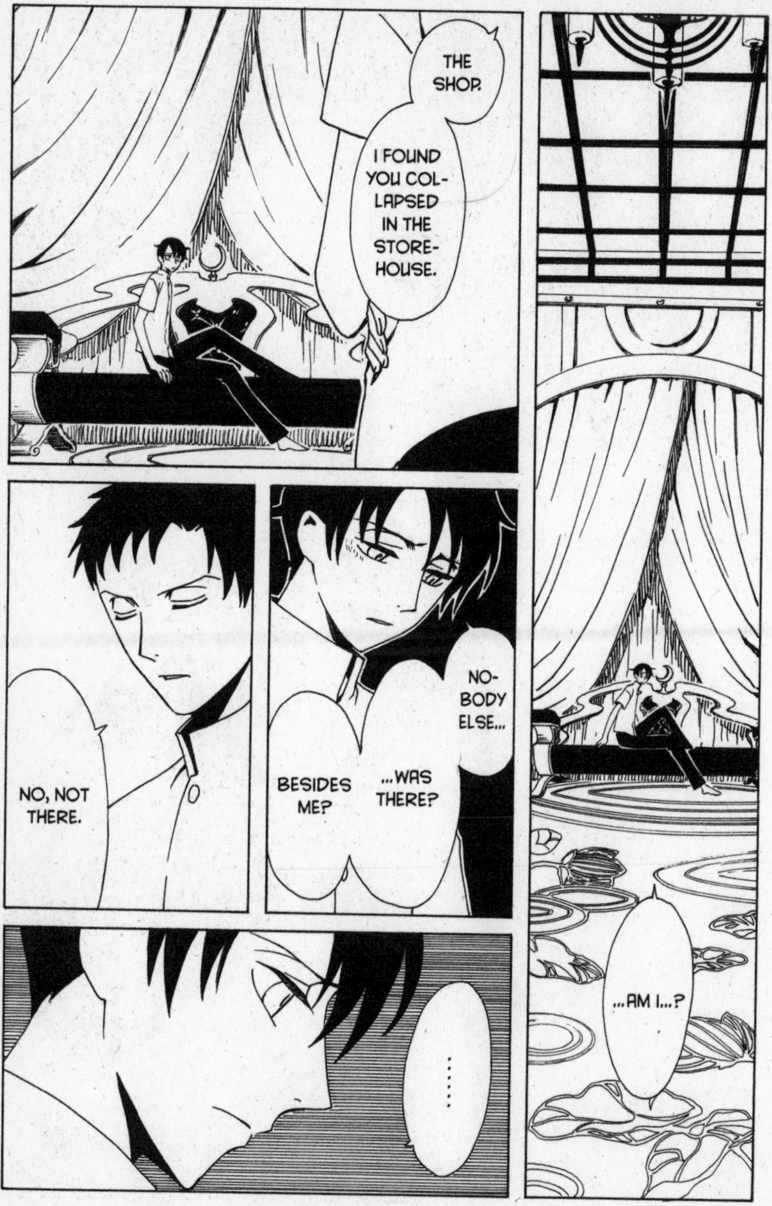
...AM I...?
THE SHOP.
I FOUND YOU COLLAPSED IN THE STOREHOUSE.
NOBODY ELSE...
...WAS THERE?
BESIDES ME?
NO, NOT THERE.
......

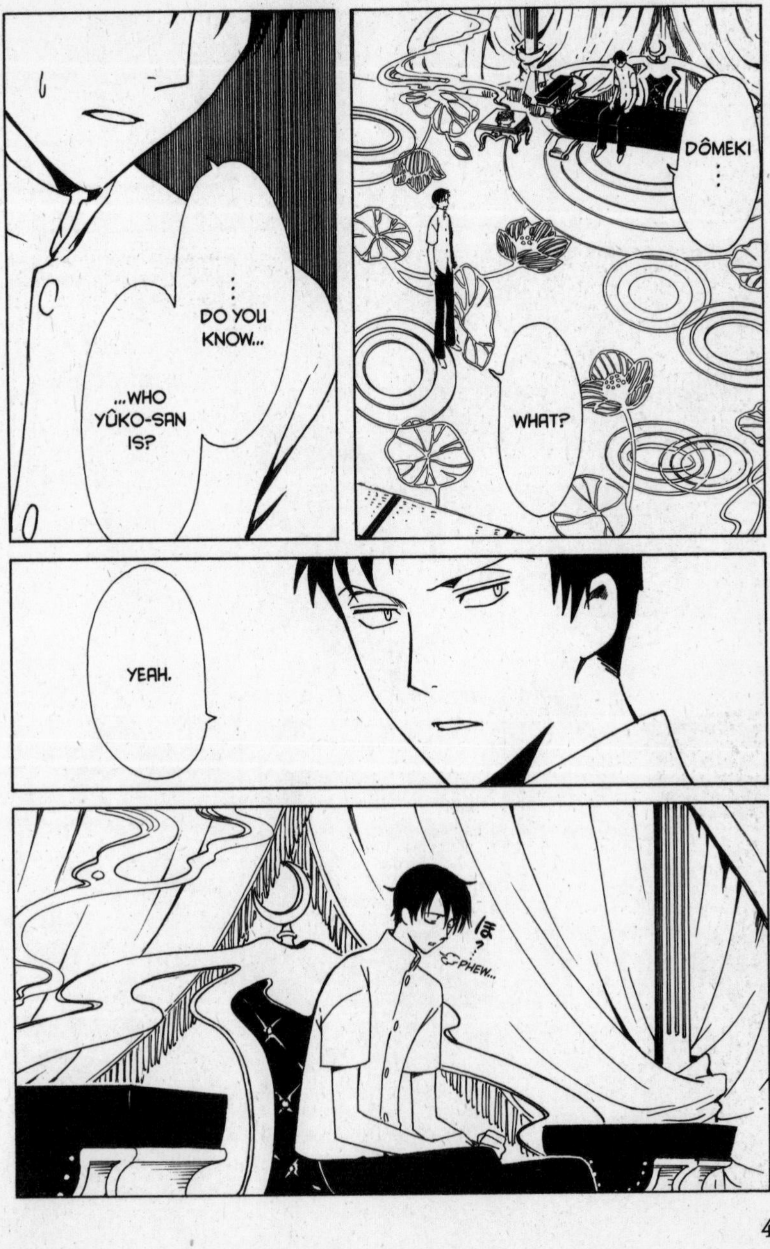
DÔMEKI
...
WHAT?
...
DO YOU KNOW...
...WHO YÛKO-SAN IS?
YEAH.
ほっ
PHEW...

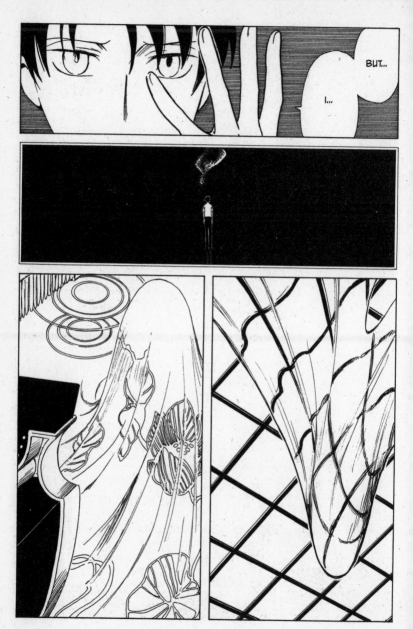

BUT...

I...

5

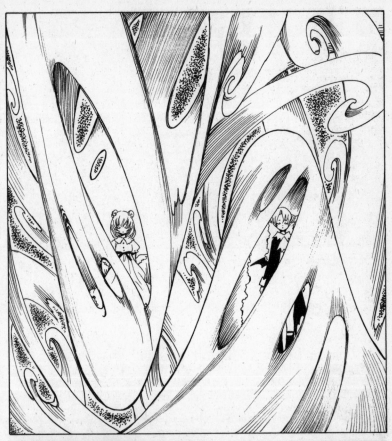

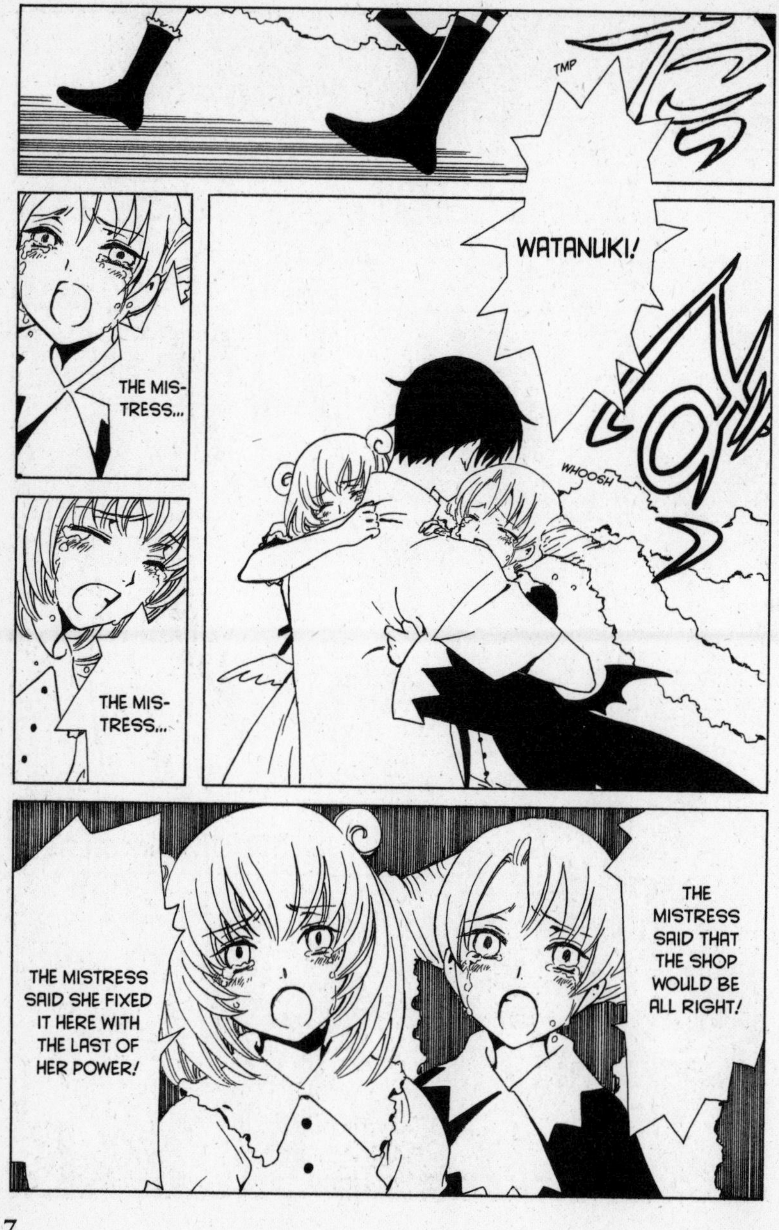
TMP
WATANUKI!
WHOOSH
THE MIS-TRESS...
THE MIS-TRESS...
THE MISTRESS SAID THAT THE SHOP WOULD BE ALL RIGHT!
THE MISTRESS SAID SHE FIXED IT HERE WITH THE LAST OF HER POWER!

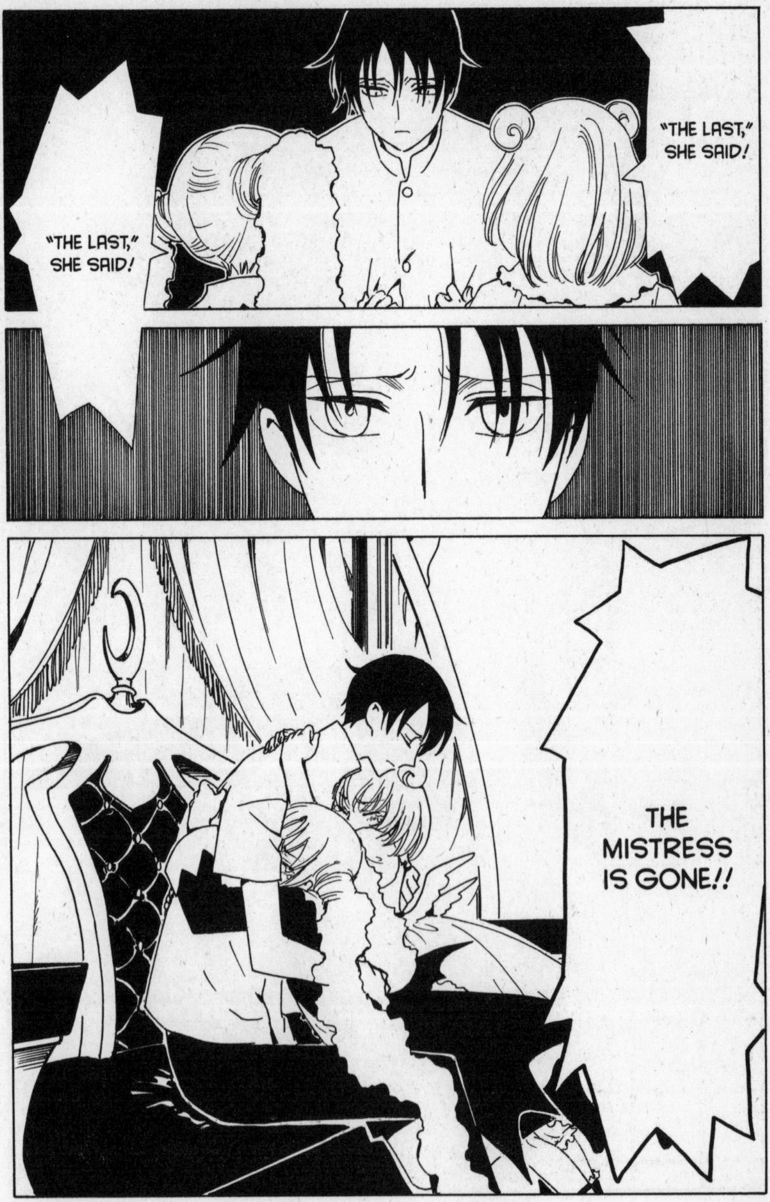
"THE LAST," SHE SAID!
"THE LAST," SHE SAID!
THE MISTRESS IS GONE!!

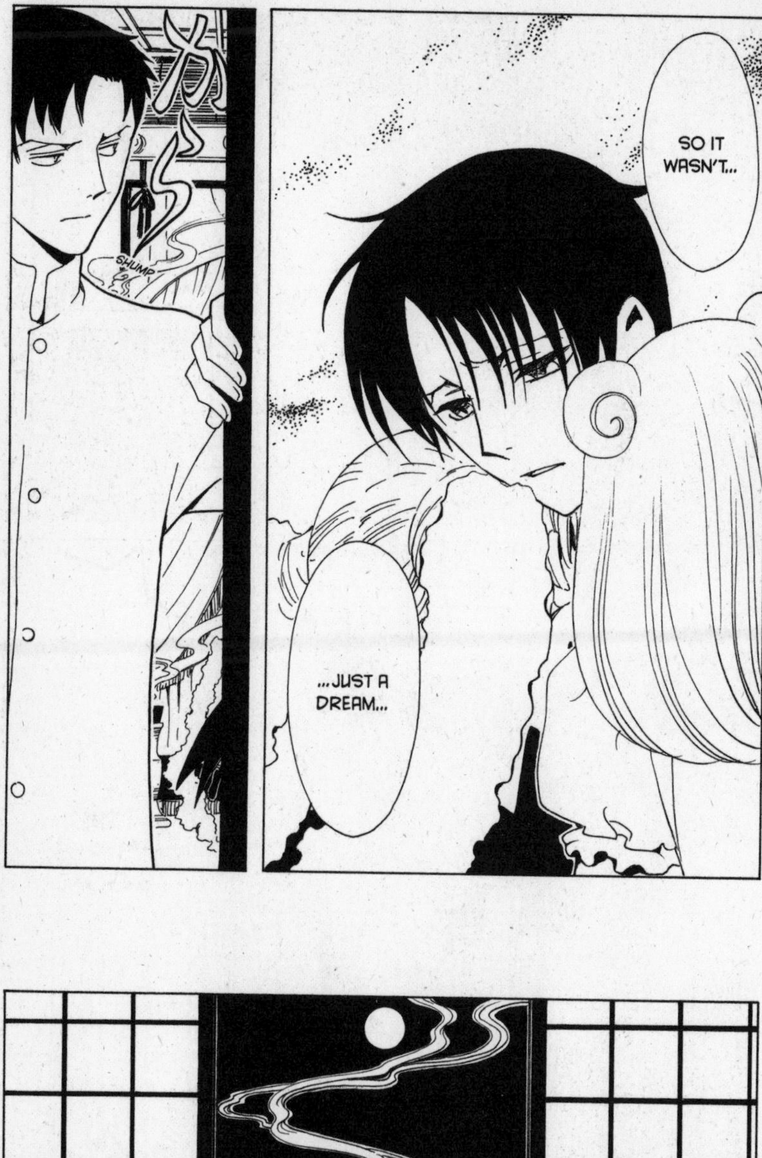
SO IT WASN'T...
...JUST A DREAM...
SHUMP

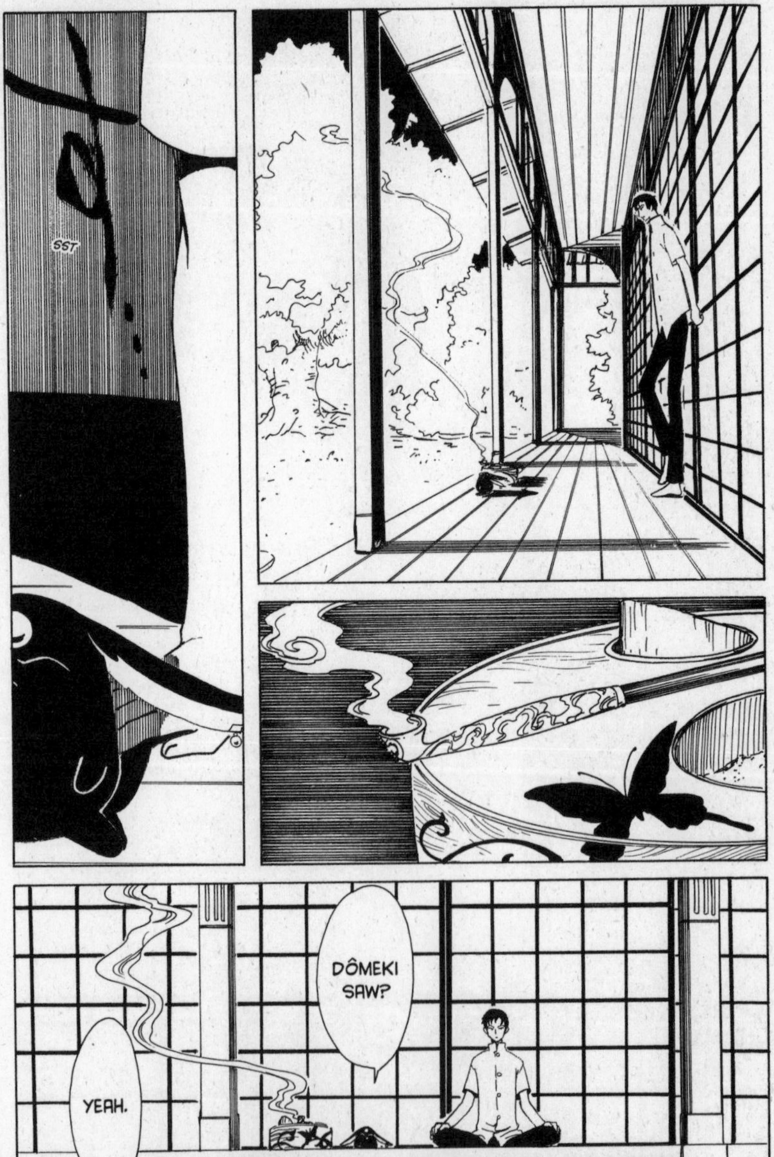
SST
DÔMEKI SAW?
YEAH.

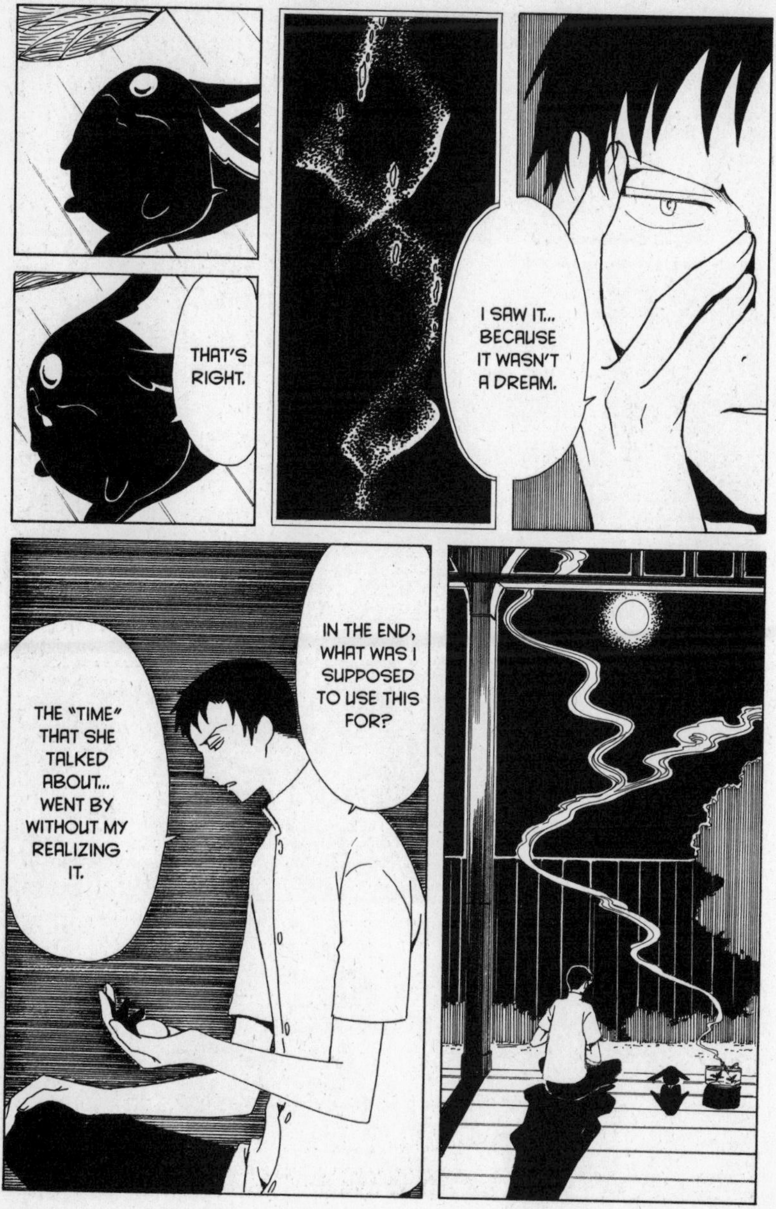
I SAW IT... BECAUSE IT WASN'T A DREAM.
THAT'S RIGHT.
IN THE END, WHAT WAS I SUPPOSED TO USE THIS FOR?
THE "TIME" THAT SHE TALKED ABOUT... WENT BY WITHOUT MY REALIZING IT.

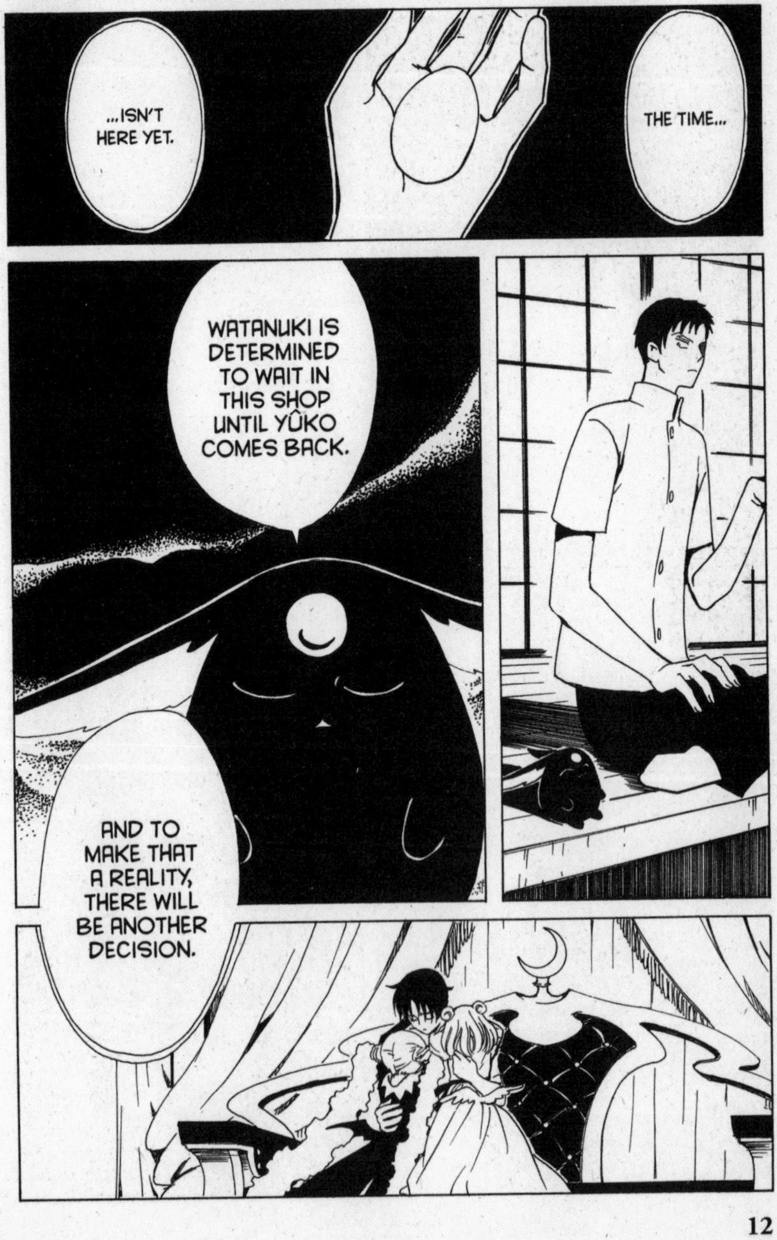
THE TIME...
...ISN'T HERE YET.
WATANUKI IS DETERMINED TO WAIT IN THIS SHOP UNTIL YÛKO COMES BACK.
AND TO MAKE THAT A REALITY, THERE WILL BE ANOTHER DECISION.

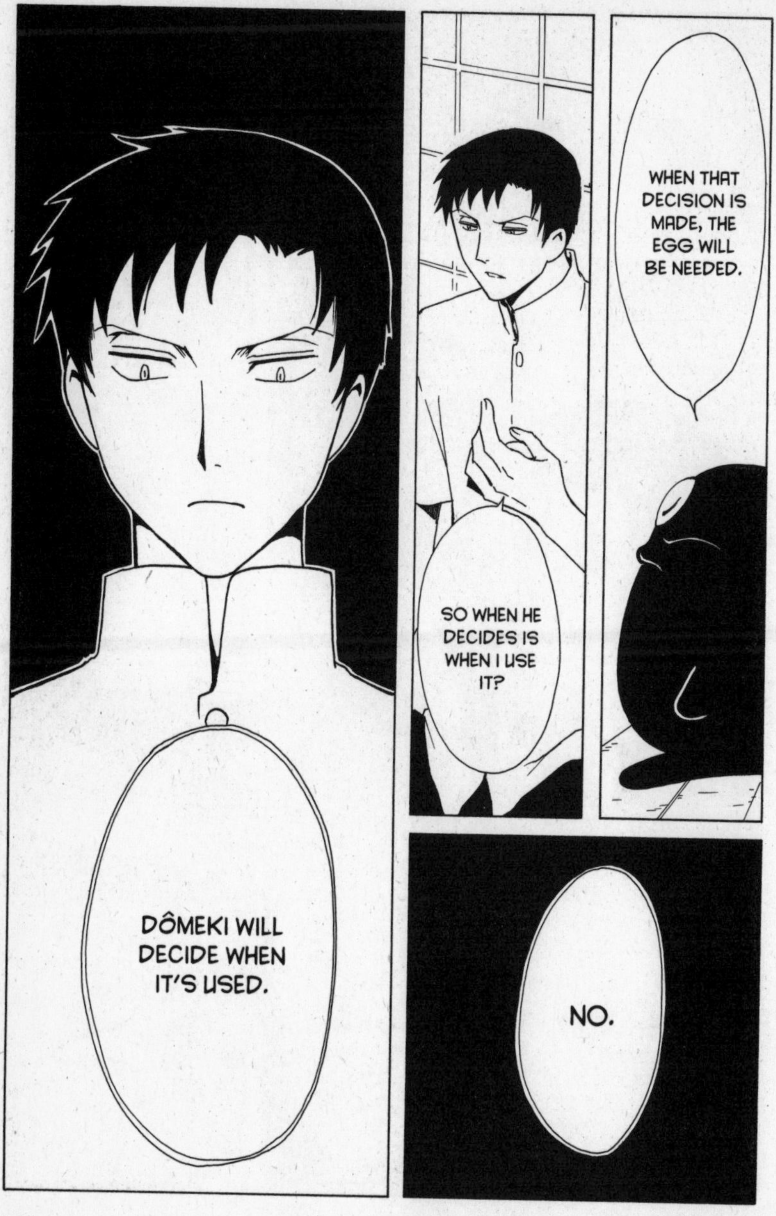
WHEN THAT DECISION IS MADE, THE EGG WILL BE NEEDED.
SO WHEN HE DECIDES IS WHEN I USE IT?
NO.
DÔMEKI WILL DECIDE WHEN IT'S USED.

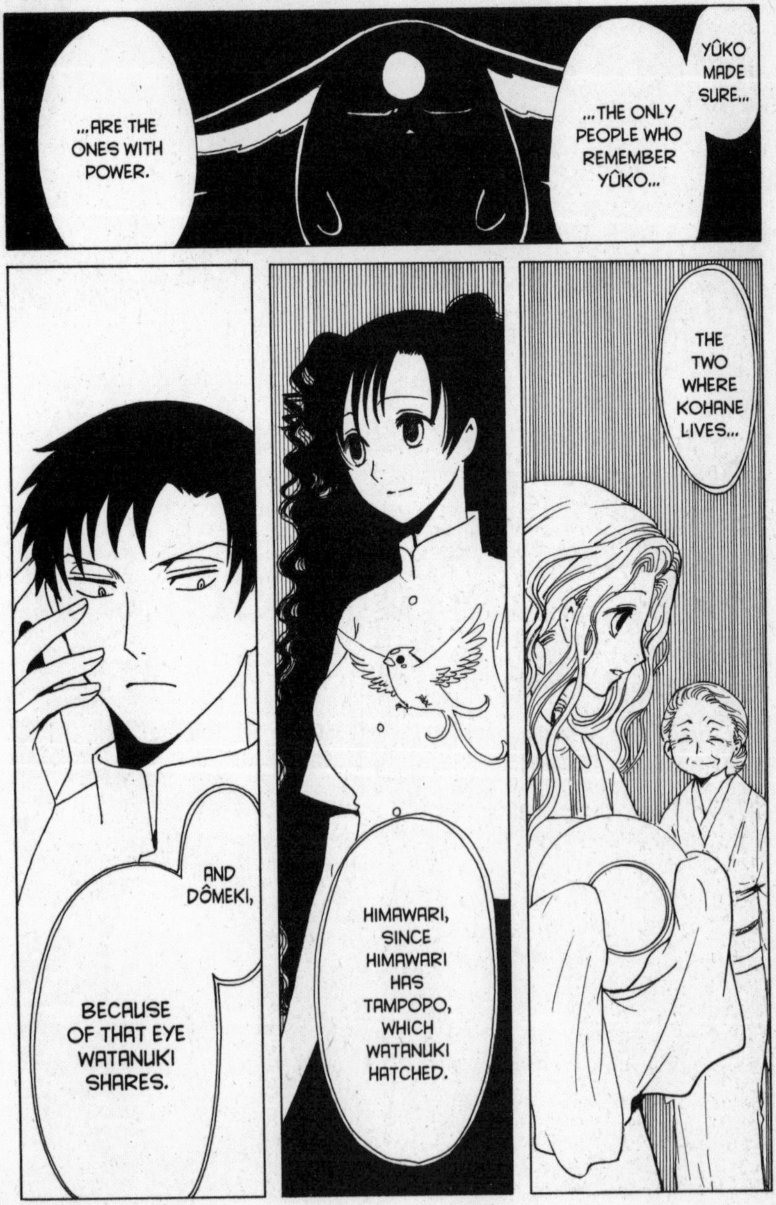
YÛKO MADE SURE...
...THE ONLY PEOPLE WHO REMEMBER YÛKO...
...ARE THE ONES WITH POWER.
THE TWO WHERE KOHANE LIVES...
HIMAWARI, SINCE HIMAWARI HAS TAMPOPO, WHICH WATANUKI HATCHED.
AND DÔMEKI,
BECAUSE OF THAT EYE WATANUKI SHARES.

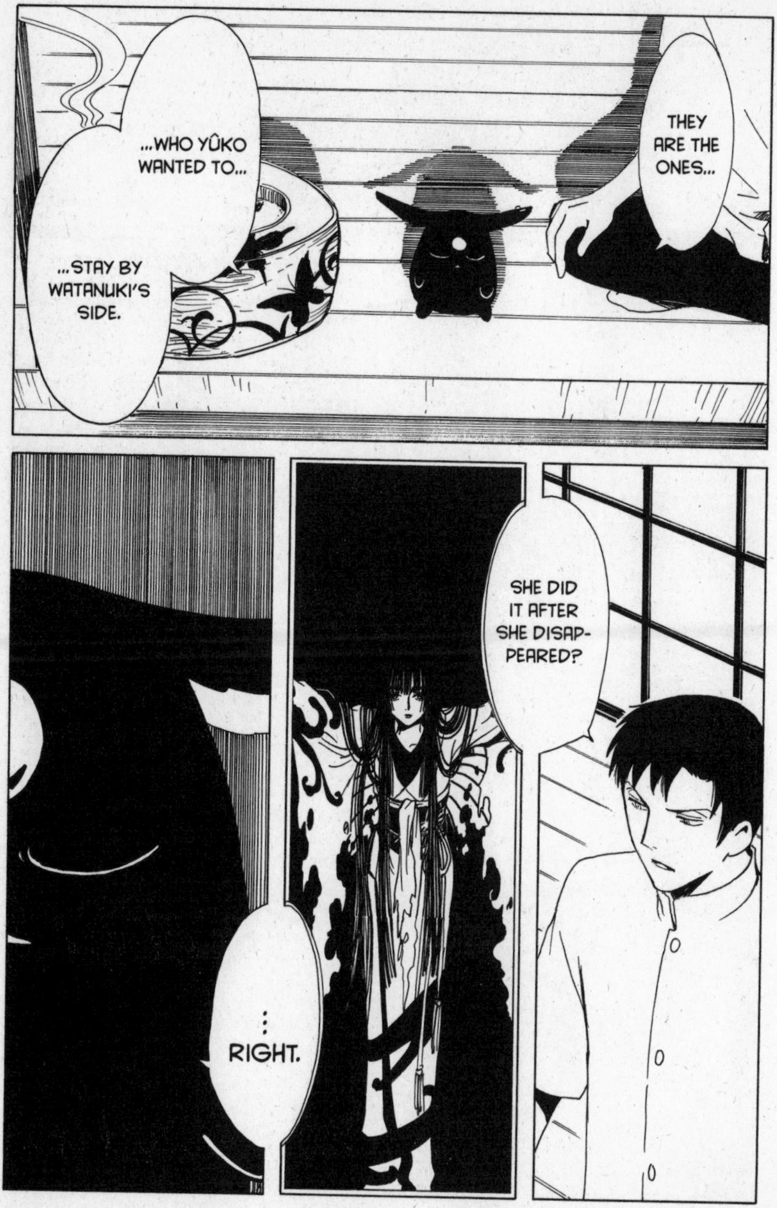
THEY ARE THE ONES...
...WHO YÛKO WANTED TO...
...STAY BY WATANUKI'S SIDE.
SHE DID IT AFTER SHE DISAPPEARED?
... RIGHT.

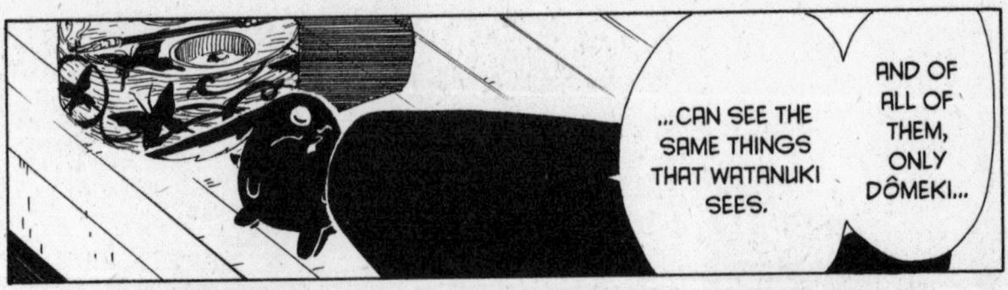
AND OF ALL OF THEM, ONLY DÔMEKI...
...CAN SEE THE SAME THINGS THAT WATANUKI SEES.
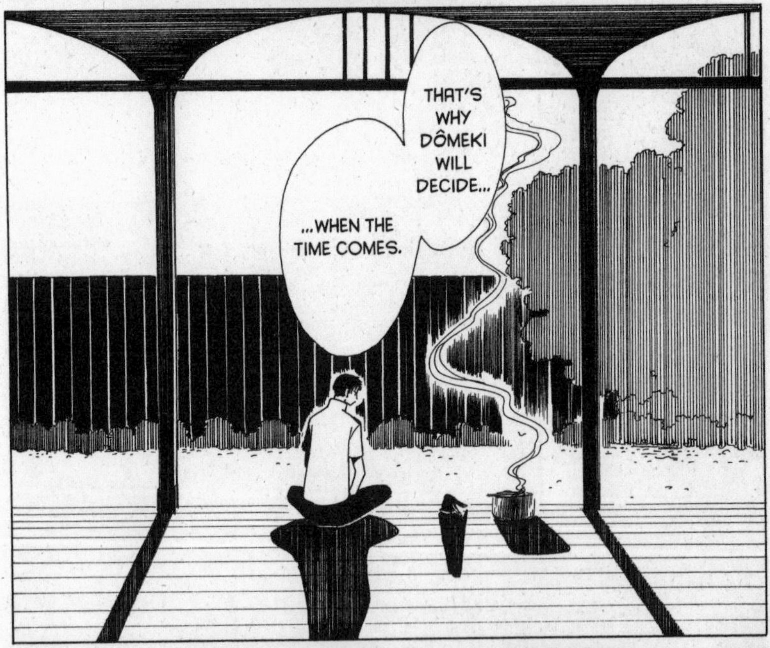
THAT'S WHY DÔMEKI WILL DECIDE...
...WHEN THE TIME COMES.
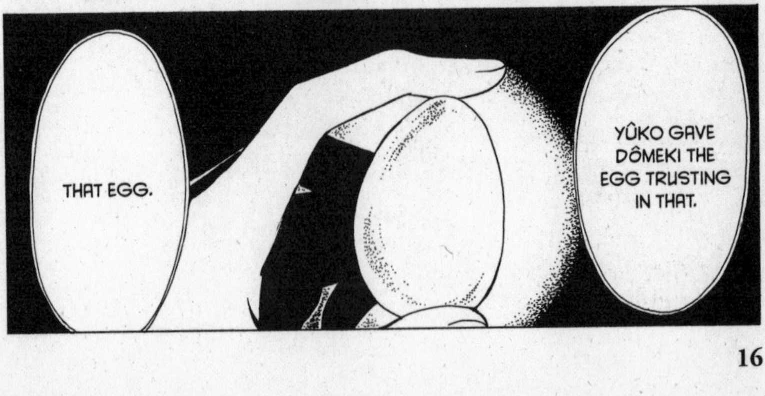
YÛKO GAVE DÔMEKI THE EGG TRUSTING IN THAT.
THAT EGG.

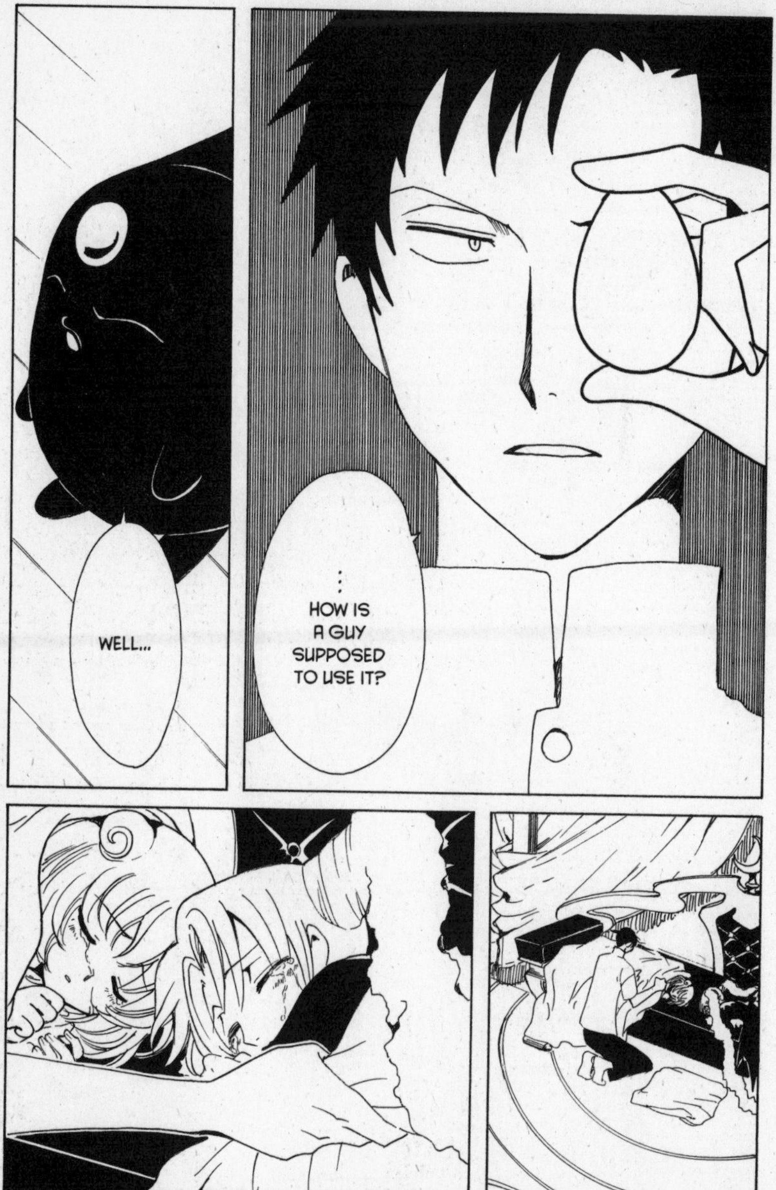
...
HOW IS A GUY SUPPOSED TO USE IT?
WELL...

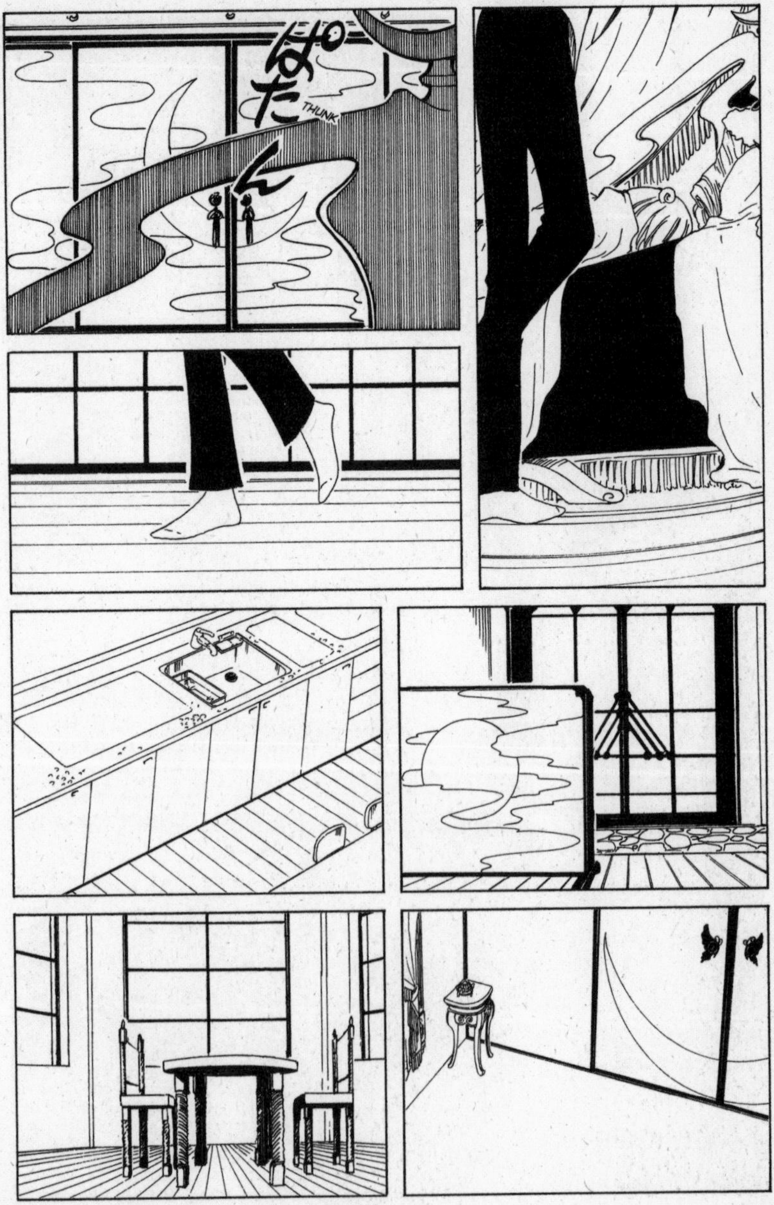
ぱたん
THUNK

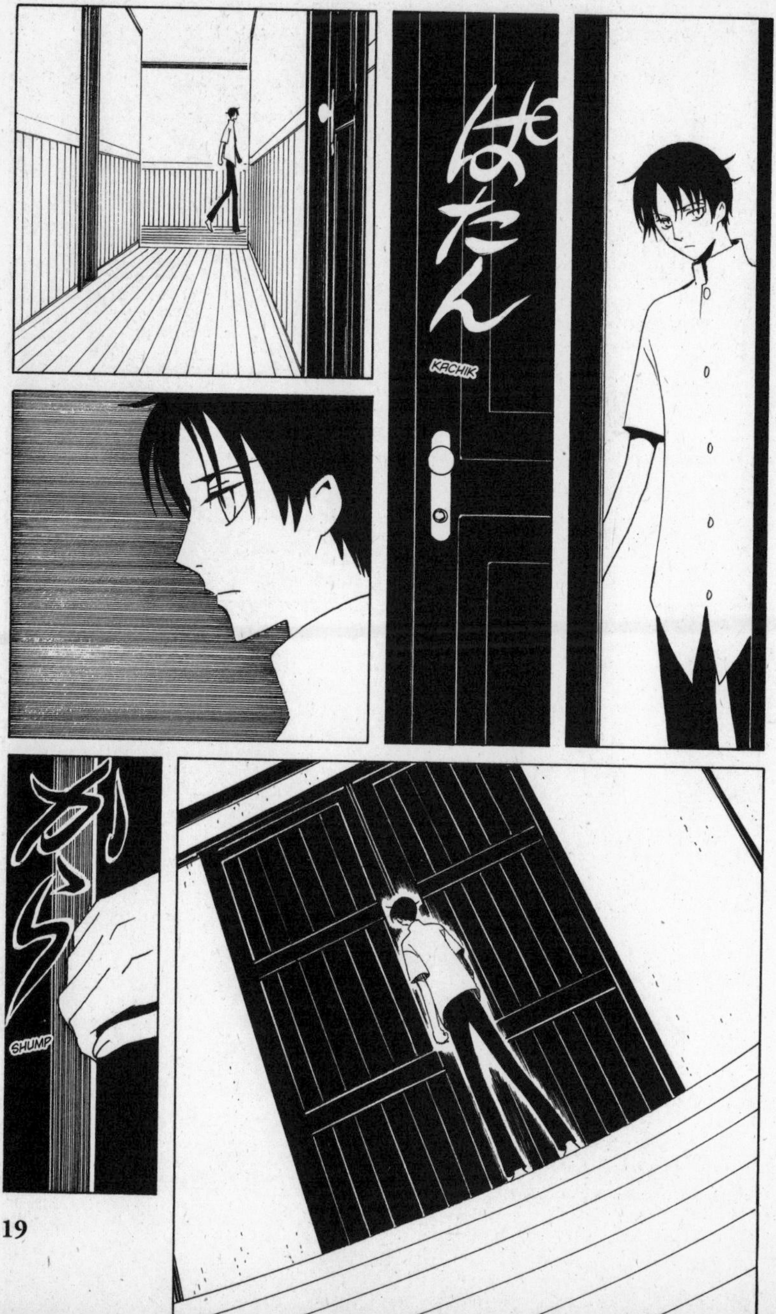
ぱたん
KACHIK
から
SHUMP

SHLUUM
しゅる

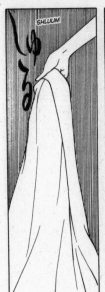

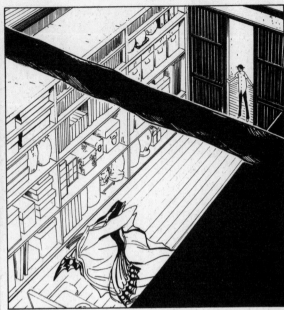

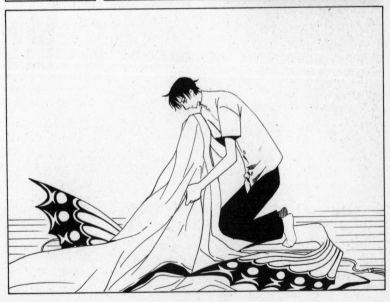

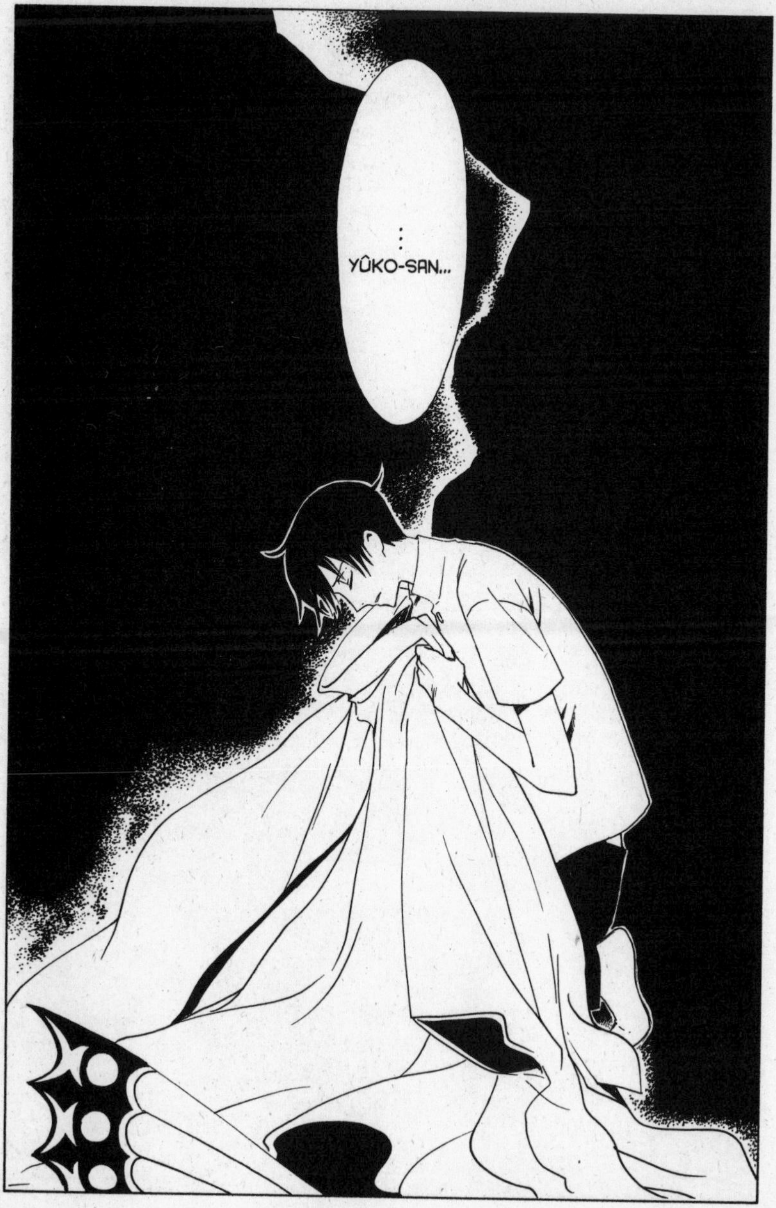
: YÛKO-SAN...

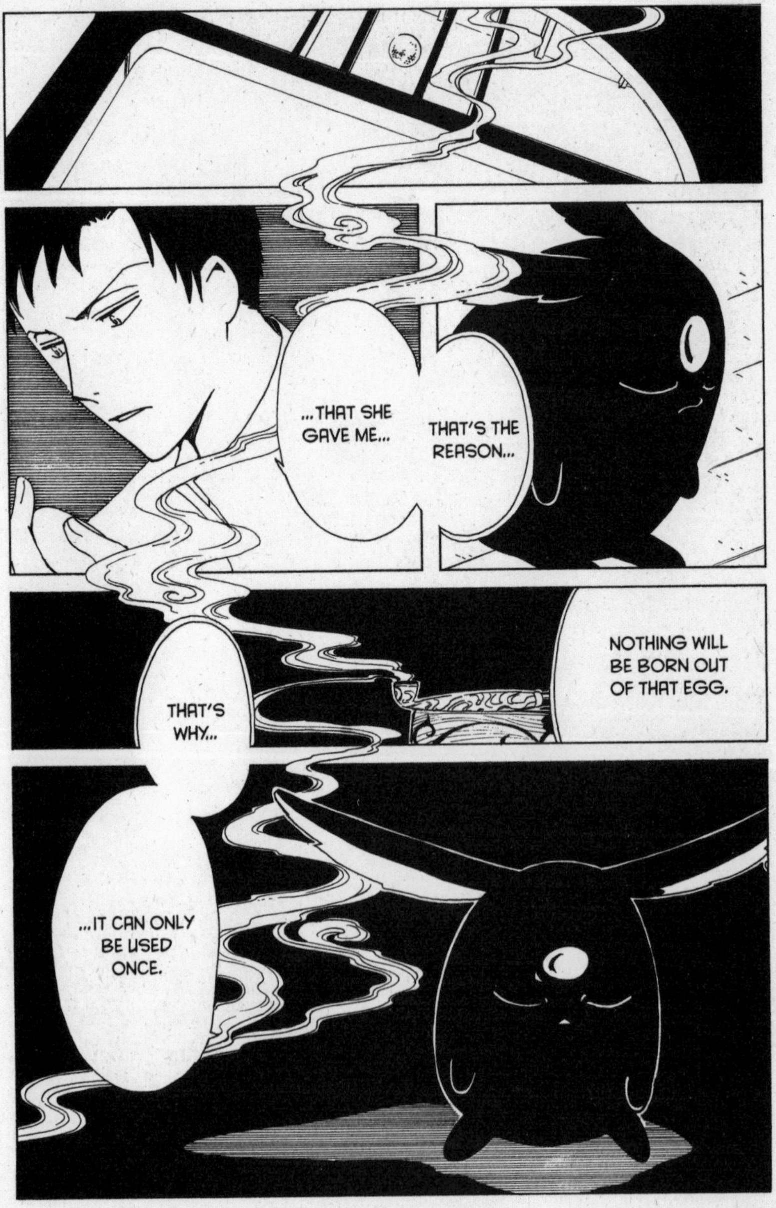
THAT'S THE REASON...
...THAT SHE GAVE ME...
NOTHING WILL BE BORN OUT OF THAT EGG.
THAT'S WHY...
...IT CAN ONLY BE USED ONCE.

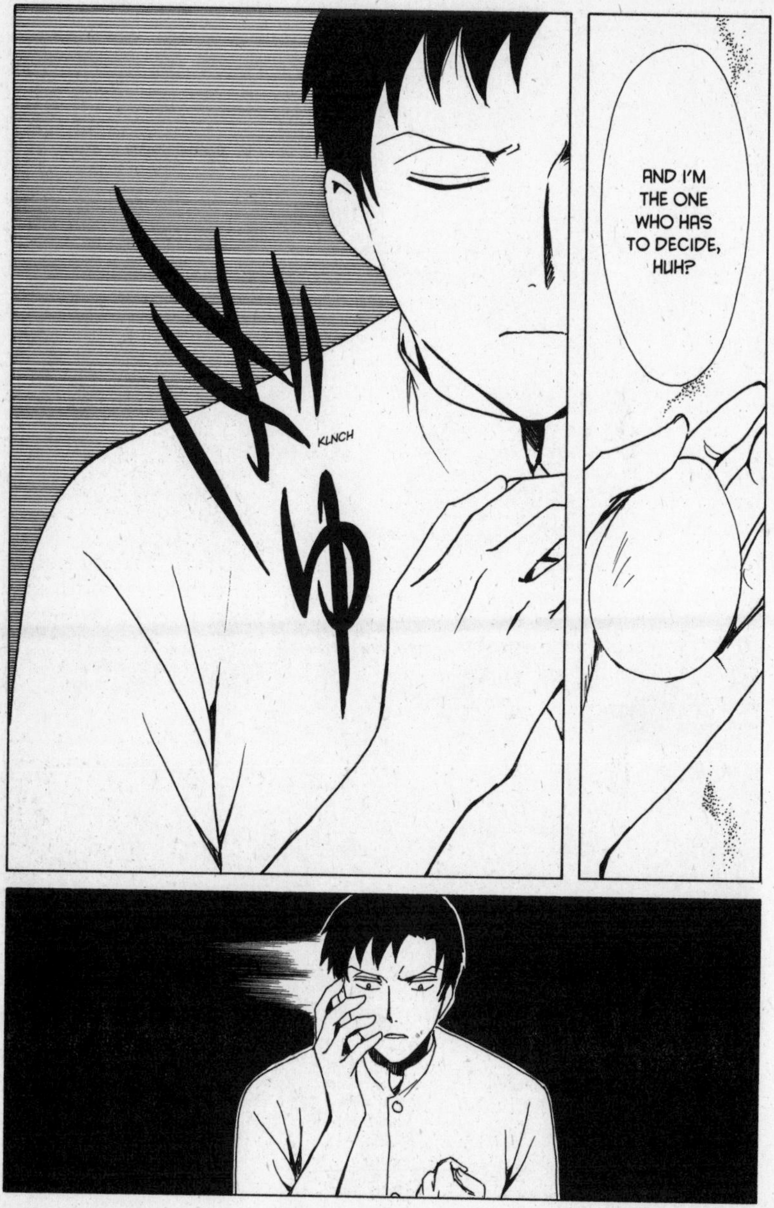
AND I'M THE ONE WHO HAS TO DECIDE, HUH?
KLNCH

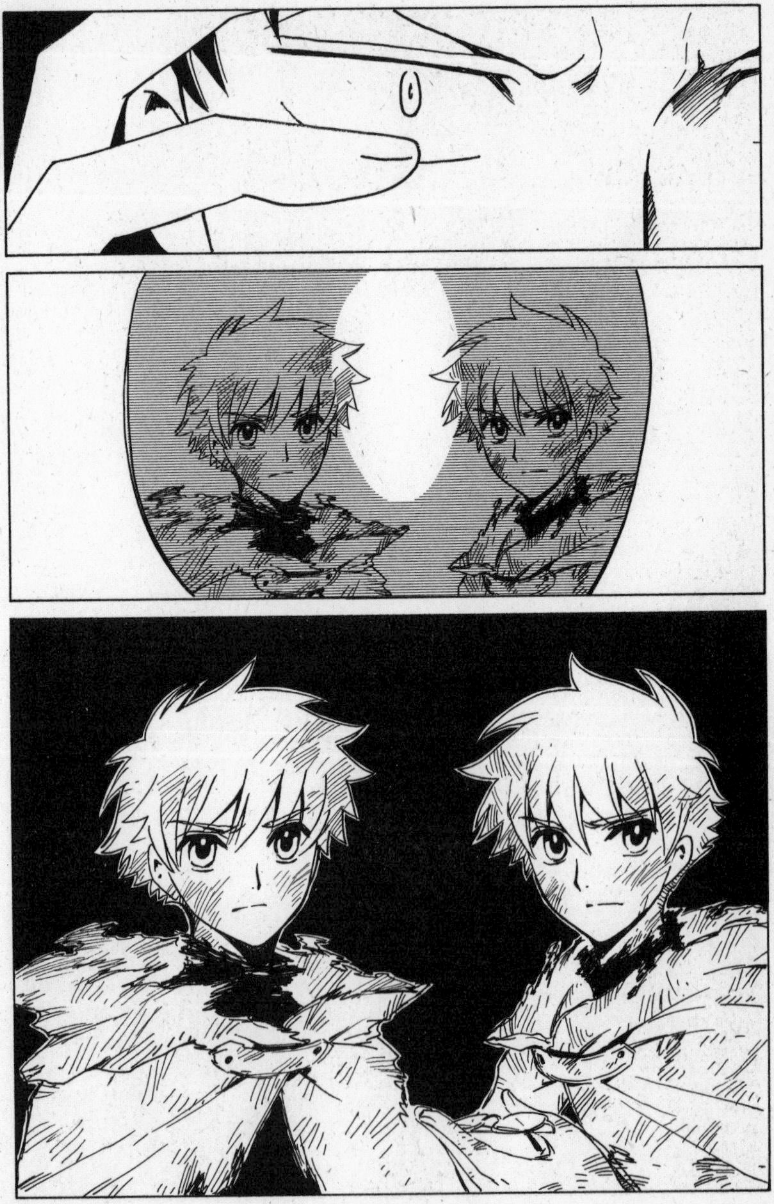

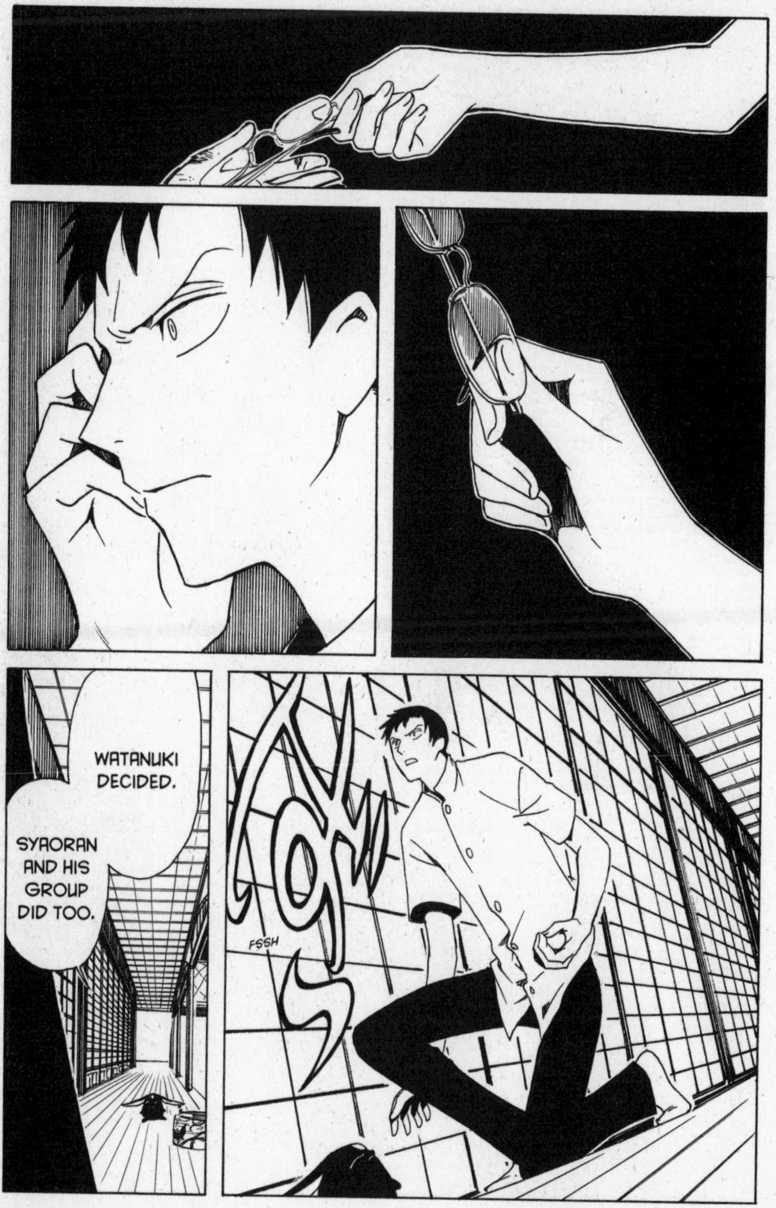
FSSH
WATANUKI DECIDED.
SYAORAN AND HIS GROUP DID TOO.

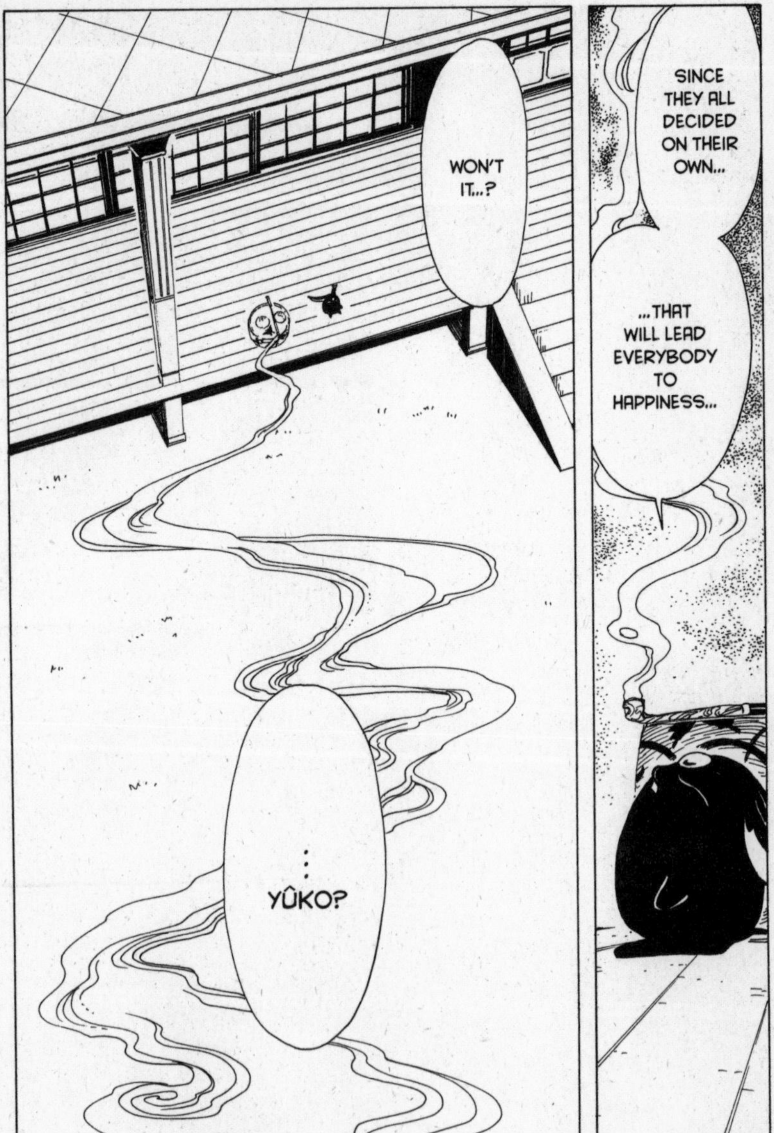
SINCE THEY ALL DECIDED ON THEIR OWN...
...THAT WILL LEAD EVERYBODY TO HAPPINESS...
WON'T IT...?
... YÛKO?

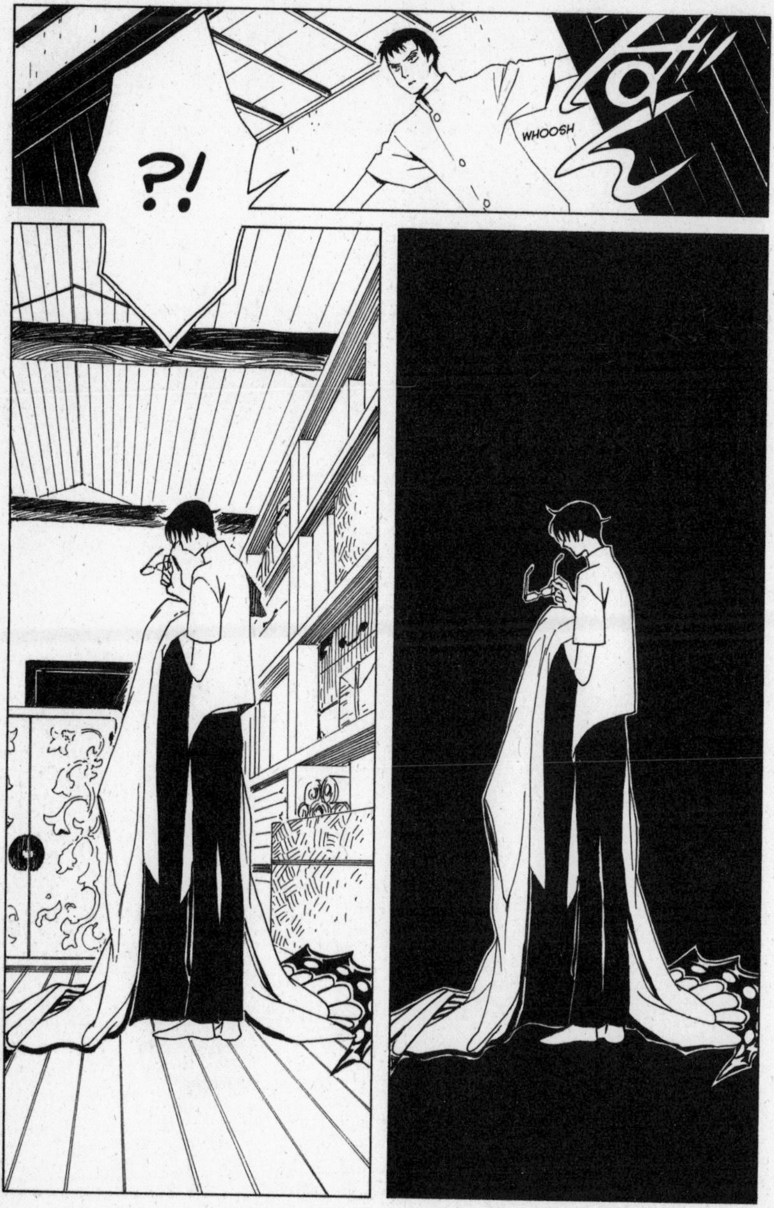
WHOOSH
?!

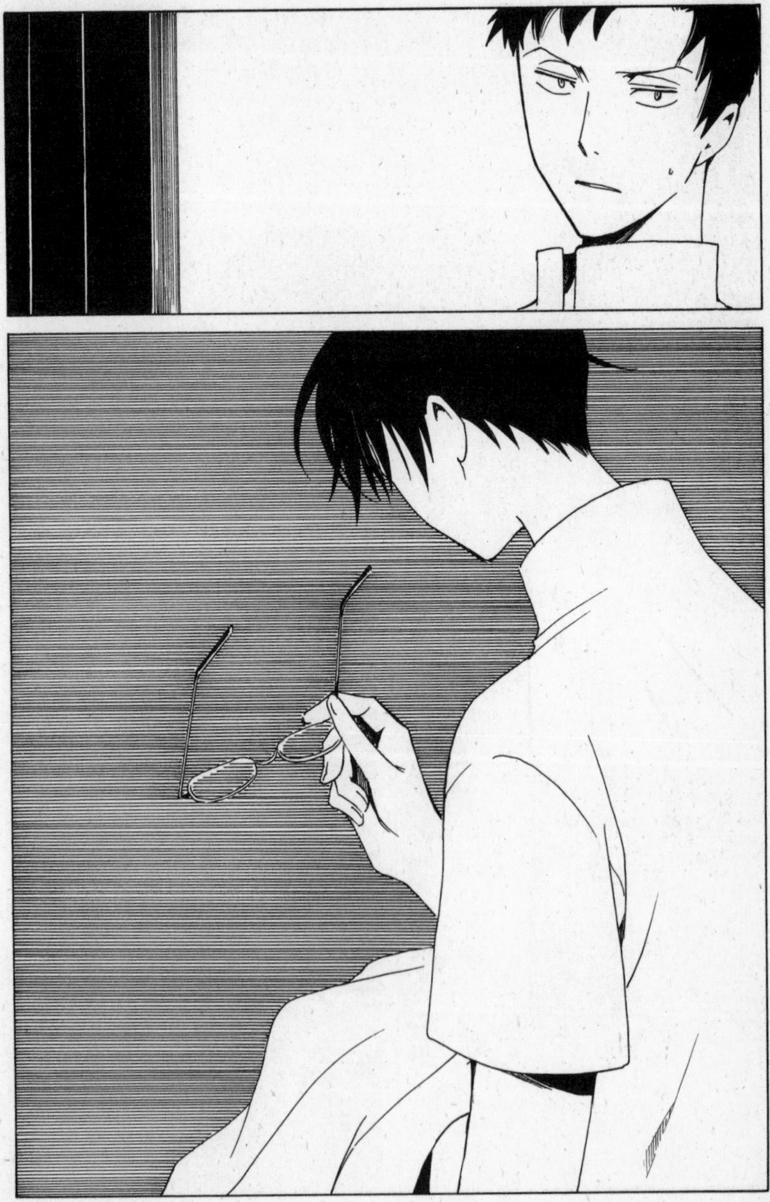

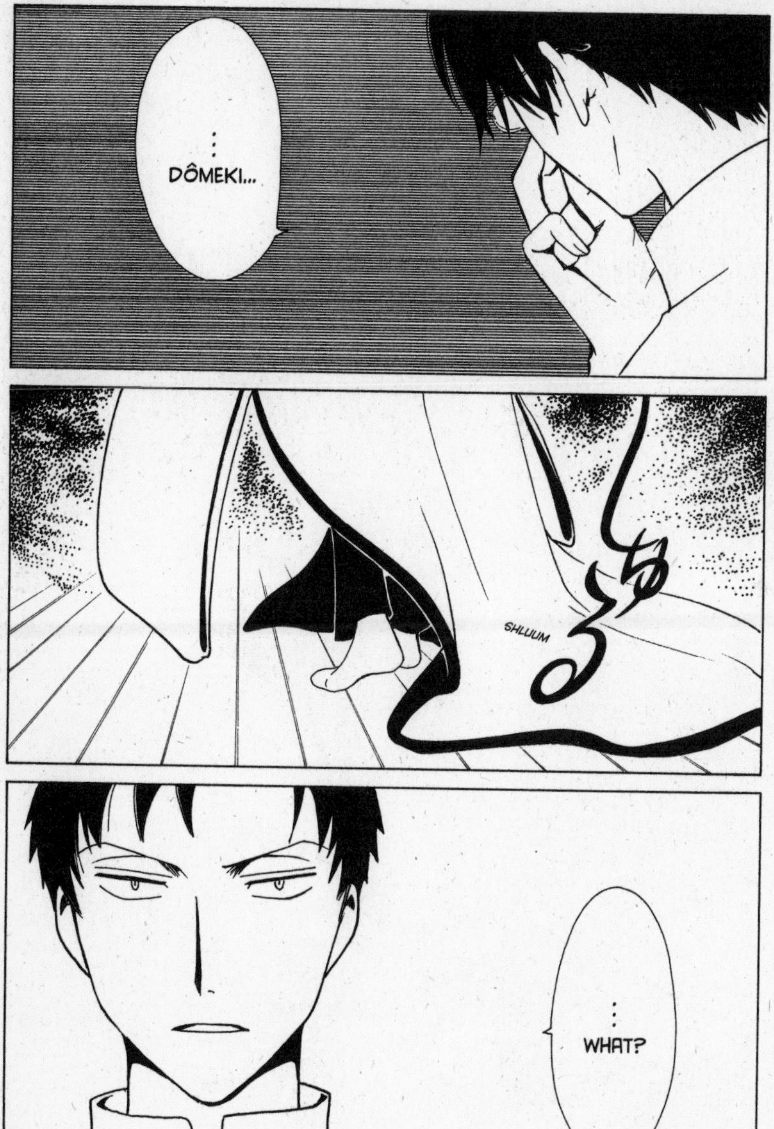

...DÔMEKI...
SHLUUM
...WHAT?

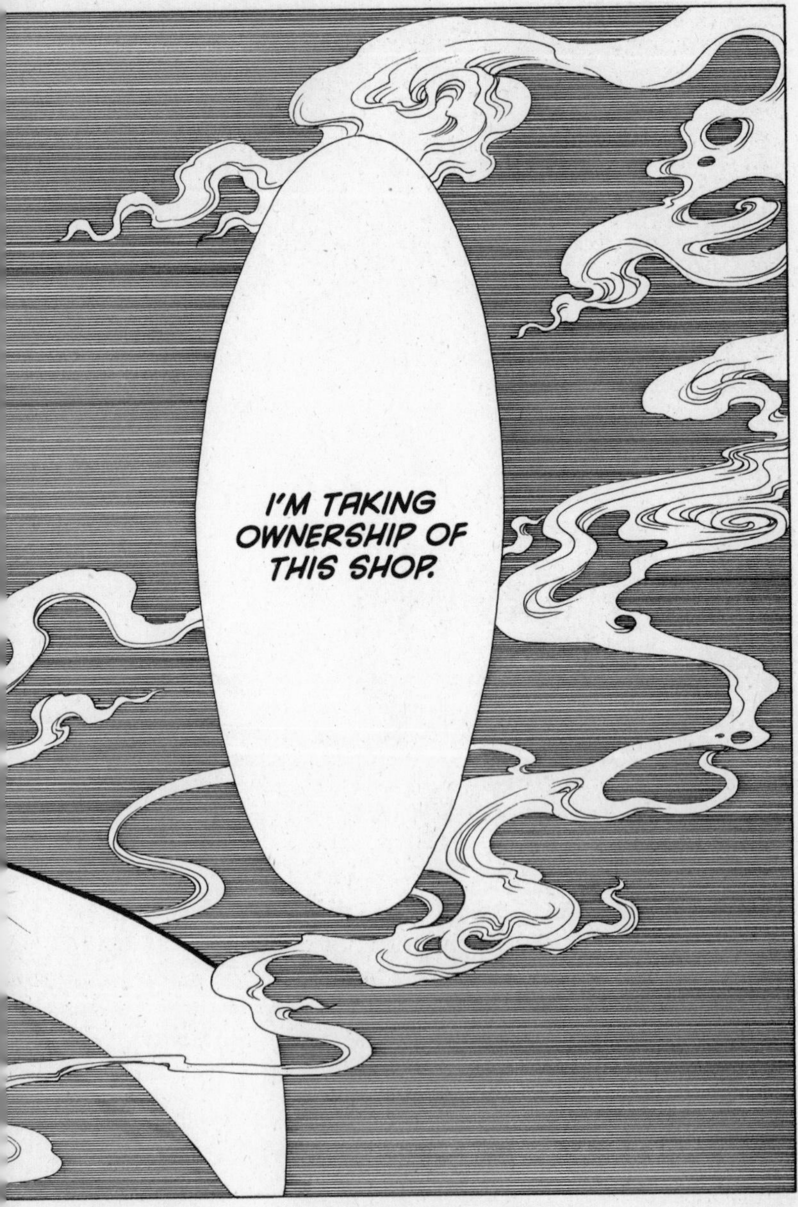
I'M TAKING OWNERSHIP OF THIS SHOP.

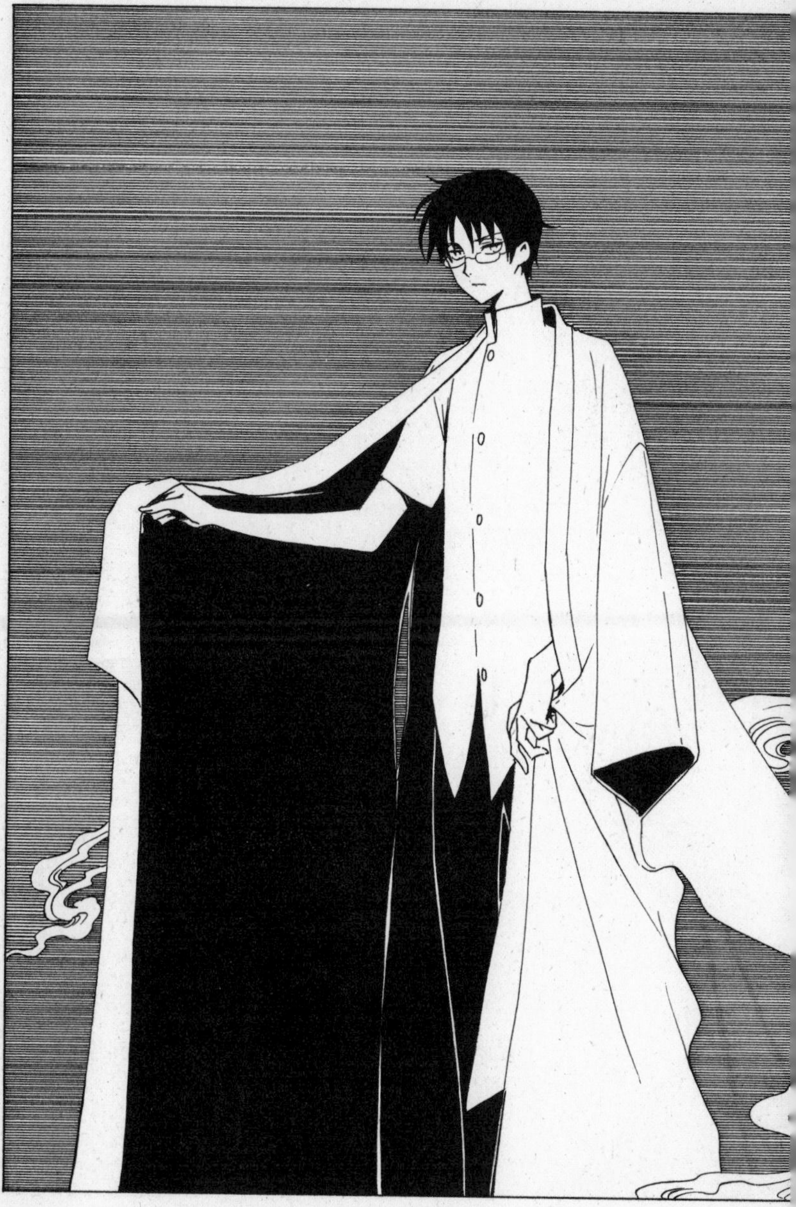

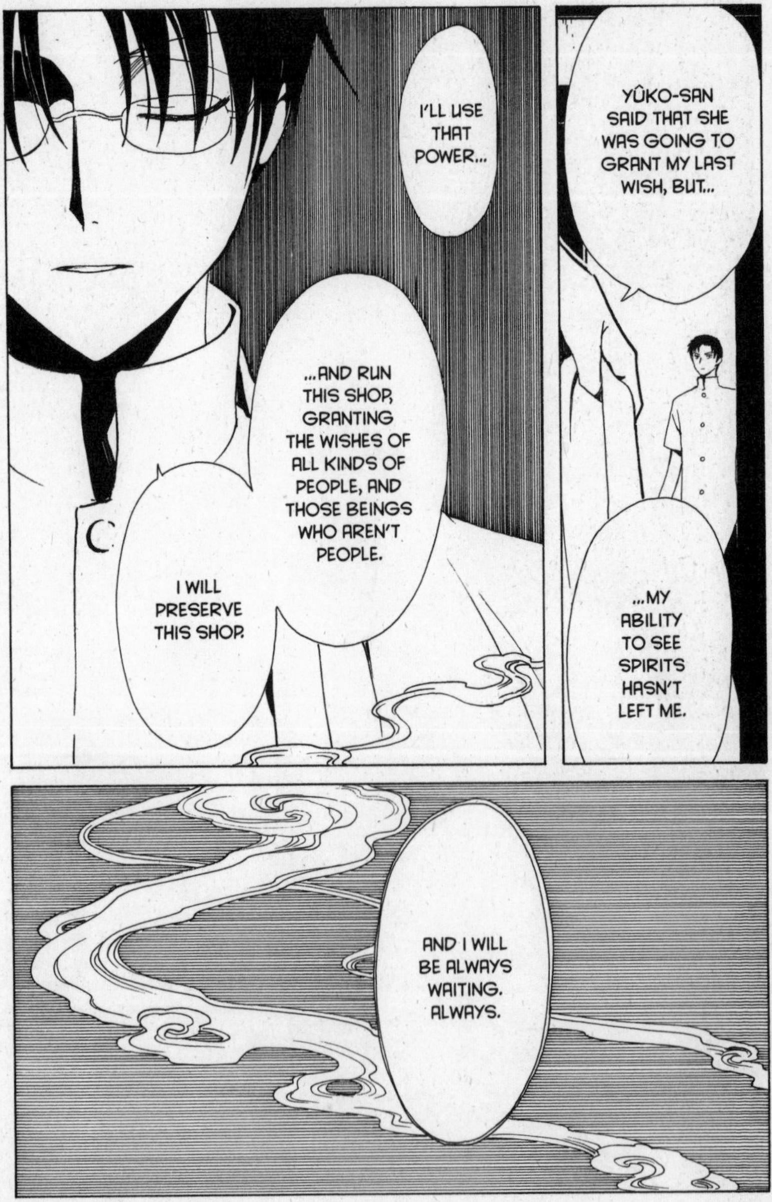
YÛKO-SAN SAID THAT SHE WAS GOING TO GRANT MY LAST WISH, BUT...
...MY ABILITY TO SEE SPIRITS HASN'T LEFT ME.
I'LL USE THAT POWER...
...AND RUN THIS SHOP, GRANTING THE WISHES OF ALL KINDS OF PEOPLE, AND THOSE BEINGS WHO AREN'T PEOPLE.
I WILL PRESERVE THIS SHOP.
AND I WILL BE ALWAYS WAITING. ALWAYS.

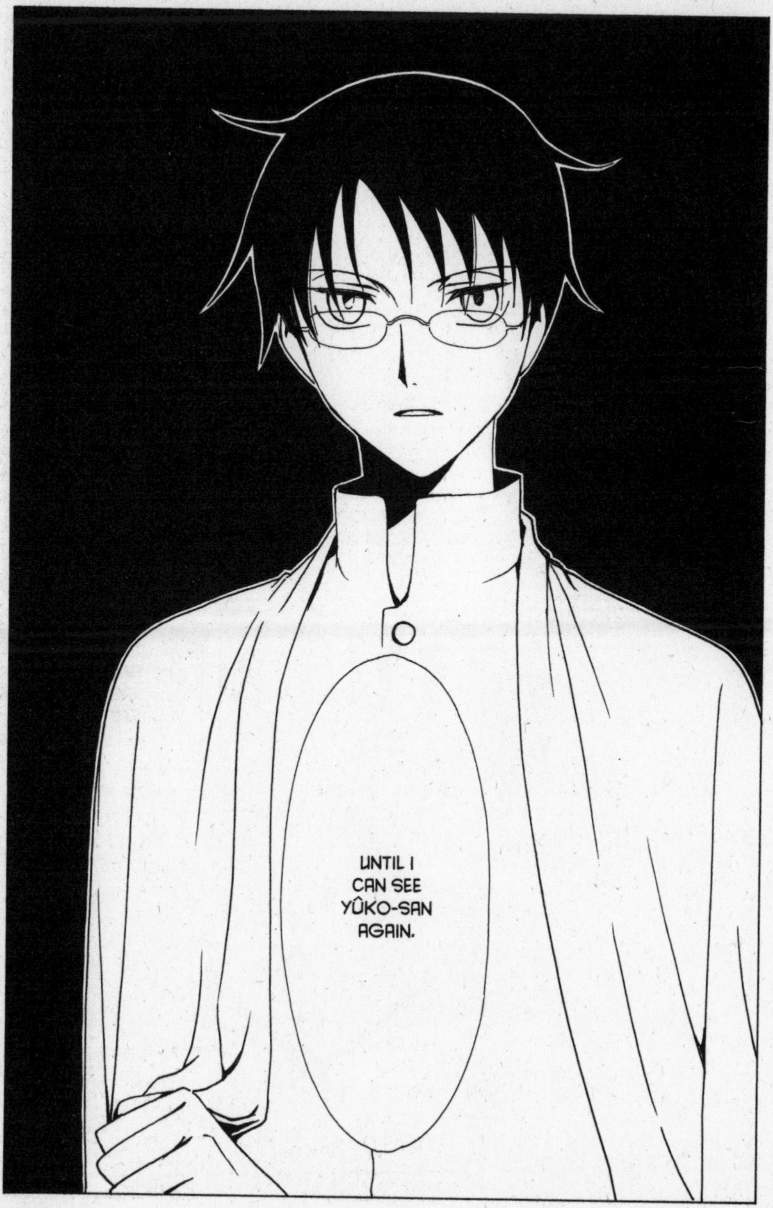
UNTIL I CAN SEE YÛKO-SAN AGAIN.

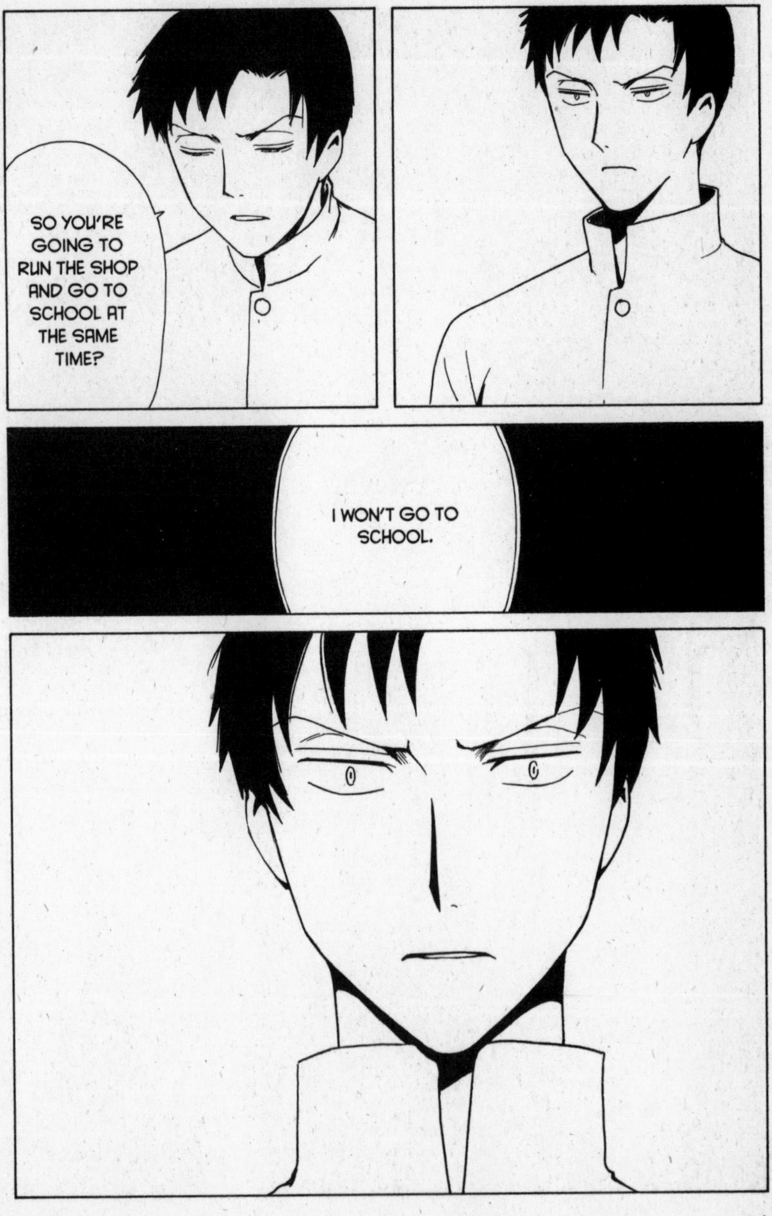
SO YOU'RE GOING TO RUN THE SHOP AND GO TO SCHOOL AT THE SAME TIME?
I WON'T GO TO SCHOOL.

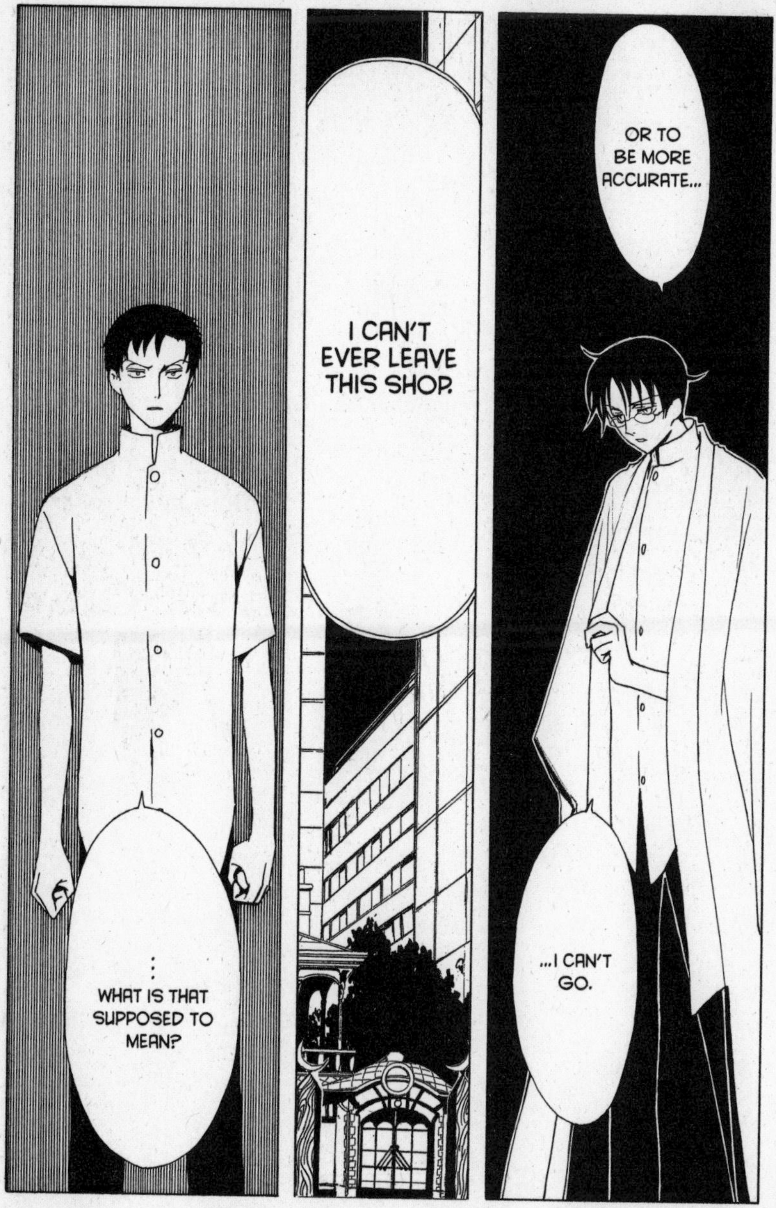
OR TO BE MORE ACCURATE...
...I CAN'T GO.
I CAN'T EVER LEAVE THIS SHOP.
... WHAT IS THAT SUPPOSED TO MEAN?

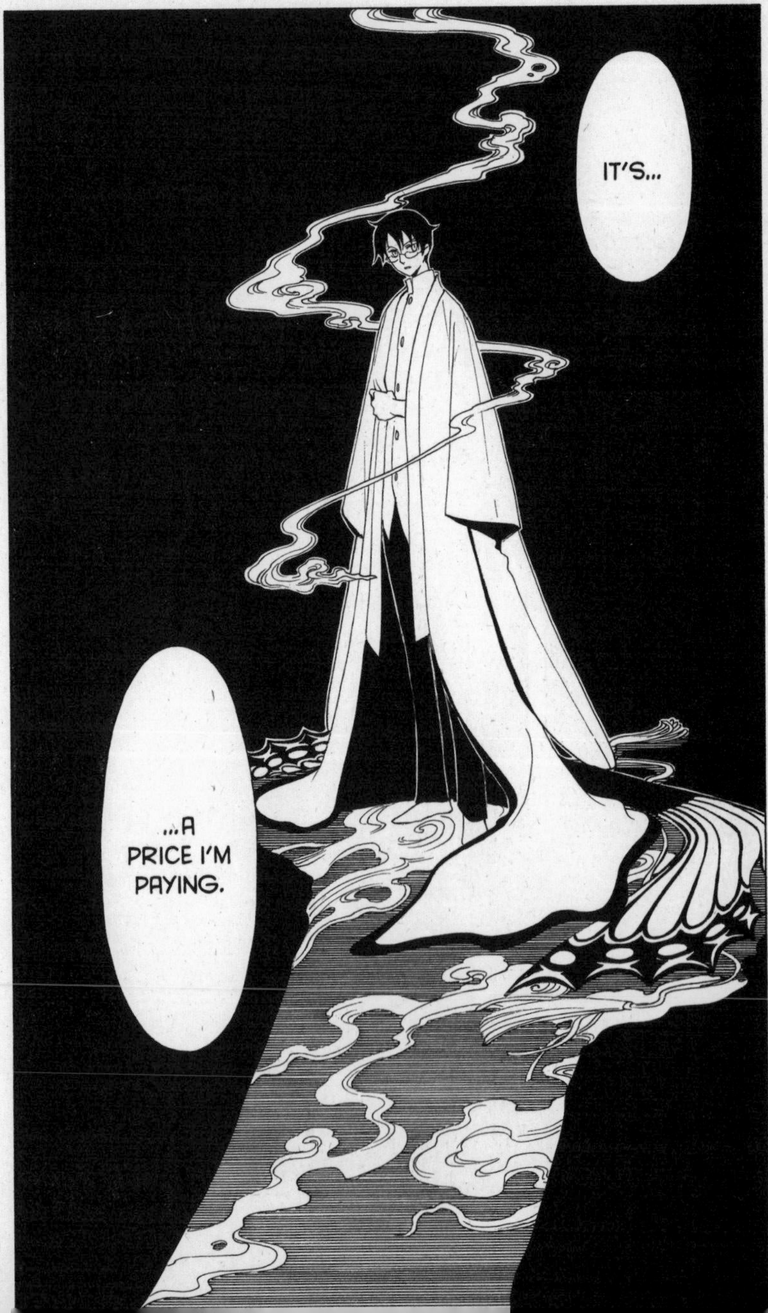
IT'S...
...A PRICE I'M PAYING.

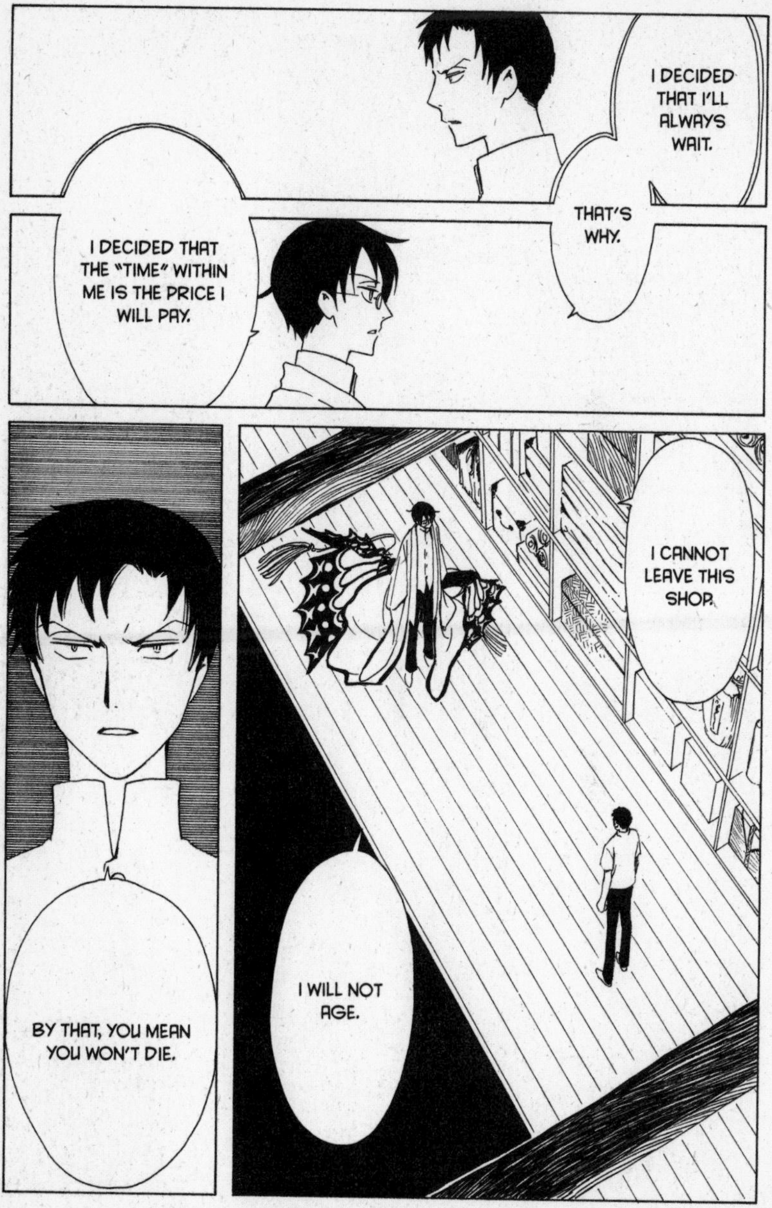
I DECIDED THAT I'LL ALWAYS WAIT.
THAT'S WHY.
I DECIDED THAT THE "TIME" WITHIN ME IS THE PRICE I WILL PAY.
I CANNOT LEAVE THIS SHOP.
I WILL NOT AGE.
BY THAT, YOU MEAN YOU WON'T DIE.

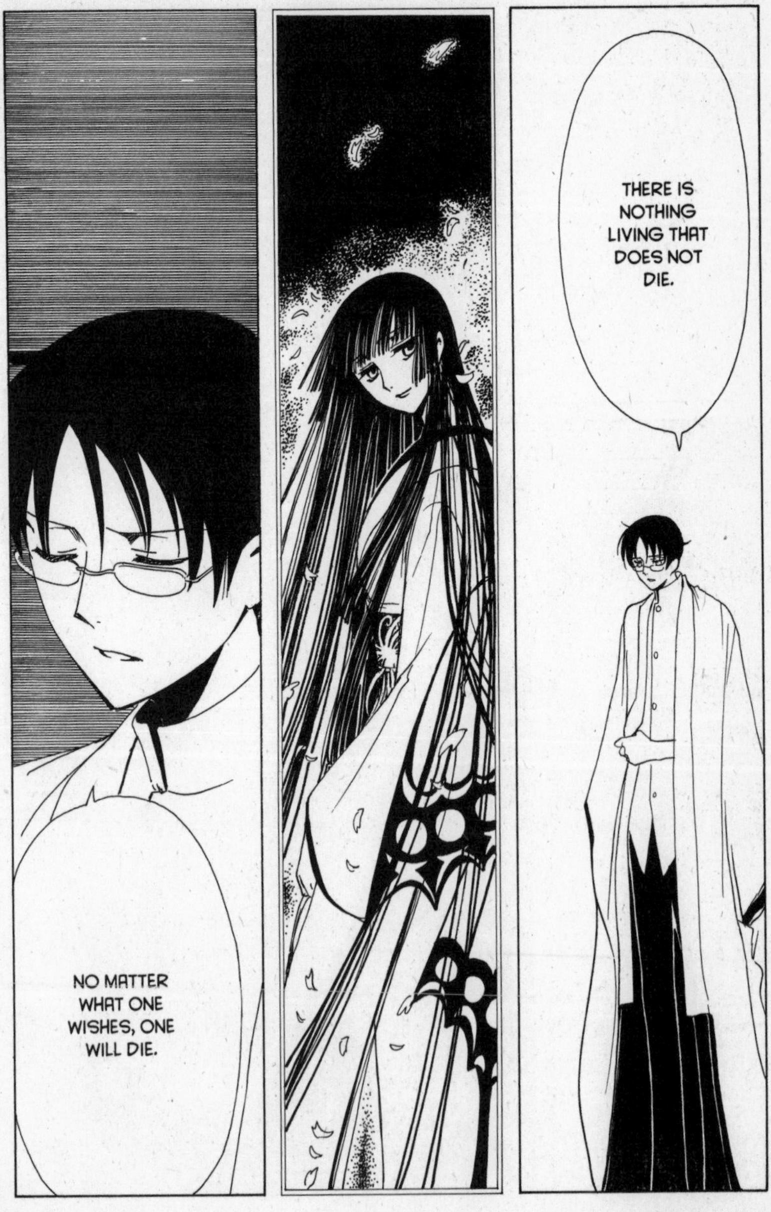
THERE IS NOTHING LIVING THAT DOES NOT DIE.
NO MATTER WHAT ONE WISHES, ONE WILL DIE.

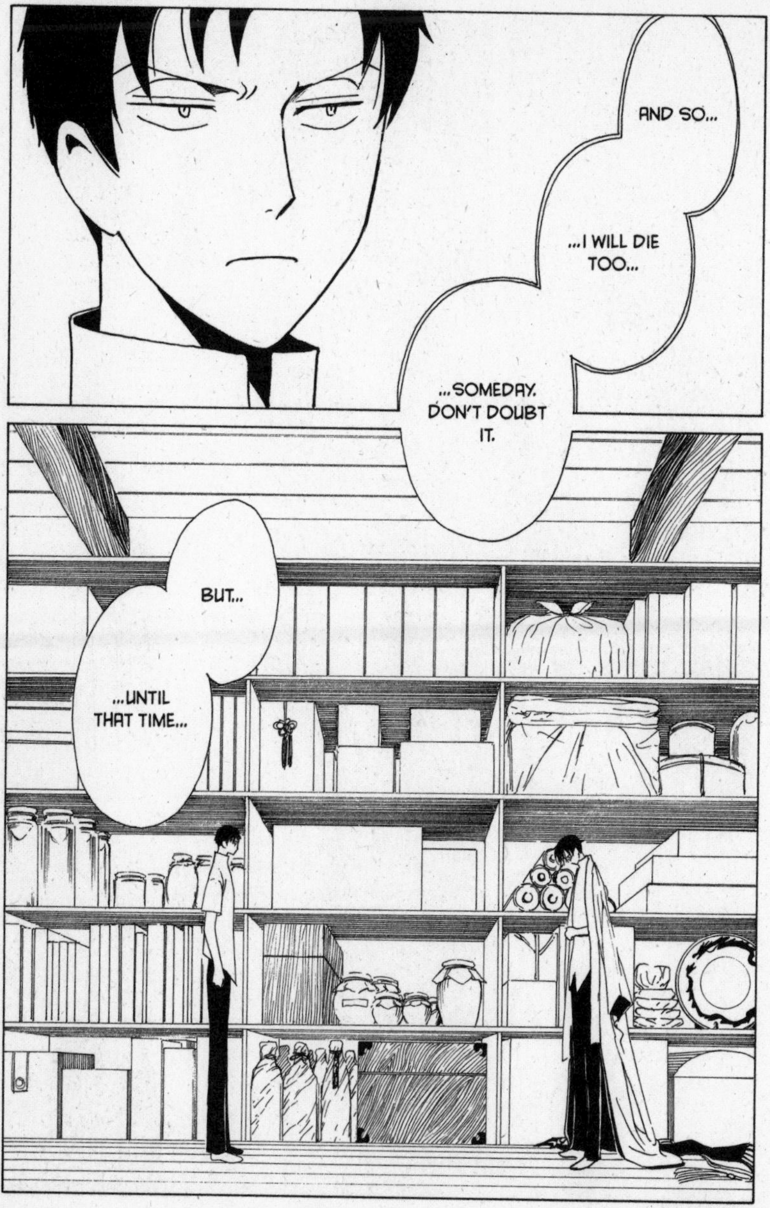
AND SO...
...I WILL DIE TOO...
...SOMEDAY. DON'T DOUBT IT.
BUT...
...UNTIL THAT TIME...

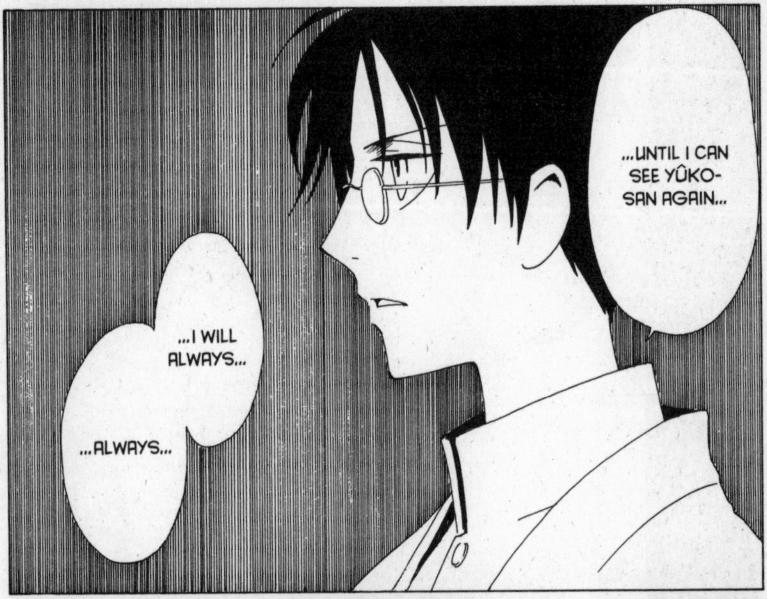
...UNTIL I CAN SEE YÛKO-SAN AGAIN...
...I WILL ALWAYS...
...ALWAYS...
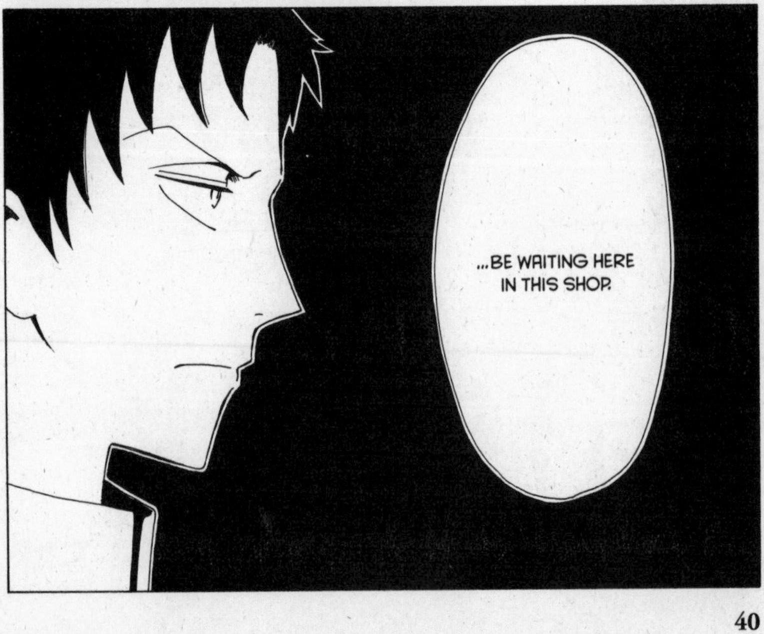
...BE WAITING HERE IN THIS SHOP.

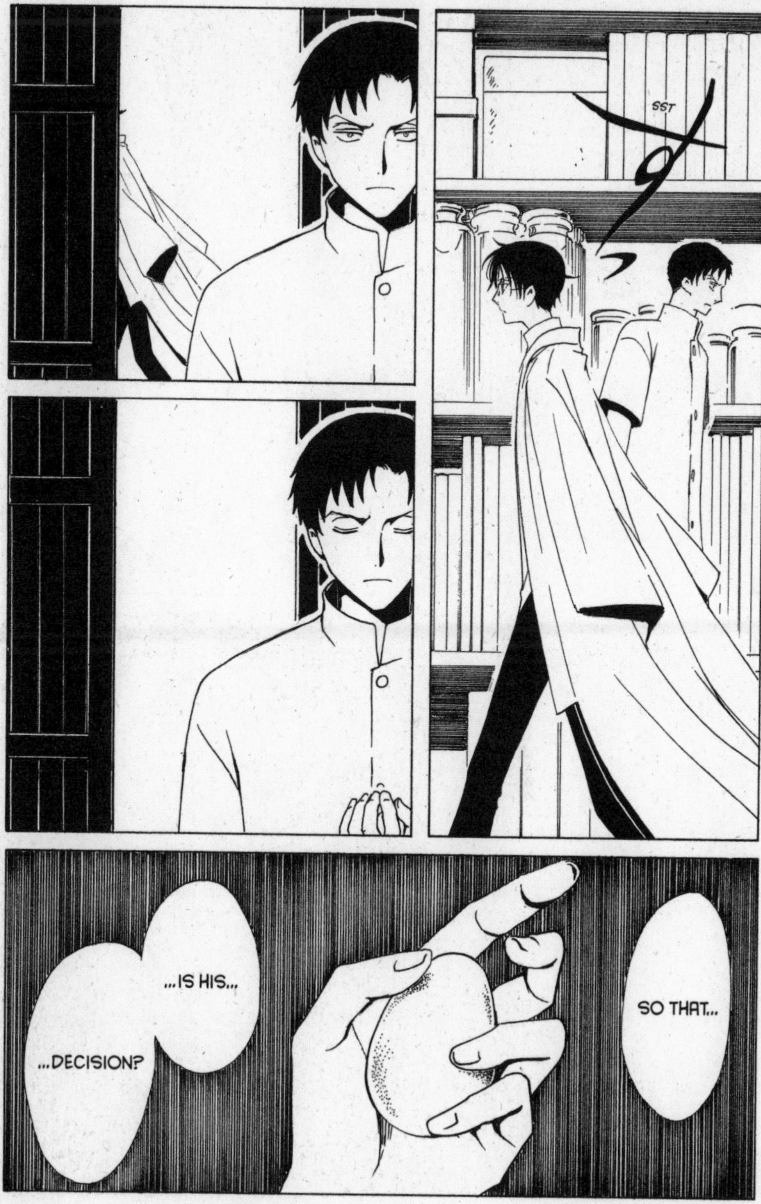
SST
SO THAT...
...IS HIS...
...DECISION?

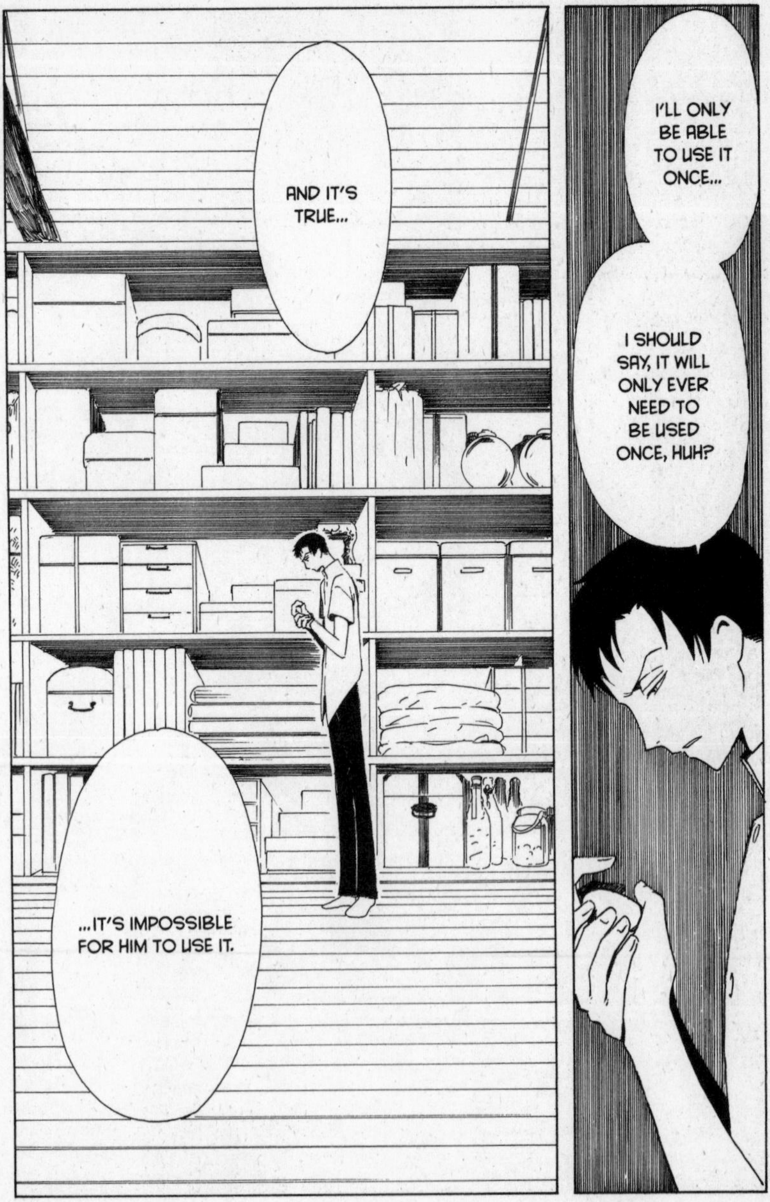
I'LL ONLY BE ABLE TO USE IT ONCE...
I SHOULD SAY, IT WILL ONLY EVER NEED TO BE USED ONCE, HUH?
AND IT'S TRUE...
...IT'S IMPOSSIBLE FOR HIM TO USE IT.

TONK
SSSS
げほ
KAFF
げほ
KAFF
げほ
KAFF
けほ
KOFF...

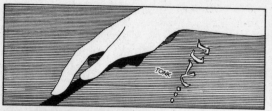

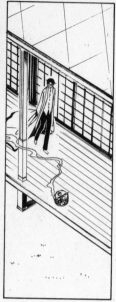

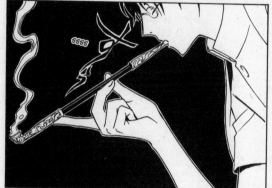

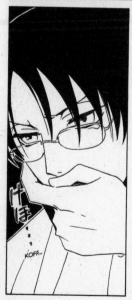

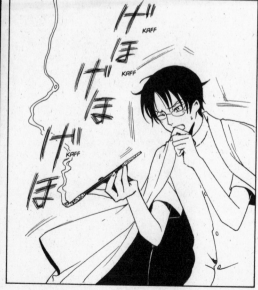

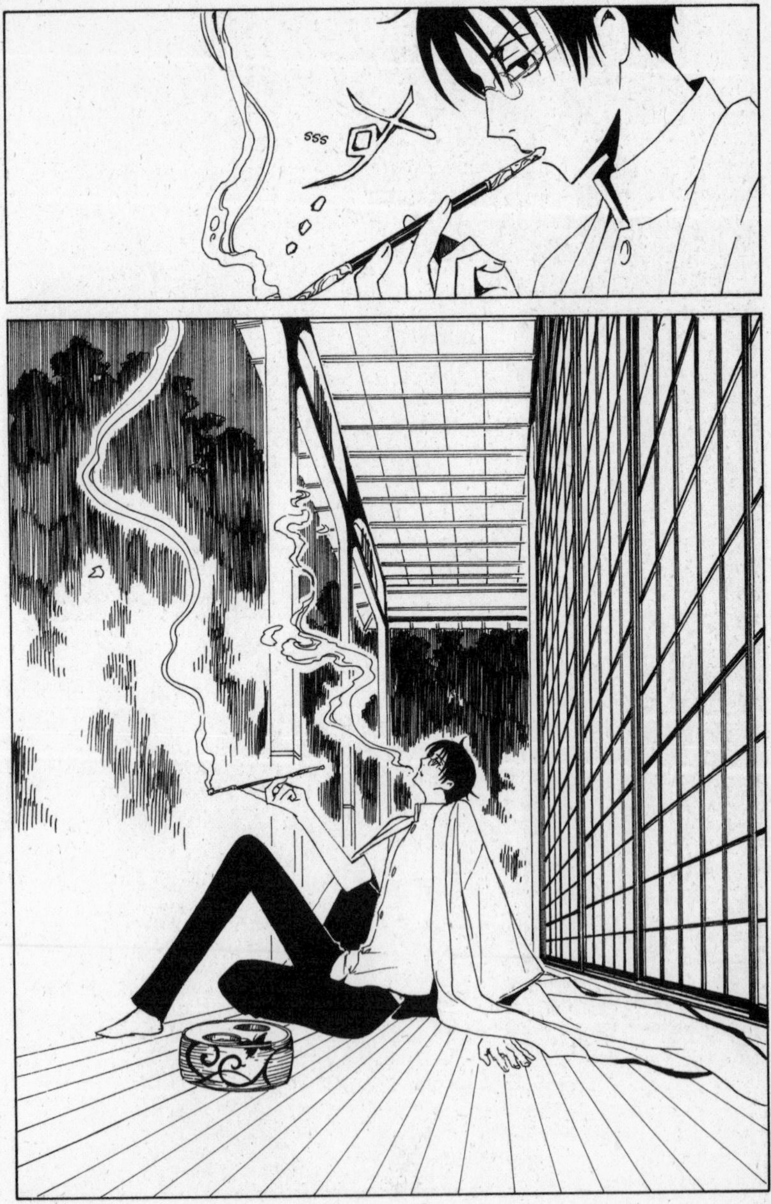
sss

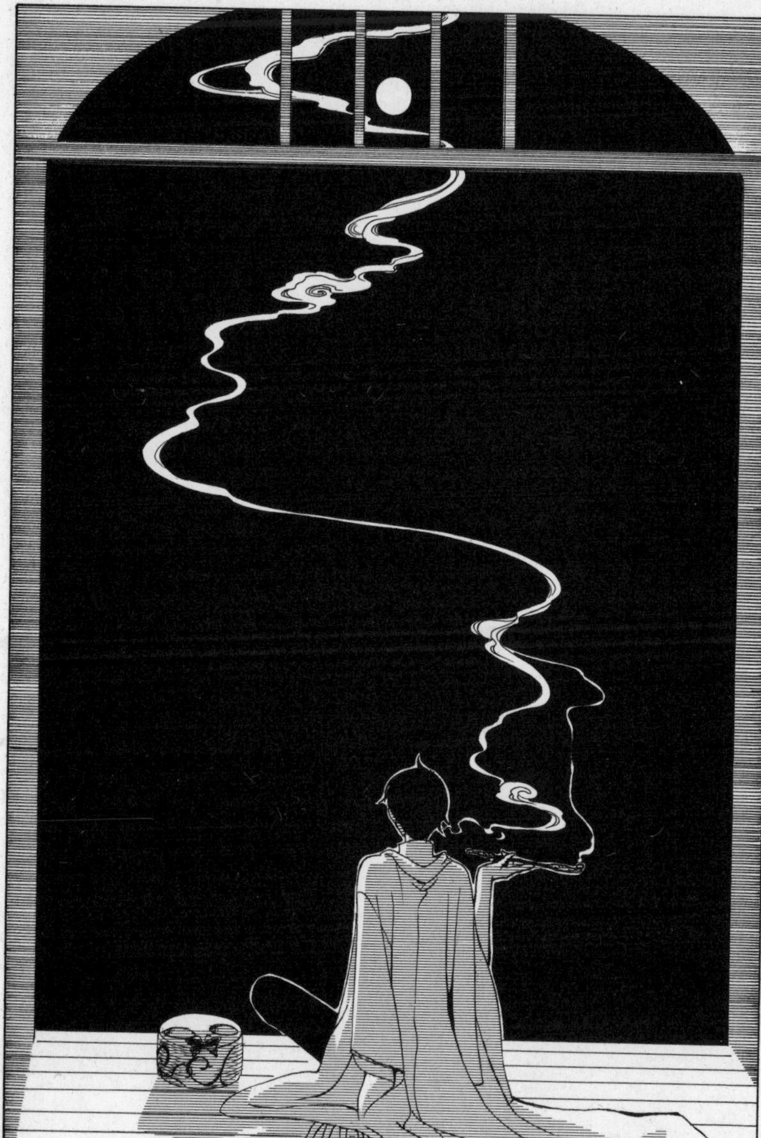

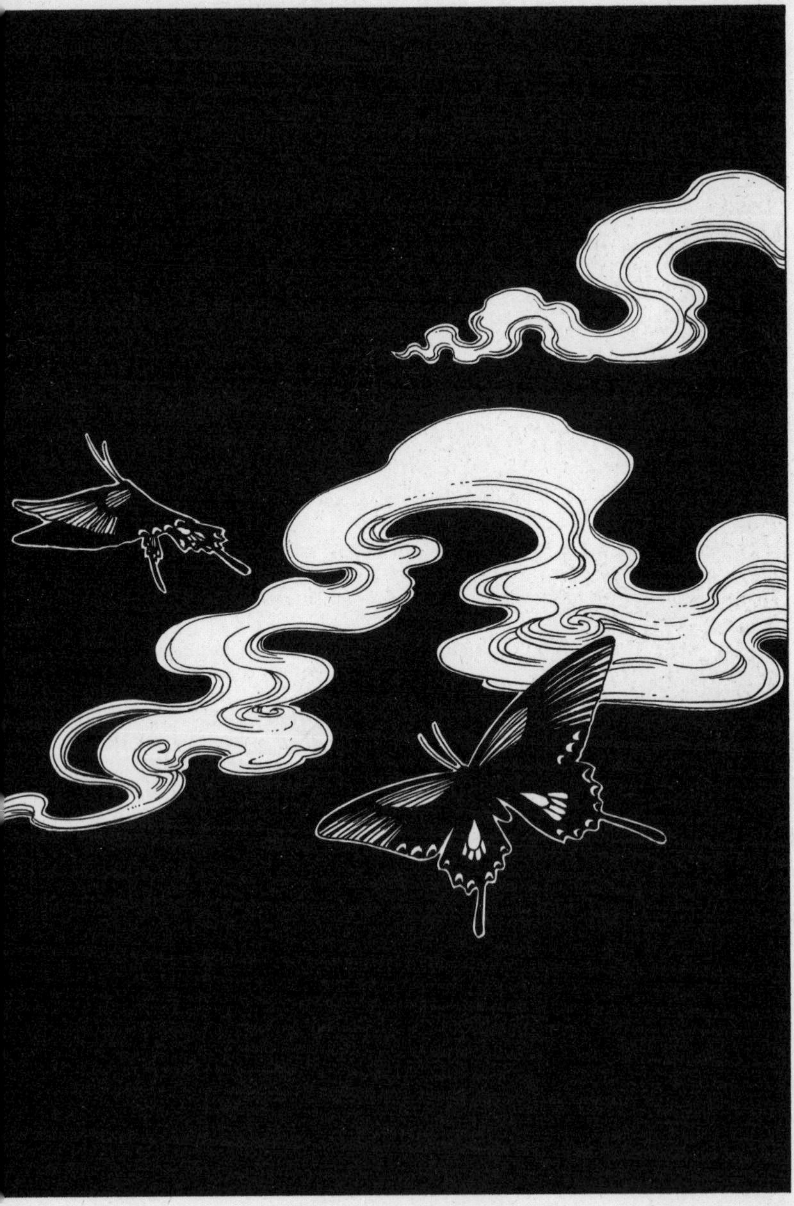

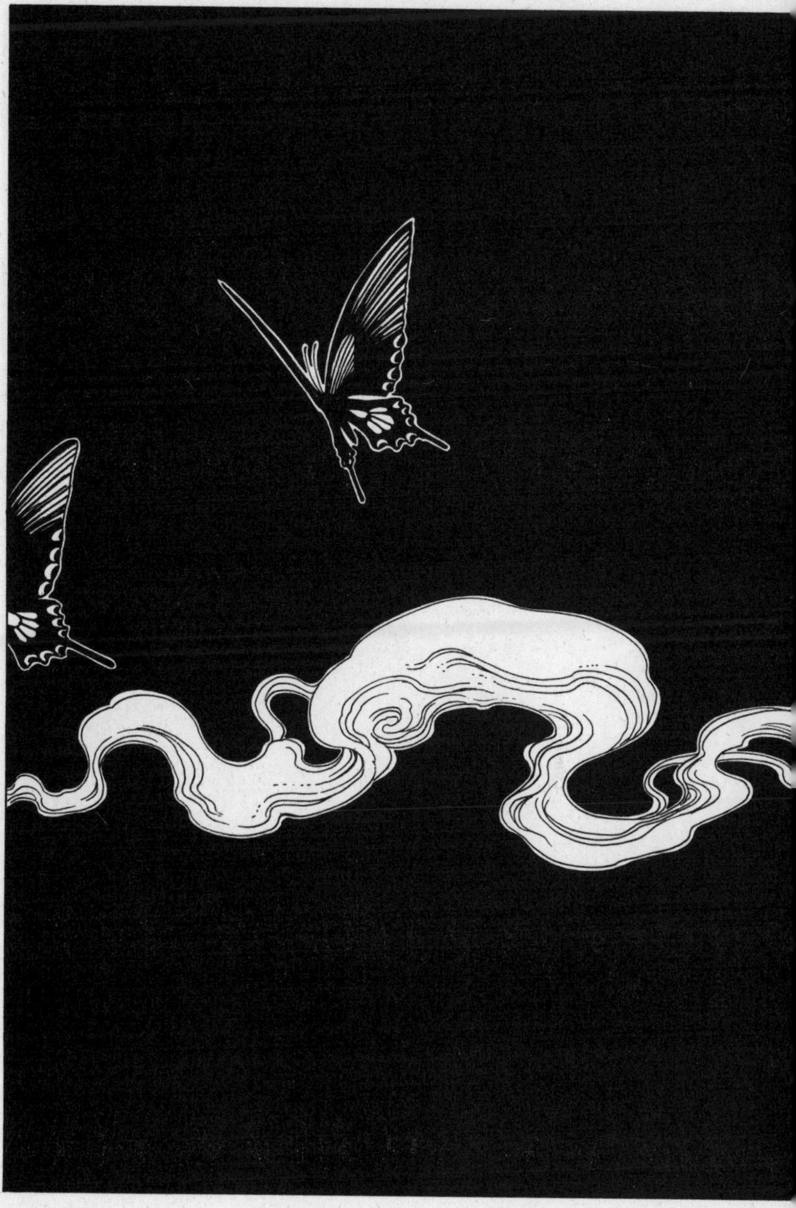

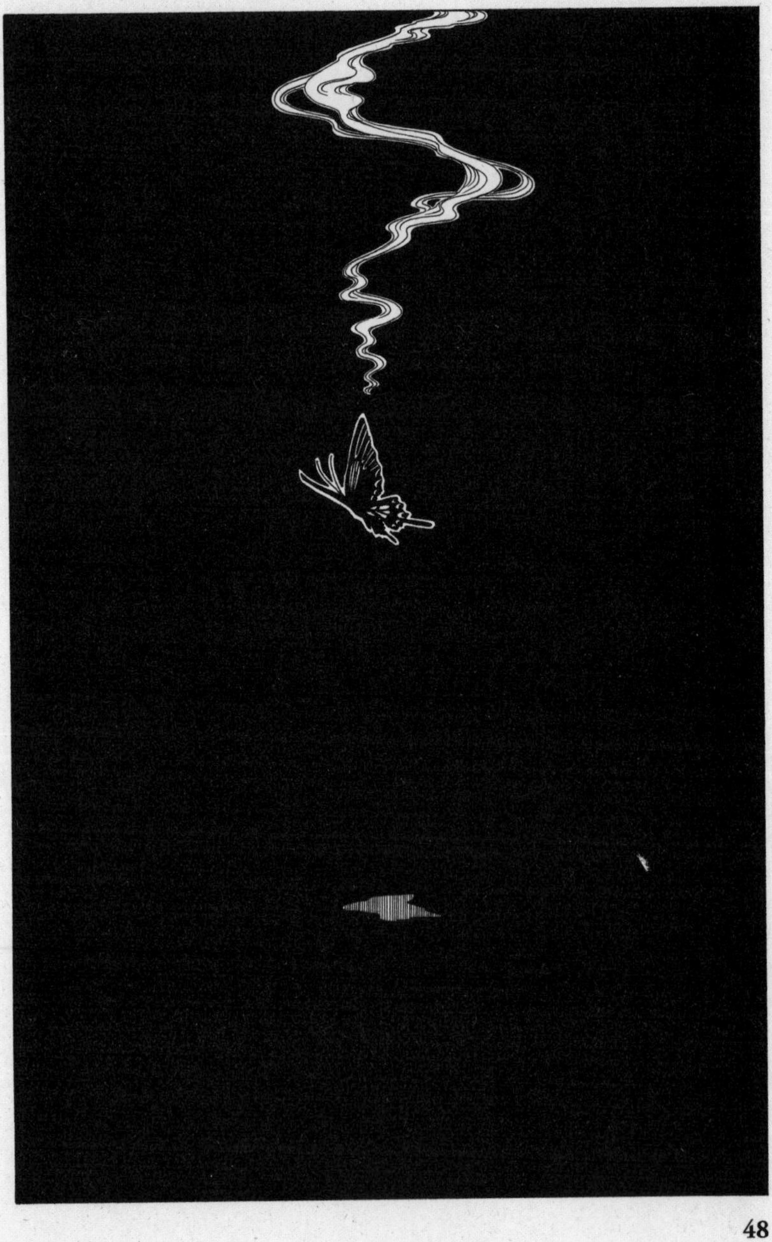

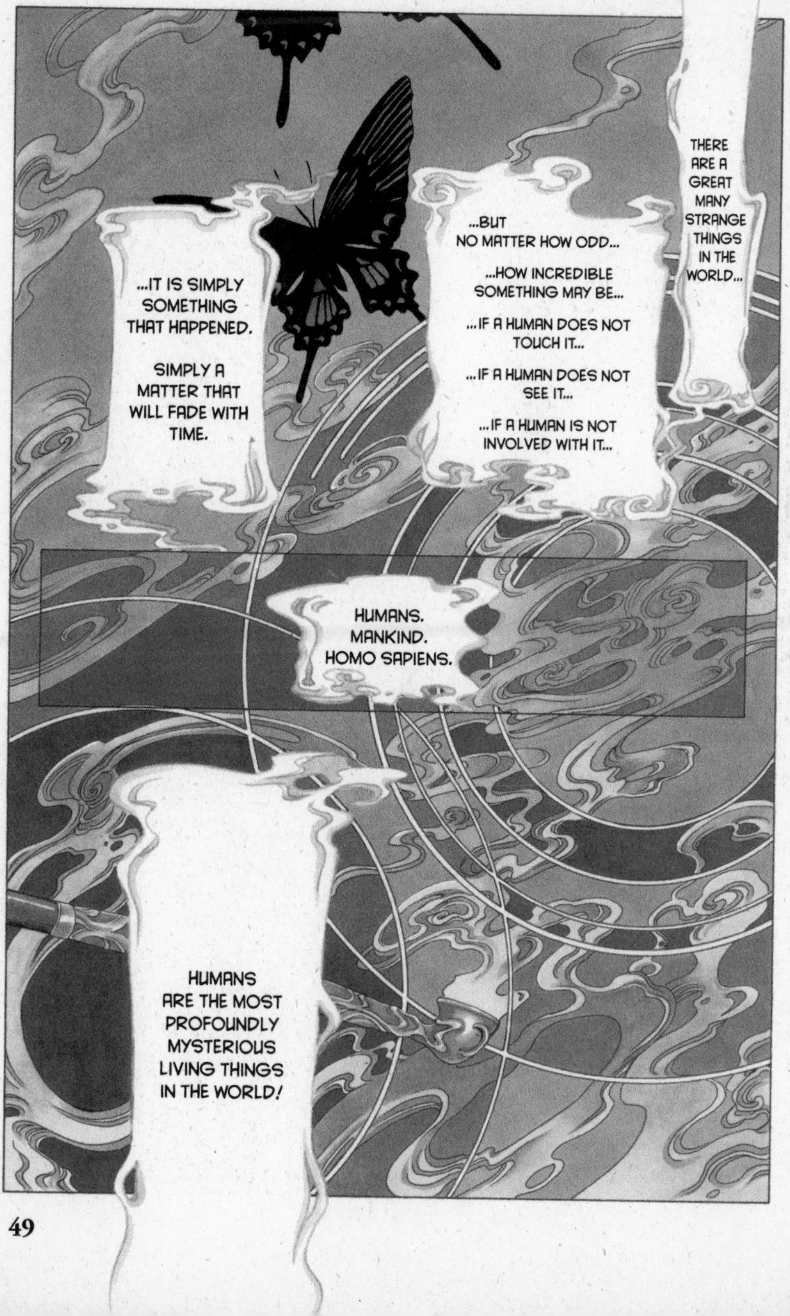
THERE ARE A GREAT MANY STRANGE THINGS IN THE WORLD...
...BUT NO MATTER HOW ODD...
...HOW INCREDIBLE SOMETHING MAY BE...
...IF A HUMAN DOES NOT TOUCH IT...
...IF A HUMAN DOES NOT SEE IT...
...IF A HUMAN IS NOT INVOLVED WITH IT...
...IT IS SIMPLY SOMETHING THAT HAPPENED.
SIMPLY A MATTER THAT WILL FADE WITH TIME.
HUMANS. MANKIND. HOMO SAPIENS.
HUMANS ARE THE MOST PROFOUNDLY MYSTERIOUS LIVING THINGS IN THE WORLD!

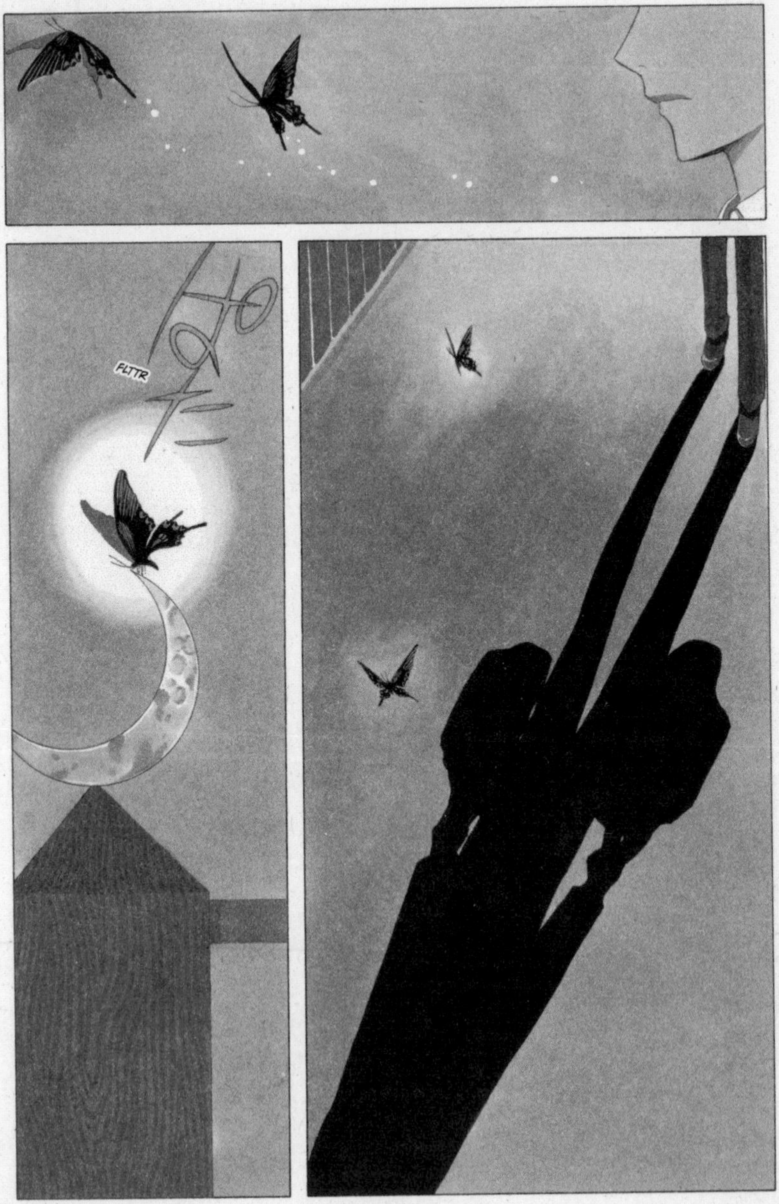
FLTTR

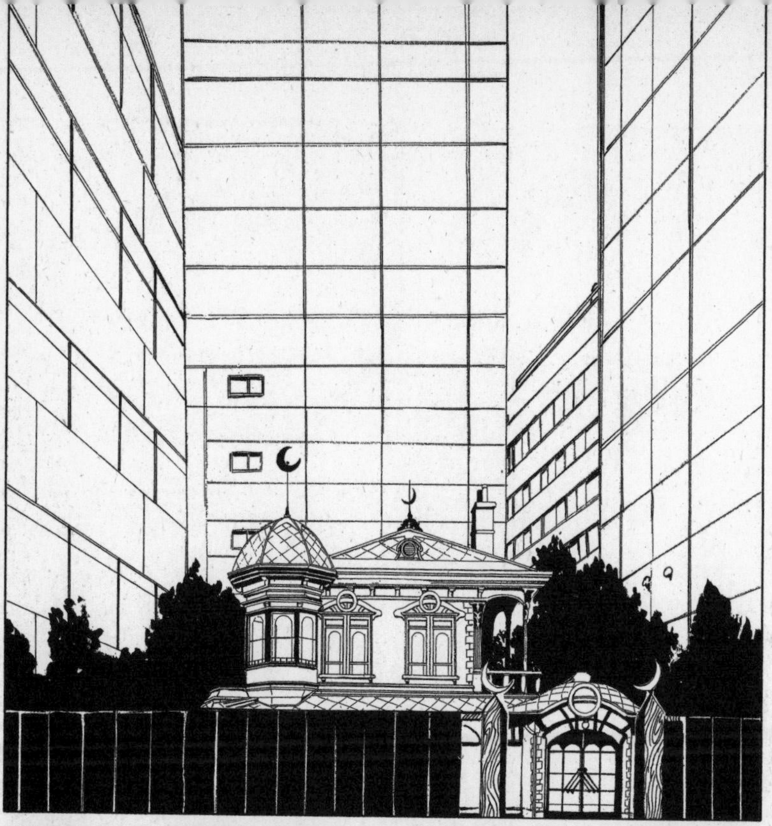

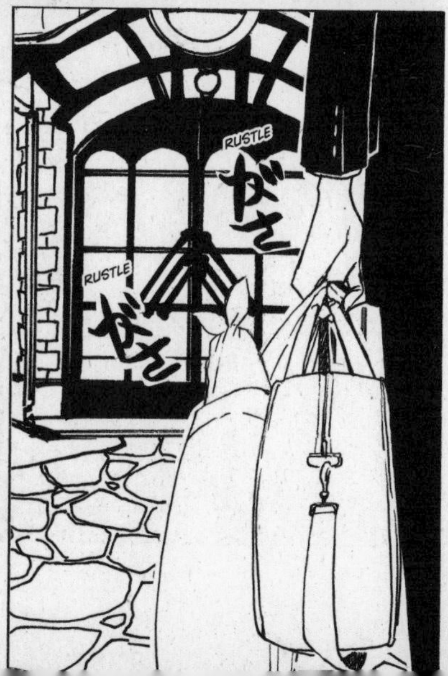
RUSTLE
がさ
RUSTLE
がさ

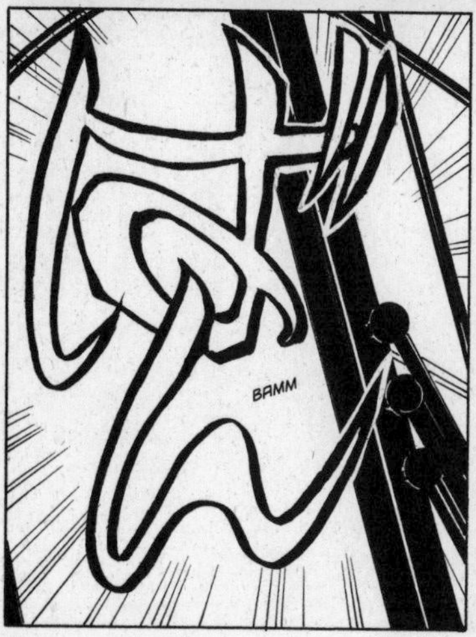
BAMM

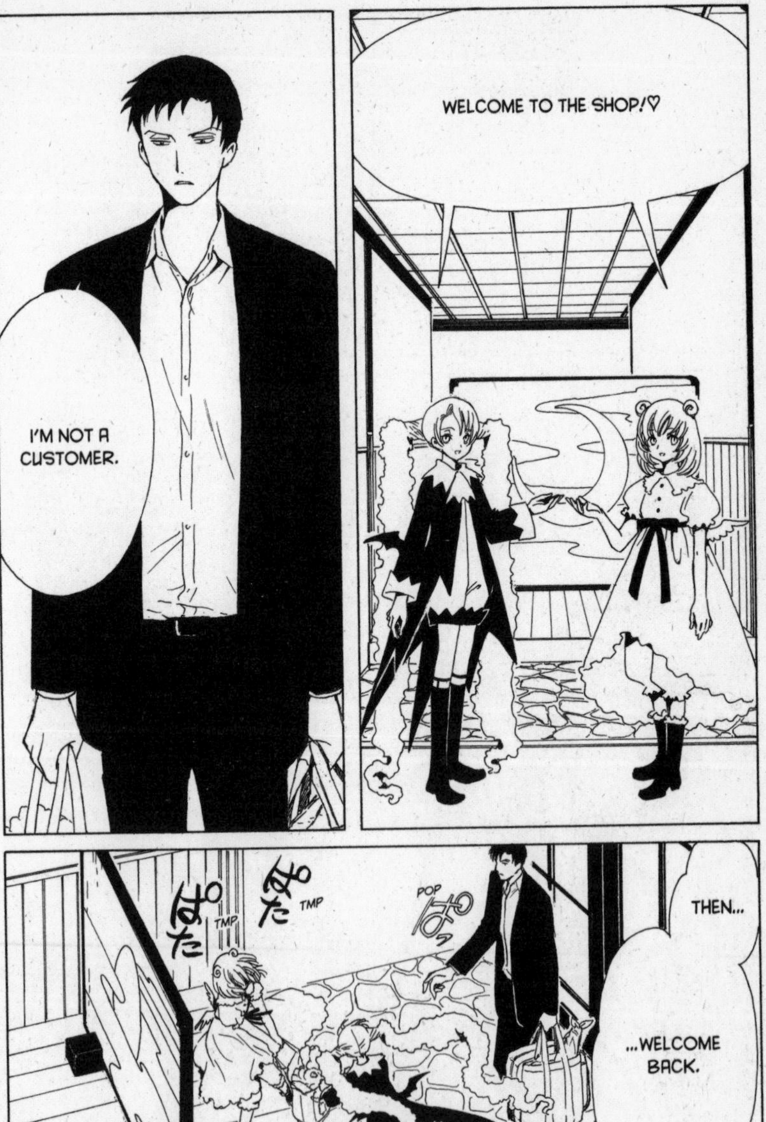
WELCOME TO THE SHOP!♡
I'M NOT A CUSTOMER.
THEN...
...WELCOME BACK.
ぱっ
POP
ぱた
TMP
ぱた
TMP

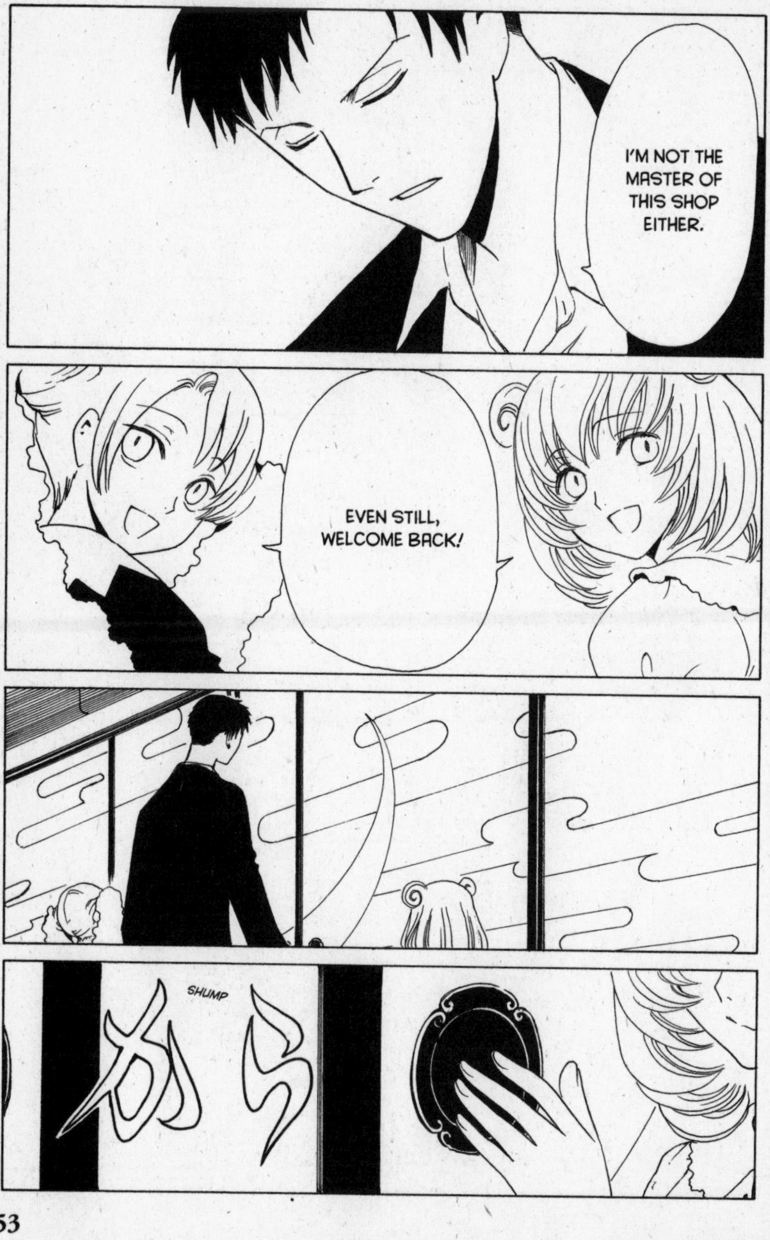
I'M NOT THE MASTER OF THIS SHOP EITHER.
EVEN STILL, WELCOME BACK!
SHUMP
から

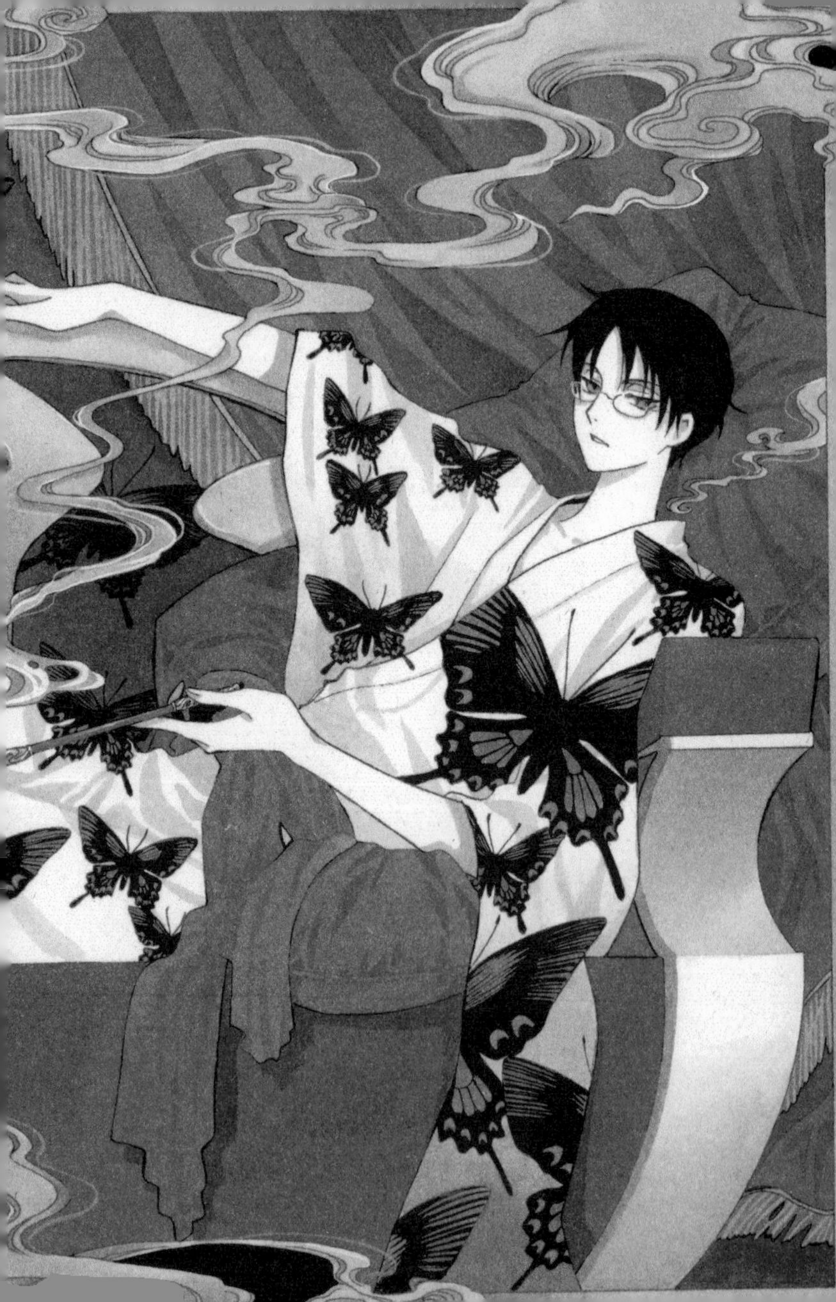

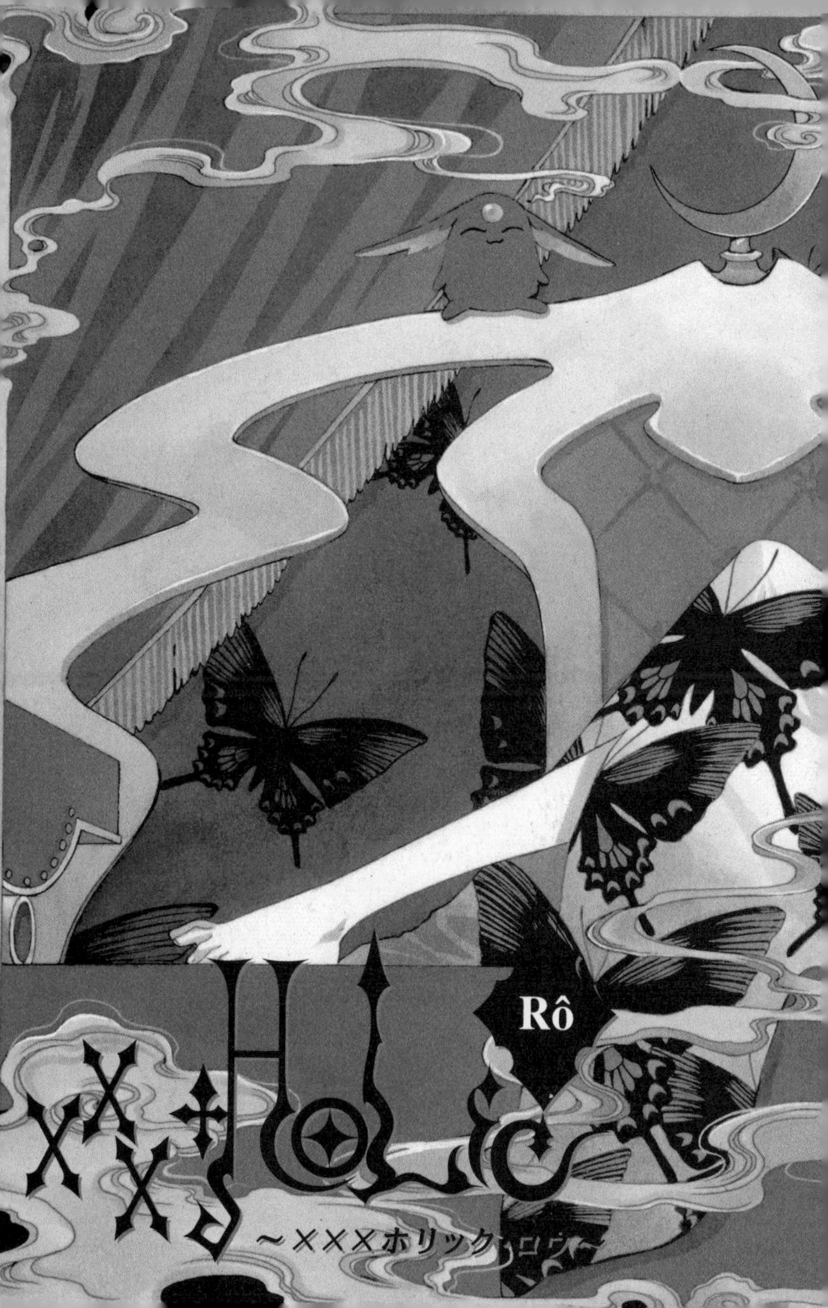
xxxHOLiC
Rô
~×××ホリック

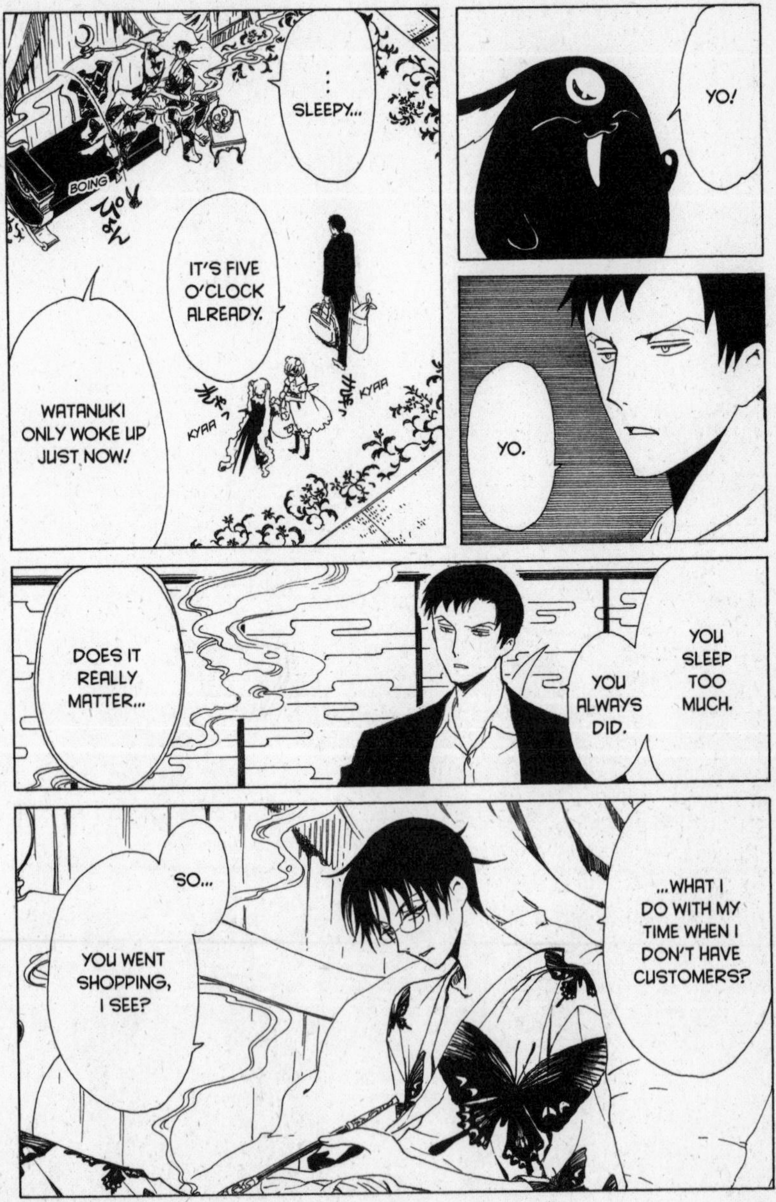
YO!
YO.
...SLEEPY...
BOING
IT'S FIVE O'CLOCK ALREADY.
KYAA
KYAA
WATANUKI ONLY WOKE UP JUST NOW!
YOU SLEEP TOO MUCH.
YOU ALWAYS DID.
DOES IT REALLY MATTER...
...WHAT I DO WITH MY TIME WHEN I DON'T HAVE CUSTOMERS?
SO...
YOU WENT SHOPPING, I SEE?

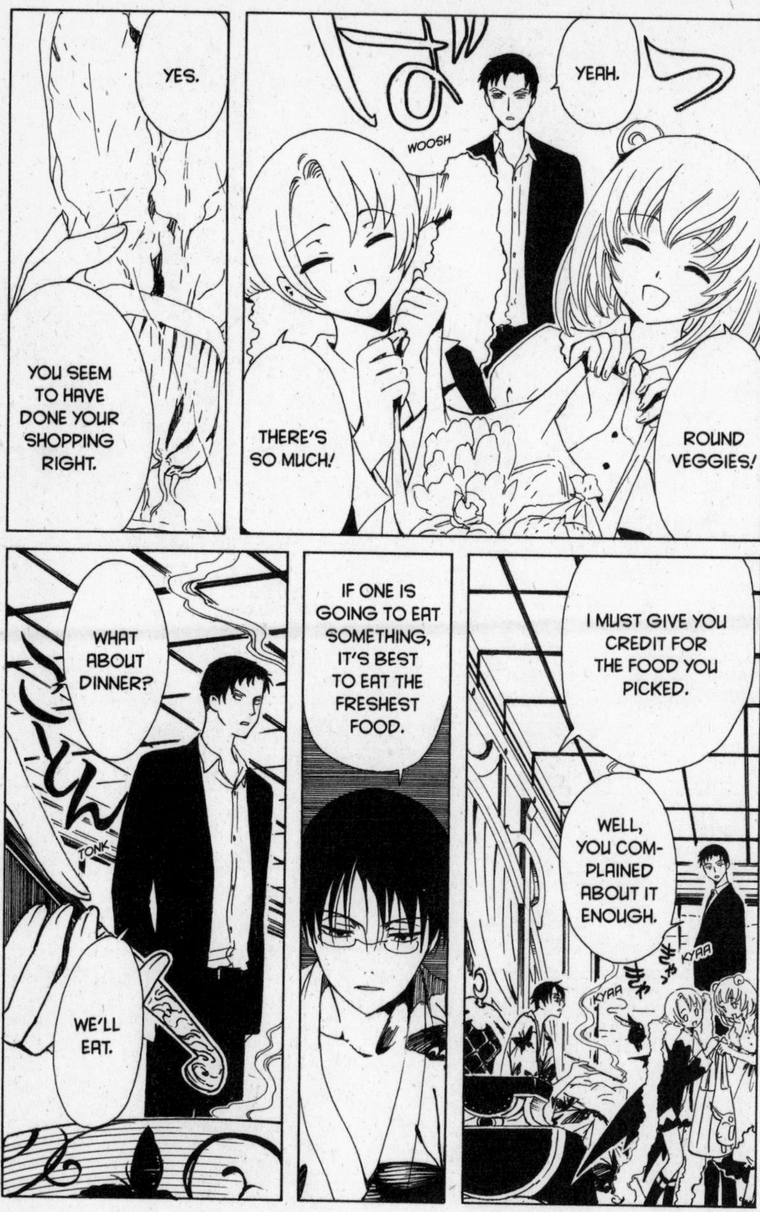
YEAH.
WOOSH
ROUND VEGGIES!
THERE'S SO MUCH!
YES.
YOU SEEM TO HAVE DONE YOUR SHOPPING RIGHT.
I MUST GIVE YOU CREDIT FOR THE FOOD YOU PICKED.
WELL, YOU COMPLAINED ABOUT IT ENOUGH.
KYAA
KYAA
IF ONE IS GOING TO EAT SOMETHING, IT'S BEST TO EAT THE FRESHEST FOOD.
WHAT ABOUT DINNER?
TONK
WE'LL EAT.

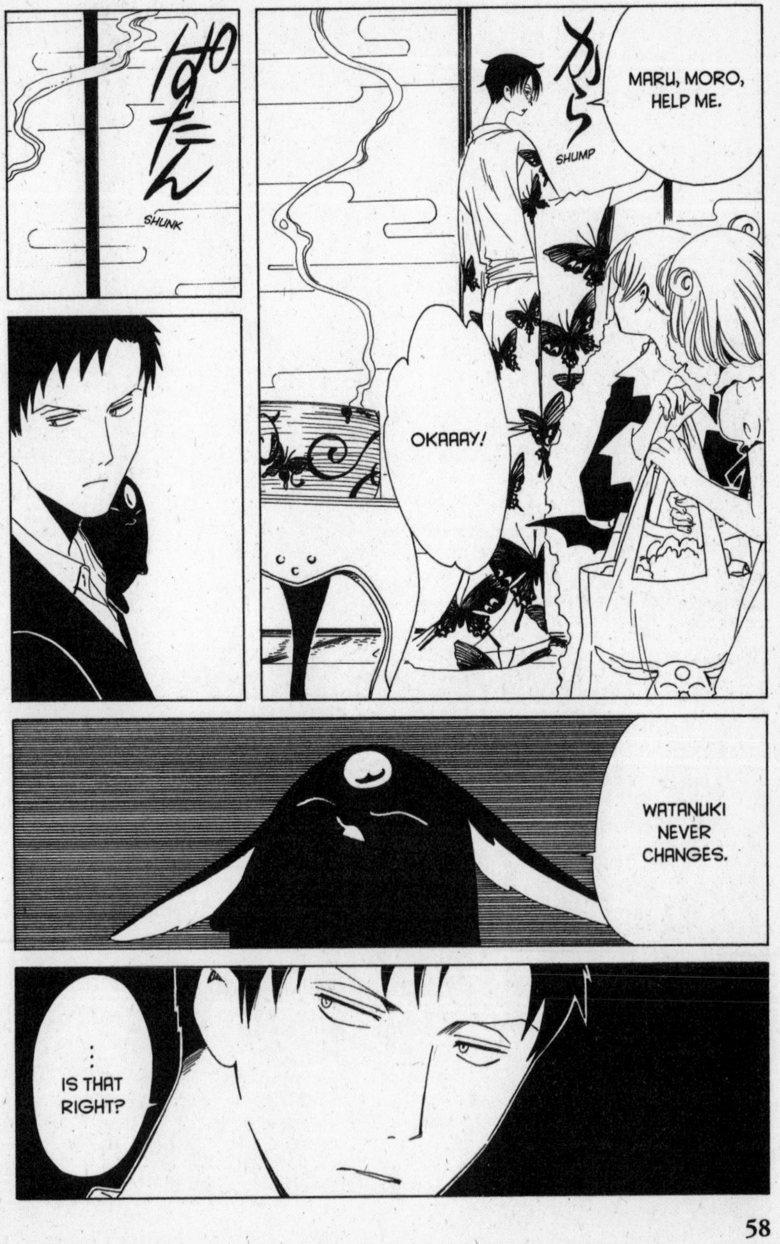
MARU, MORO, HELP ME.
から
SHUMP
OKAAAY!
ぱたん
SHUNK
WATANUKI NEVER CHANGES.
... IS THAT RIGHT?

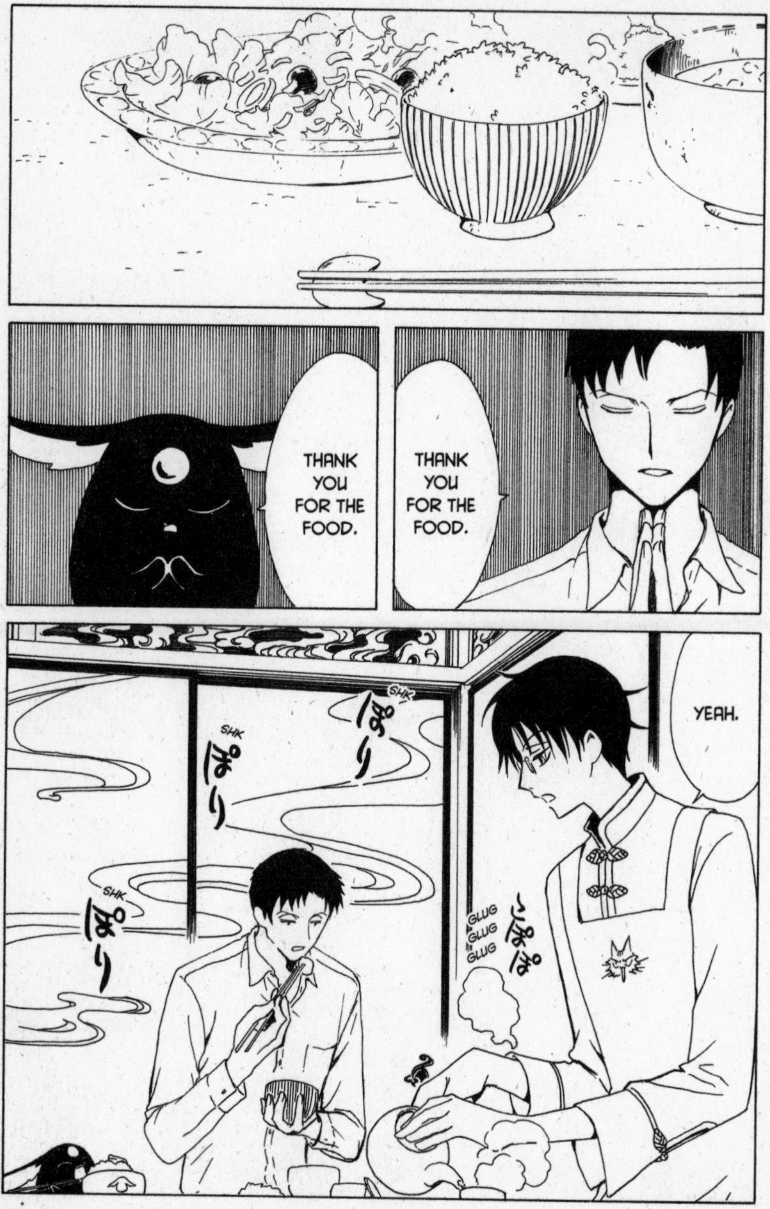
THANK YOU FOR THE FOOD.
THANK YOU FOR THE FOOD.
YEAH.
SHK
ぽり
SHK
ぽり
こぽぽ
GLUG GLUG GLUG
SHK
ぽり

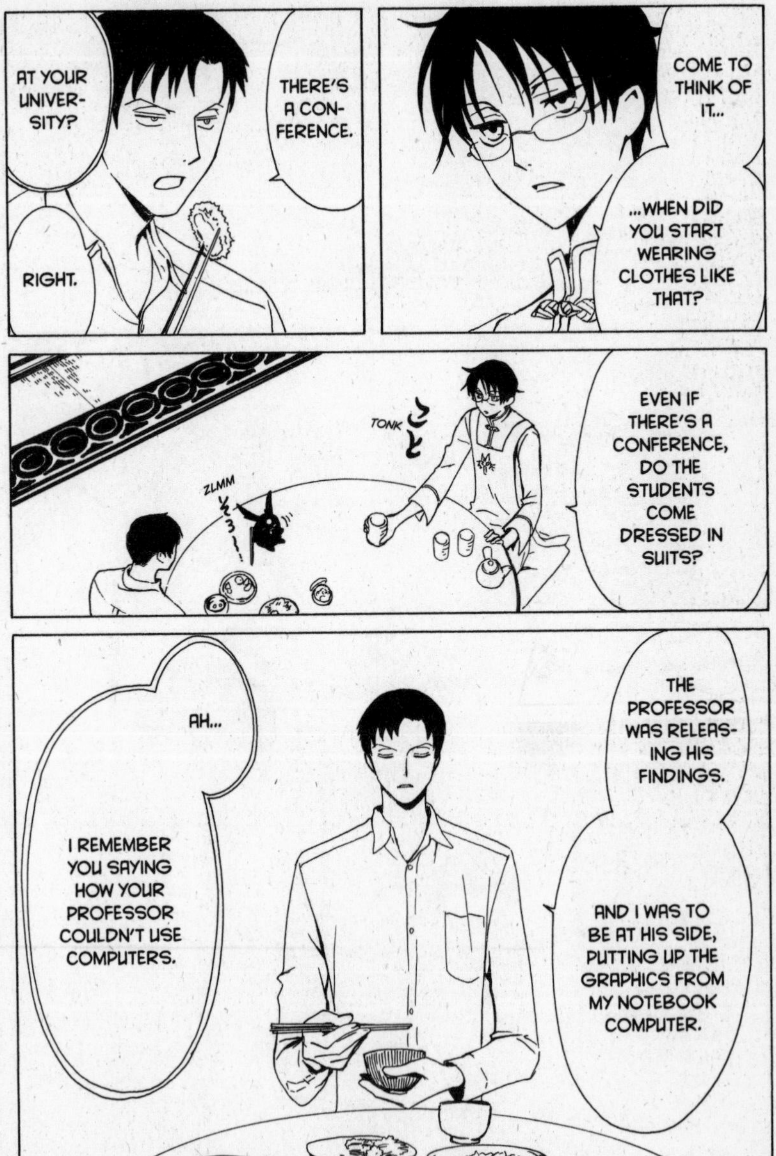
COME TO THINK OF IT...
...WHEN DID YOU START WEARING CLOTHES LIKE THAT?
THERE'S A CONFERENCE.
AT YOUR UNIVER-SITY?
RIGHT.
EVEN IF THERE'S A CONFERENCE, DO THE STUDENTS COME DRESSED IN SUITS?
TONK
ZLMM
THE PROFESSOR WAS RELEAS-ING HIS FINDINGS.
AND I WAS TO BE AT HIS SIDE, PUTTING UP THE GRAPHICS FROM MY NOTEBOOK COMPUTER.
AH...
I REMEMBER YOU SAYING HOW YOUR PROFESSOR COULDN'T USE COMPUTERS.

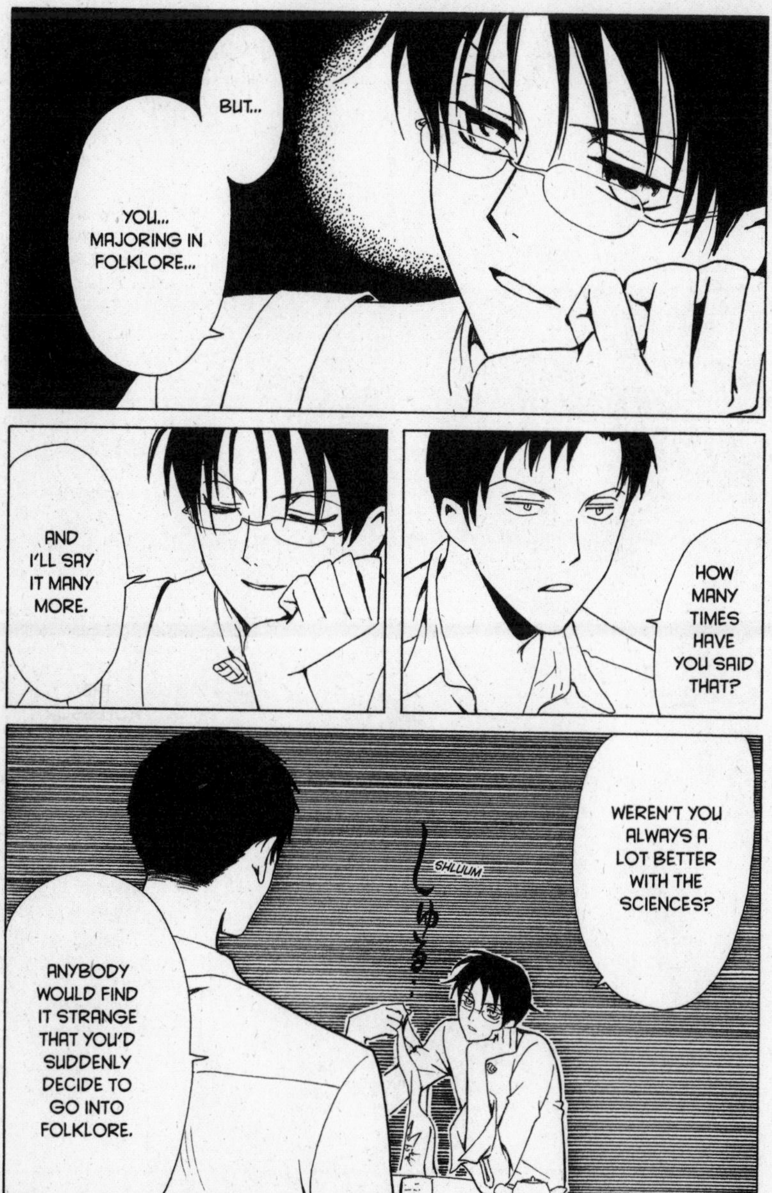
BUT...
YOU... MAJORING IN FOLKLORE...
HOW MANY TIMES HAVE YOU SAID THAT?
AND I'LL SAY IT MANY MORE.
WEREN'T YOU ALWAYS A LOT BETTER WITH THE SCIENCES?
SHLUUM
ANYBODY WOULD FIND IT STRANGE THAT YOU'D SUDDENLY DECIDE TO GO INTO FOLKLORE.

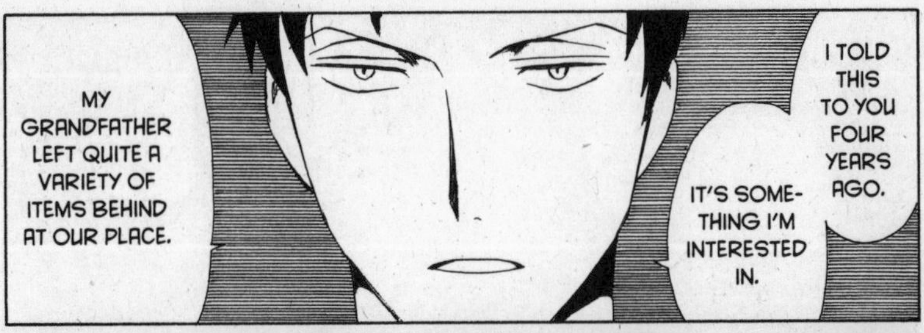
I TOLD THIS TO YOU FOUR YEARS AGO.
IT'S SOME-THING I'M INTERESTED IN.
MY GRANDFATHER LEFT QUITE A VARIETY OF ITEMS BEHIND AT OUR PLACE.

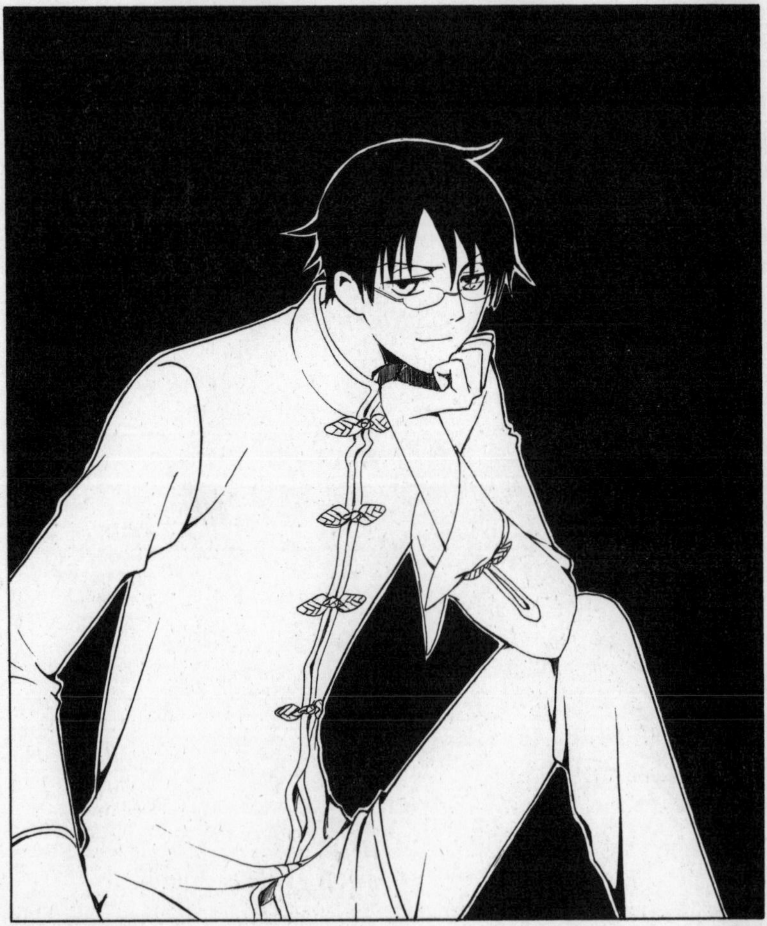

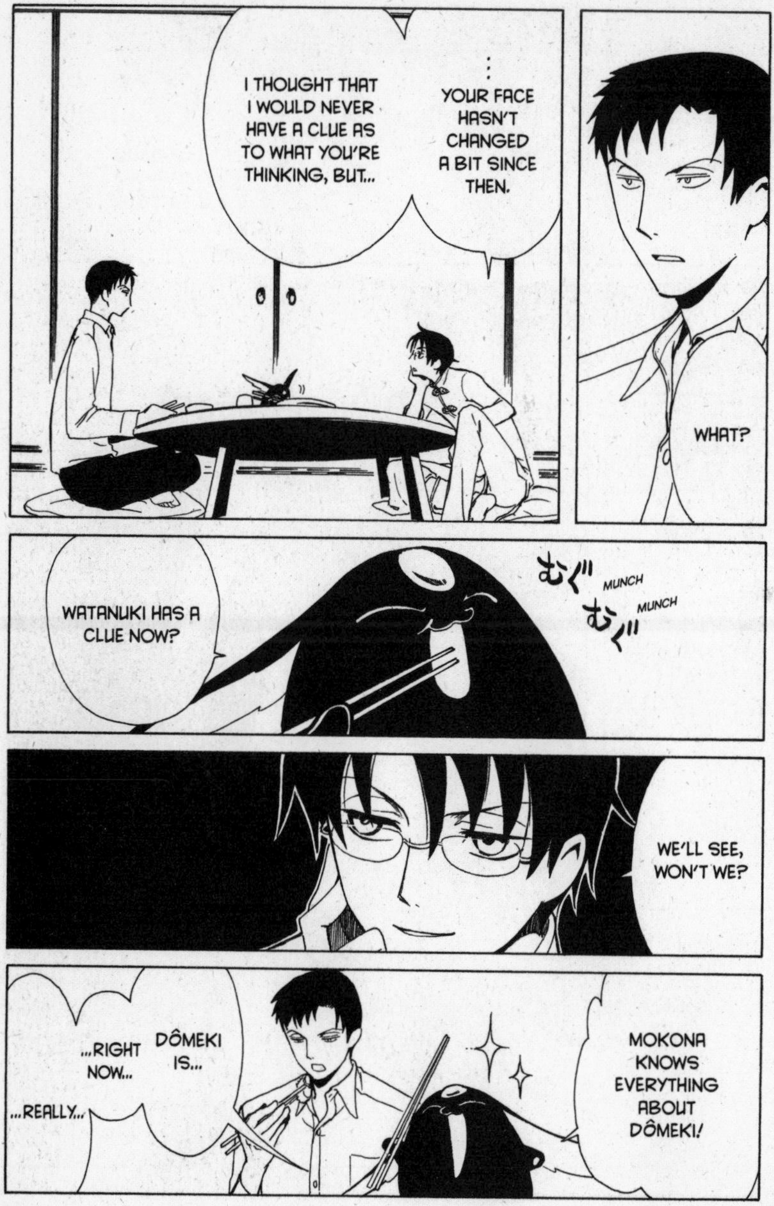

WHAT?
...
YOUR FACE HASN'T CHANGED A BIT SINCE THEN.
I THOUGHT THAT I WOULD NEVER HAVE A CLUE AS TO WHAT YOU'RE THINKING, BUT...
むぐ MUNCH
むぐ MUNCH
WATANUKI HAS A CLUE NOW?
WE'LL SEE, WON'T WE?
MOKONA KNOWS EVERYTHING ABOUT DÔMEKI!
DÔMEKI IS...
...RIGHT NOW...
...REALLY...

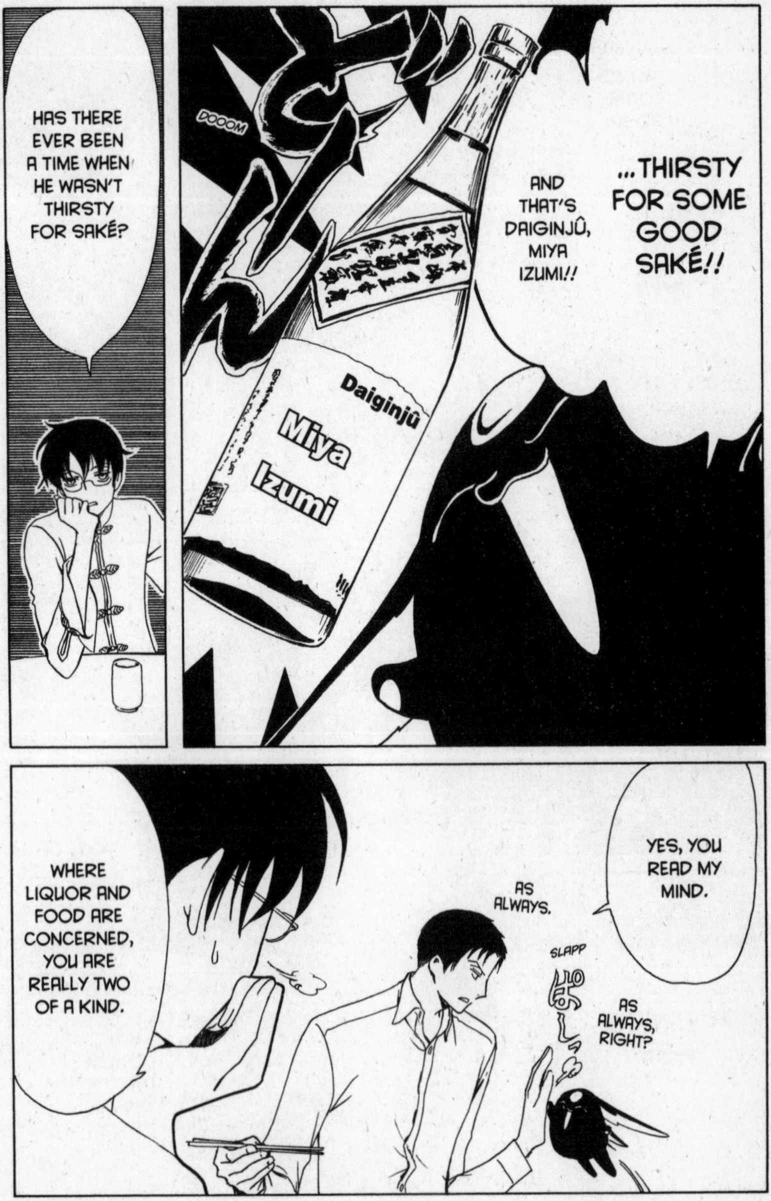
...THIRSTY FOR SOME GOOD SAKÉ!!
AND THAT'S DAIGINJÛ, MIYA IZUMI!!
DOOOM
Daiginjû
Miya Izumi
HAS THERE EVER BEEN A TIME WHEN HE WASN'T THIRSTY FOR SAKÉ?
YES, YOU READ MY MIND.
AS ALWAYS.
SLAPP
AS ALWAYS, RIGHT?
WHERE LIQUOR AND FOOD ARE CONCERNED, YOU ARE REALLY TWO OF A KIND.

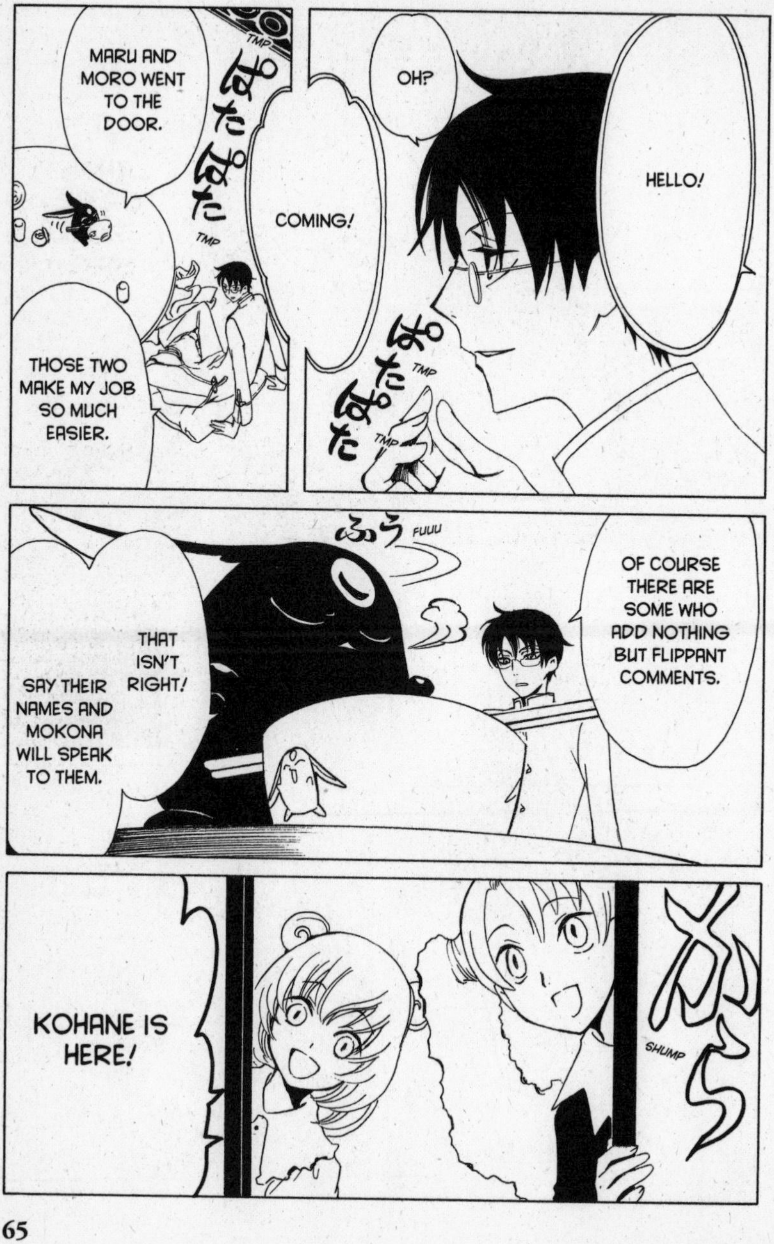
HELLO!
OH?
COMING!
ぱたぱた
TMP
TMP
ぱたぱた
TMP
TMP
MARU AND MORO WENT TO THE DOOR.
THOSE TWO MAKE MY JOB SO MUCH EASIER.
OF COURSE THERE ARE SOME WHO ADD NOTHING BUT FLIPPANT COMMENTS.
ふう
FUUU
THAT ISN'T RIGHT!
SAY THEIR NAMES AND MOKONA WILL SPEAK TO THEM.
SHUMP
KOHANE IS HERE!

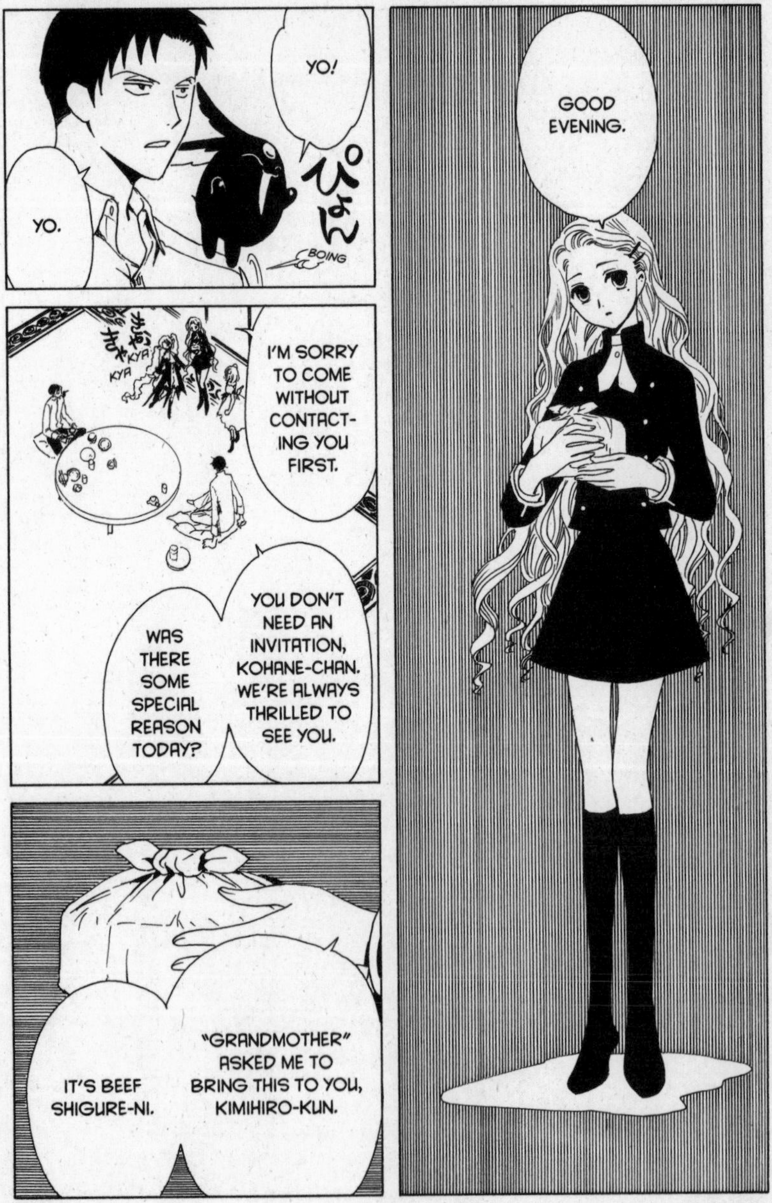

GOOD EVENING.
YO!
ぴょん
BOING
YO.
I'M SORRY TO COME WITHOUT CONTACTING YOU FIRST.
KYA KYA
YOU DON'T NEED AN INVITATION, KOHANE-CHAN. WE'RE ALWAYS THRILLED TO SEE YOU.
WAS THERE SOME SPECIAL REASON TODAY?
"GRANDMOTHER" ASKED ME TO BRING THIS TO YOU, KIMIHIRO-KUN.
IT'S BEEF SHIGURE-NI.

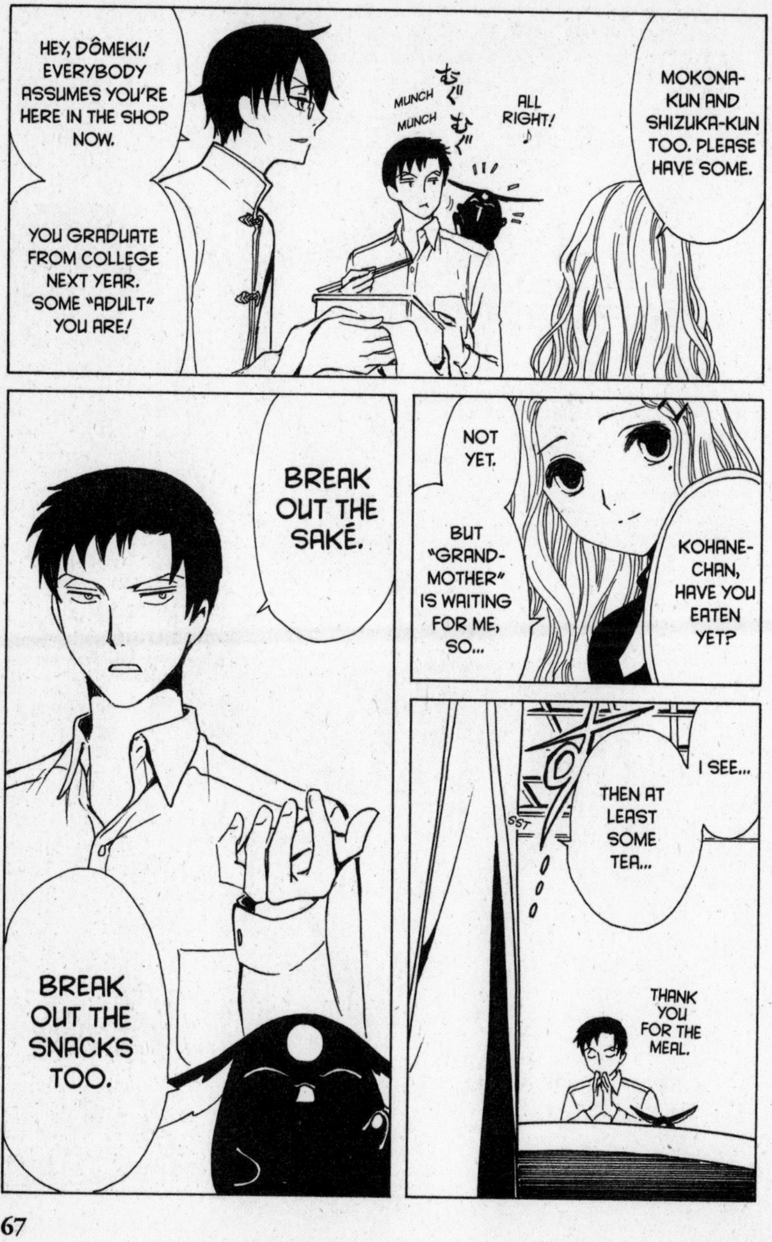
MOKONA-KUN AND SHIZUKA-KUN TOO. PLEASE HAVE SOME.
ALL RIGHT! ♪
むぐ むぐ
MUNCH MUNCH
HEY, DÔMEKI! EVERYBODY ASSUMES YOU'RE HERE IN THE SHOP NOW.
YOU GRADUATE FROM COLLEGE NEXT YEAR. SOME "ADULT" YOU ARE!
KOHANE-CHAN, HAVE YOU EATEN YET?
NOT YET.
BUT "GRANDMOTHER" IS WAITING FOR ME, SO...
I SEE...
THEN AT LEAST SOME TEA...
SST
THANK YOU FOR THE MEAL.
BREAK OUT THE SAKÉ.
BREAK OUT THE SNACKS TOO.

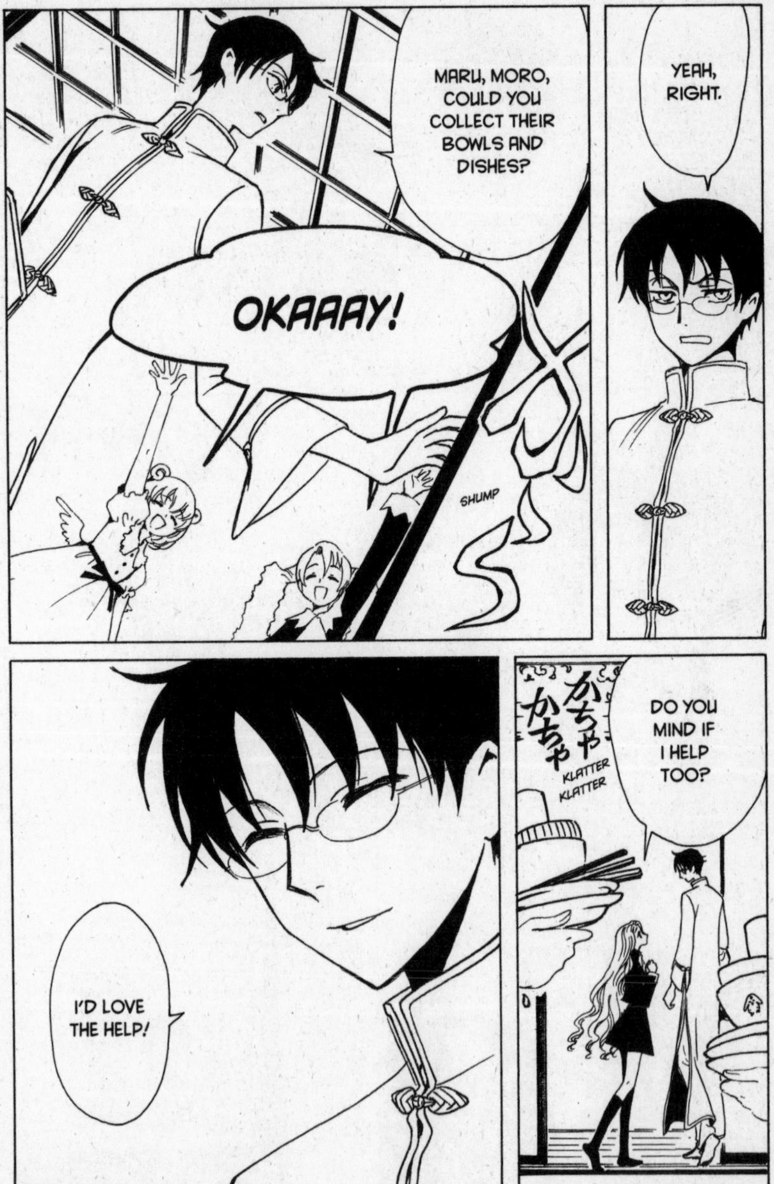
YEAH, RIGHT.
MARU, MORO, COULD YOU COLLECT THEIR BOWLS AND DISHES?
OKAAAY!
SHUMP
DO YOU MIND IF I HELP TOO?
かちゃかちゃ
KLATTER KLATTER
I'D LOVE THE HELP!

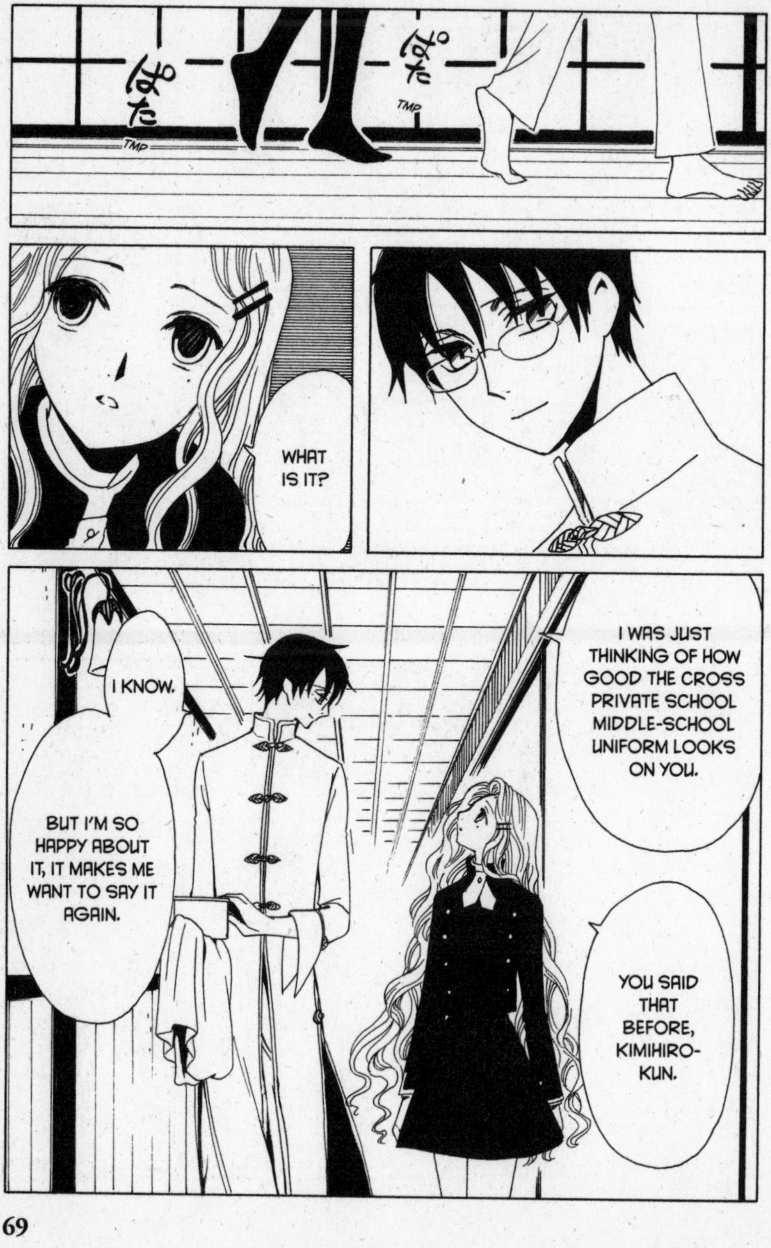
ぱた
TMP
ぱた
TMP
WHAT IS IT?
I WAS JUST THINKING OF HOW GOOD THE CROSS PRIVATE SCHOOL MIDDLE-SCHOOL UNIFORM LOOKS ON YOU.
YOU SAID THAT BEFORE, KIMIHIRO-KUN.
I KNOW.
BUT I'M SO HAPPY ABOUT IT, IT MAKES ME WANT TO SAY IT AGAIN.

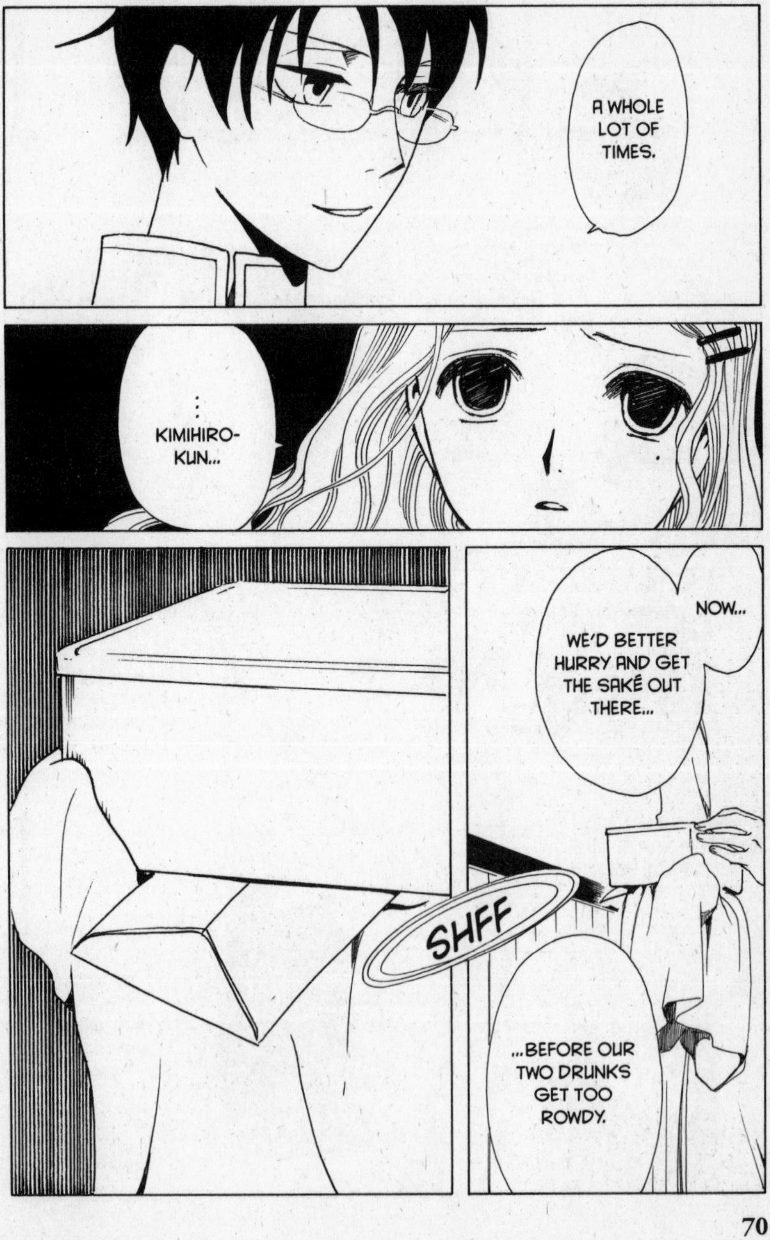
A WHOLE LOT OF TIMES.
...
KIMIHIRO-KUN...
NOW...
WE'D BETTER HURRY AND GET THE SAKÉ OUT THERE...
SHFF
...BEFORE OUR TWO DRUNKS GET TOO ROWDY.

A LETTER?

YES.

FROM YOUR "GRAND-MOTHER."

IT SAYS THAT I SHOULD EXPECT A CUSTOMER AT THE SHOP TOMORROW.

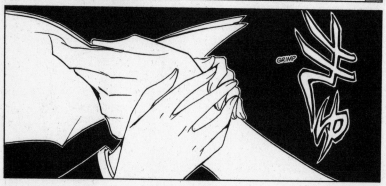

GRIMP!

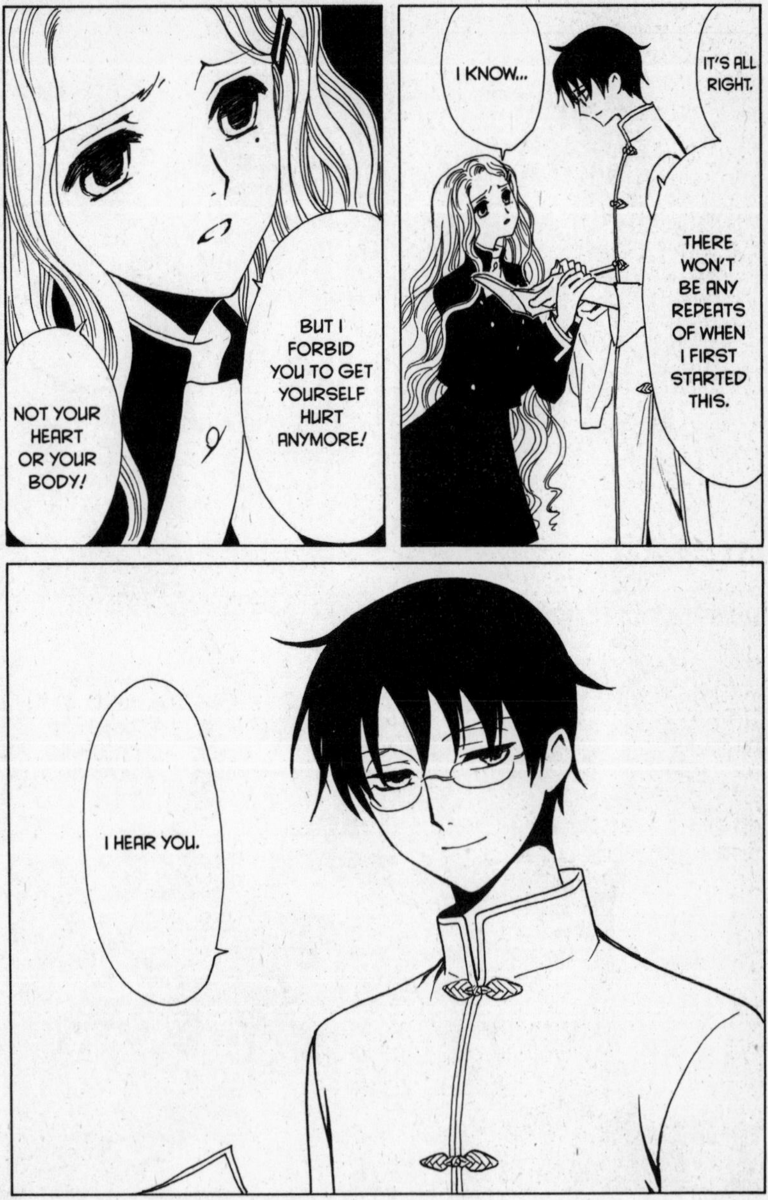
IT'S ALL RIGHT.
I KNOW...
THERE WON'T BE ANY REPEATS OF WHEN I FIRST STARTED THIS.
BUT I FORBID YOU TO GET YOURSELF HURT ANYMORE!
NOT YOUR HEART OR YOUR BODY!
I HEAR YOU.

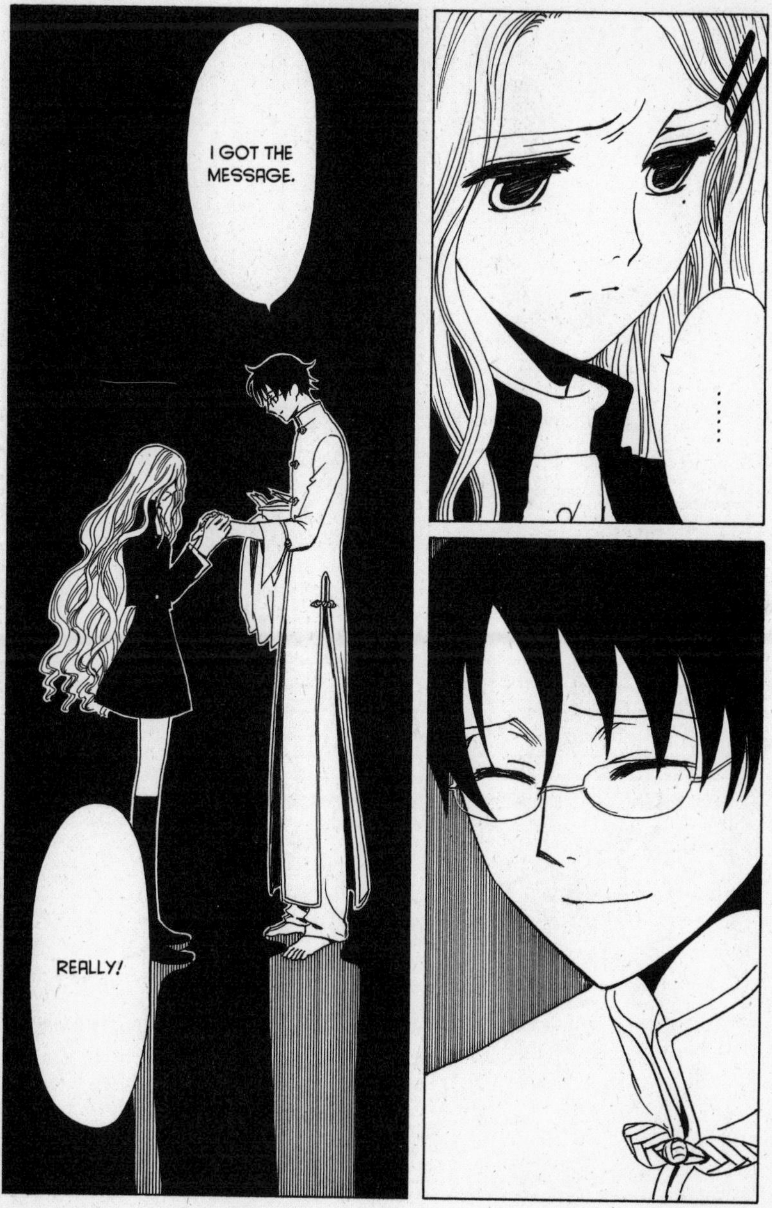
......
I GOT THE MESSAGE.
REALLY!

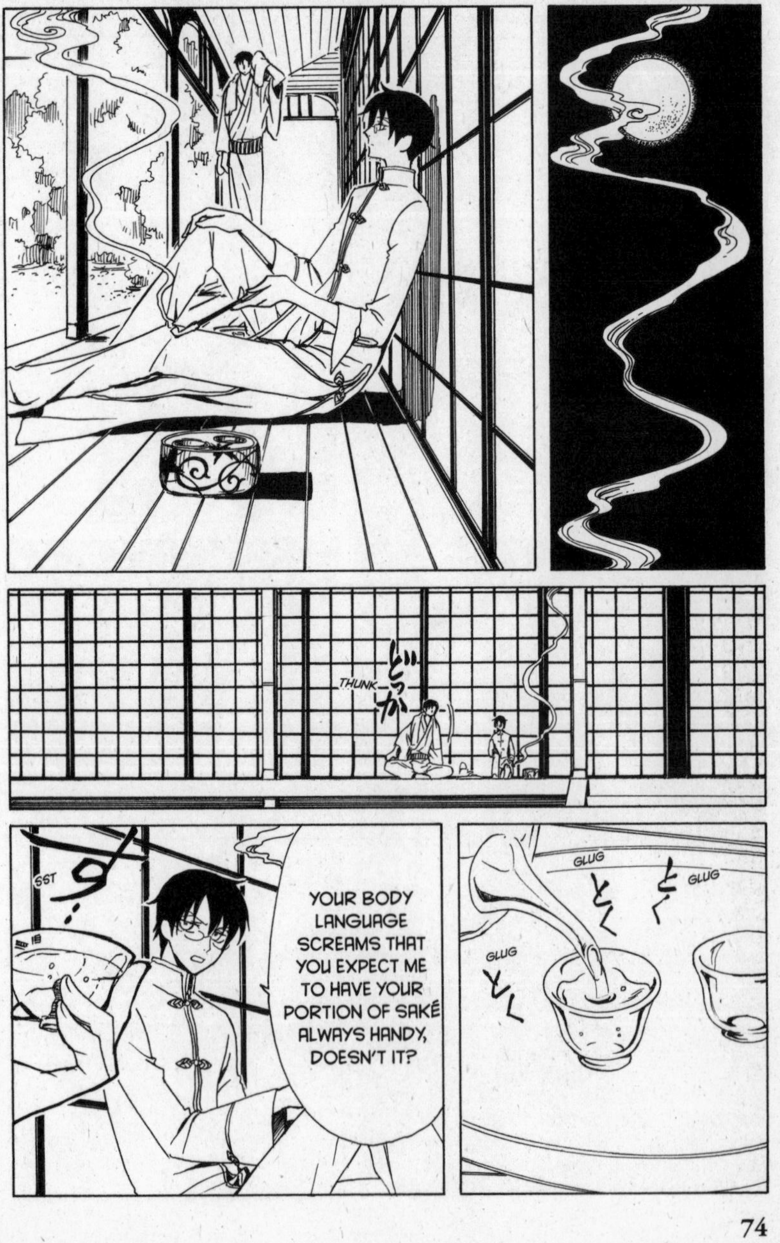
どっか
THUNK
GLUG
とく
GLUG
とく
GLUG
とく
SST
YOUR BODY LANGUAGE SCREAMS THAT YOU EXPECT ME TO HAVE YOUR PORTION OF SAKÉ ALWAYS HANDY, DOESN'T IT?

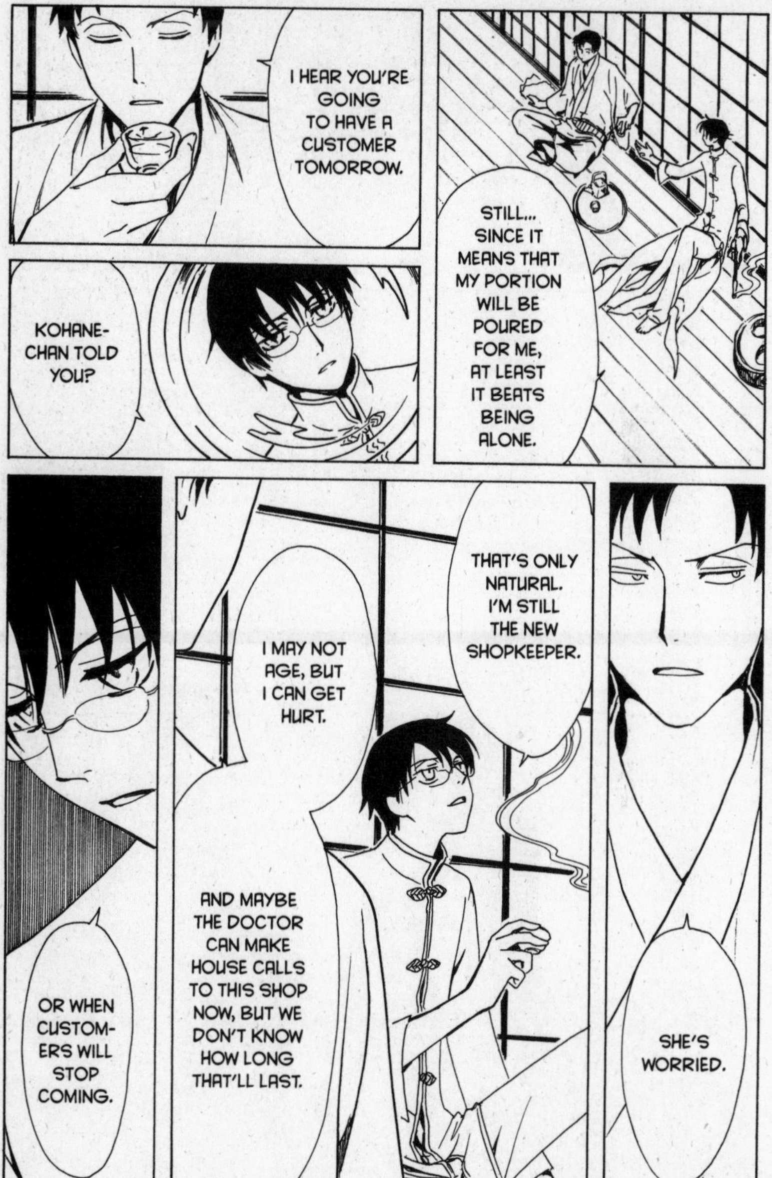
STILL... SINCE IT MEANS THAT MY PORTION WILL BE POURED FOR ME, AT LEAST IT BEATS BEING ALONE.
I HEAR YOU'RE GOING TO HAVE A CUSTOMER TOMORROW.
KOHANE-CHAN TOLD YOU?
SHE'S WORRIED.
THAT'S ONLY NATURAL. I'M STILL THE NEW SHOPKEEPER.
I MAY NOT AGE, BUT I CAN GET HURT.
AND MAYBE THE DOCTOR CAN MAKE HOUSE CALLS TO THIS SHOP NOW, BUT WE DON'T KNOW HOW LONG THAT'LL LAST.
OR WHEN CUSTOM-ERS WILL STOP COMING.

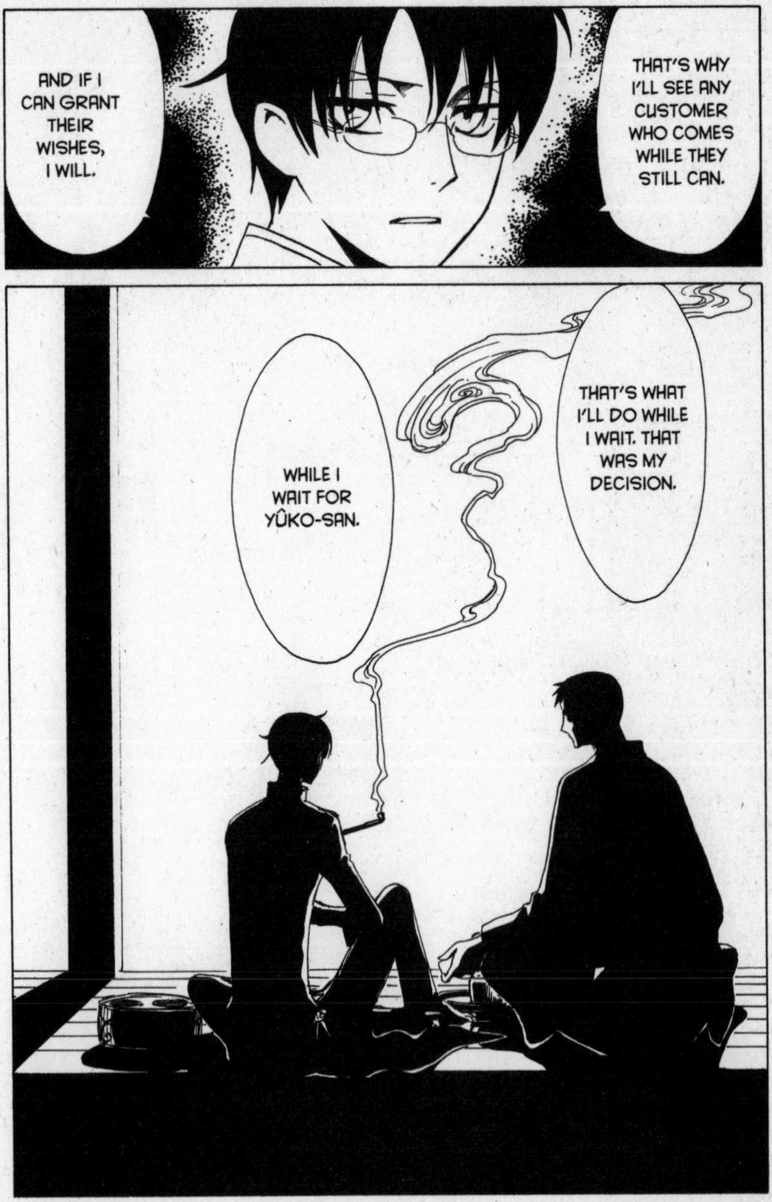
THAT'S WHY I'LL SEE ANY CUSTOMER WHO COMES WHILE THEY STILL CAN.
AND IF I CAN GRANT THEIR WISHES, I WILL.
THAT'S WHAT I'LL DO WHILE I WAIT. THAT WAS MY DECISION.
WHILE I WAIT FOR YÛKO-SAN.

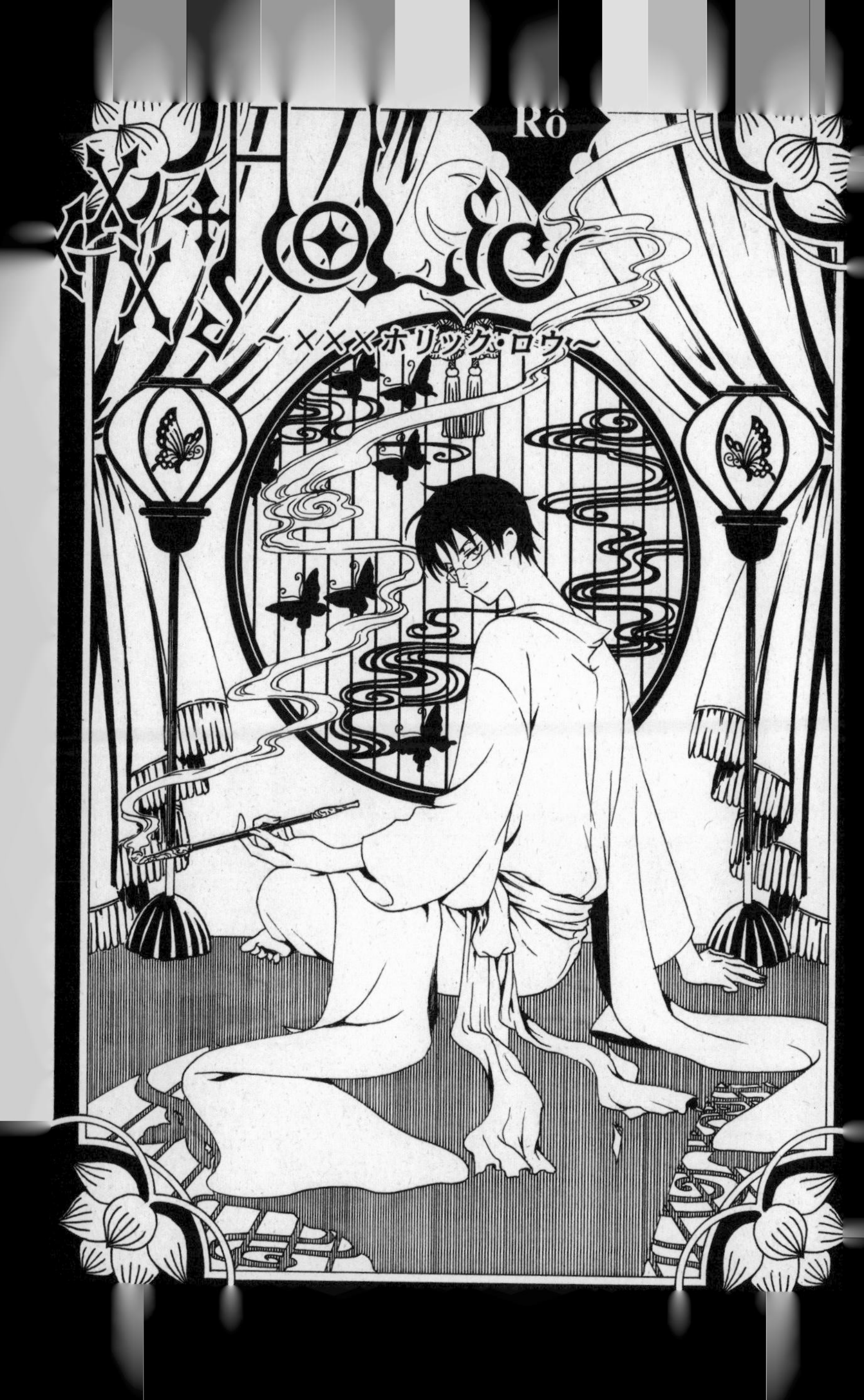

Rō
xxxHOLiC
〜×××ホリック·ロウ〜

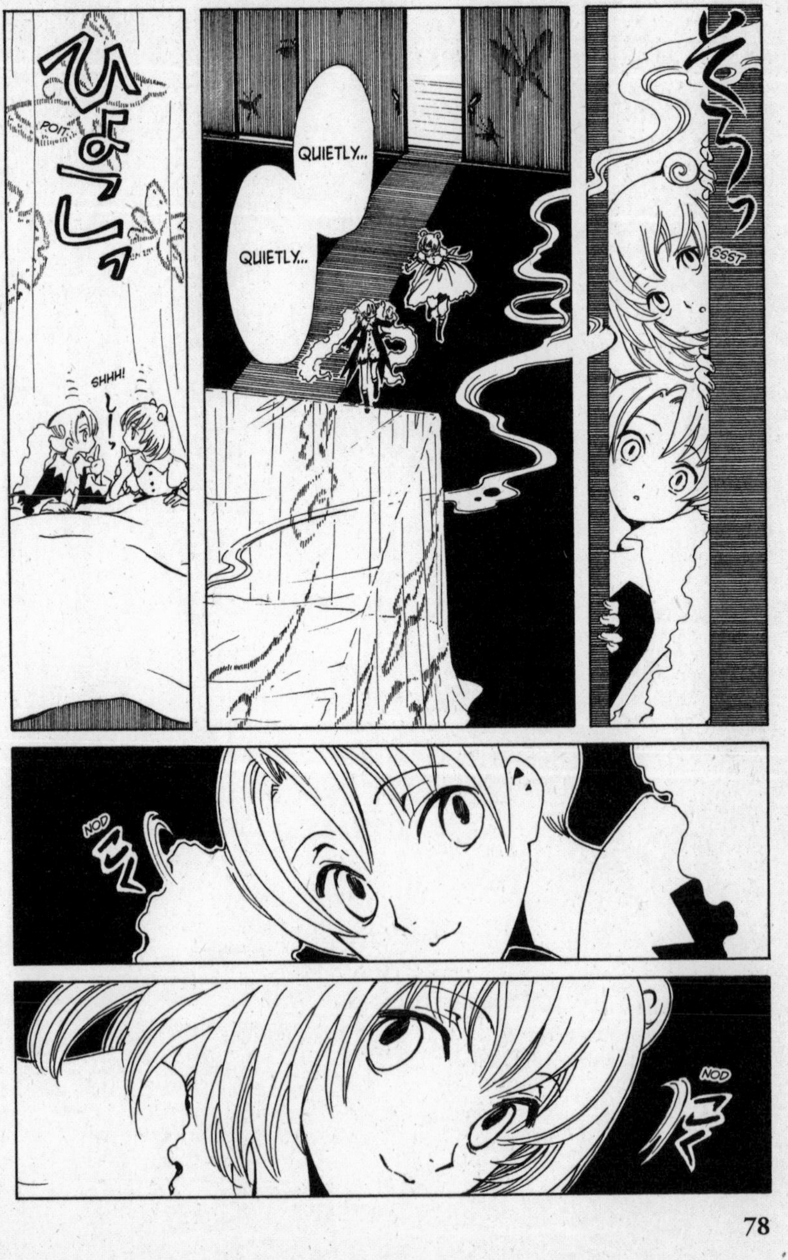
SSST
QUIETLY...
QUIETLY...
POIT
SHHH!
NOD
NOD

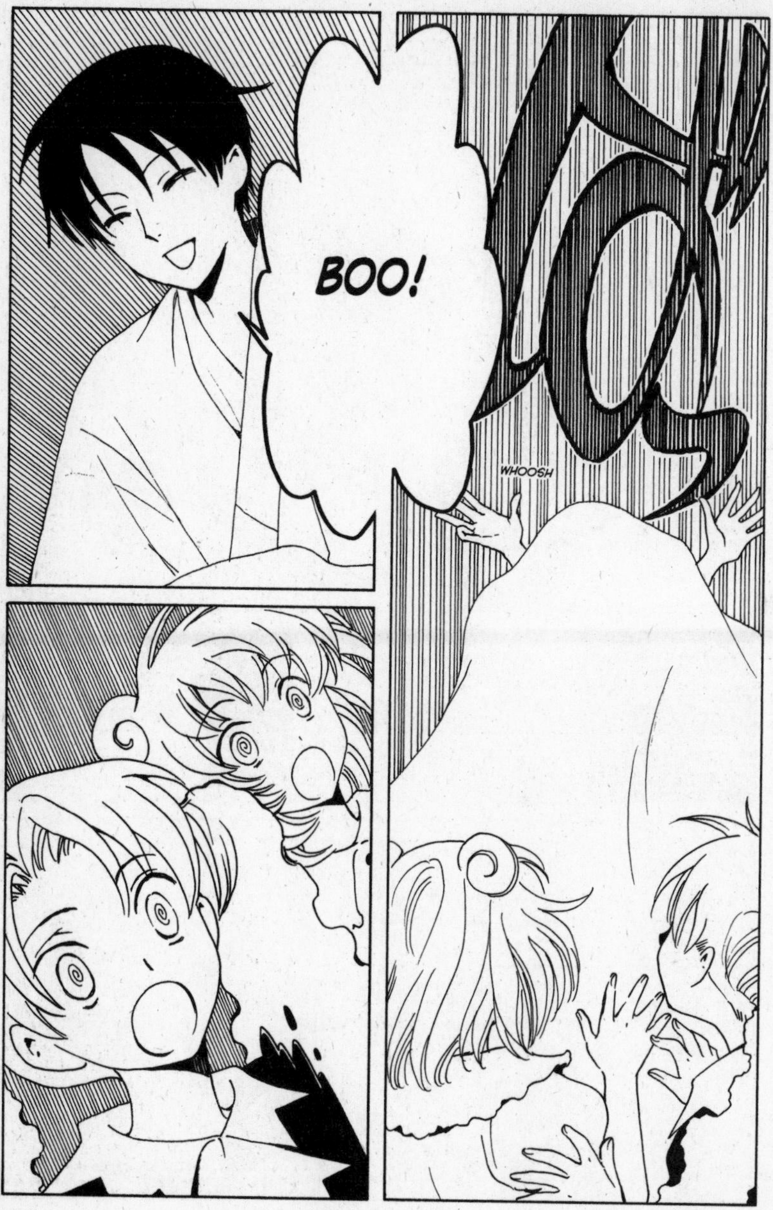
WHOOSH
BOO!

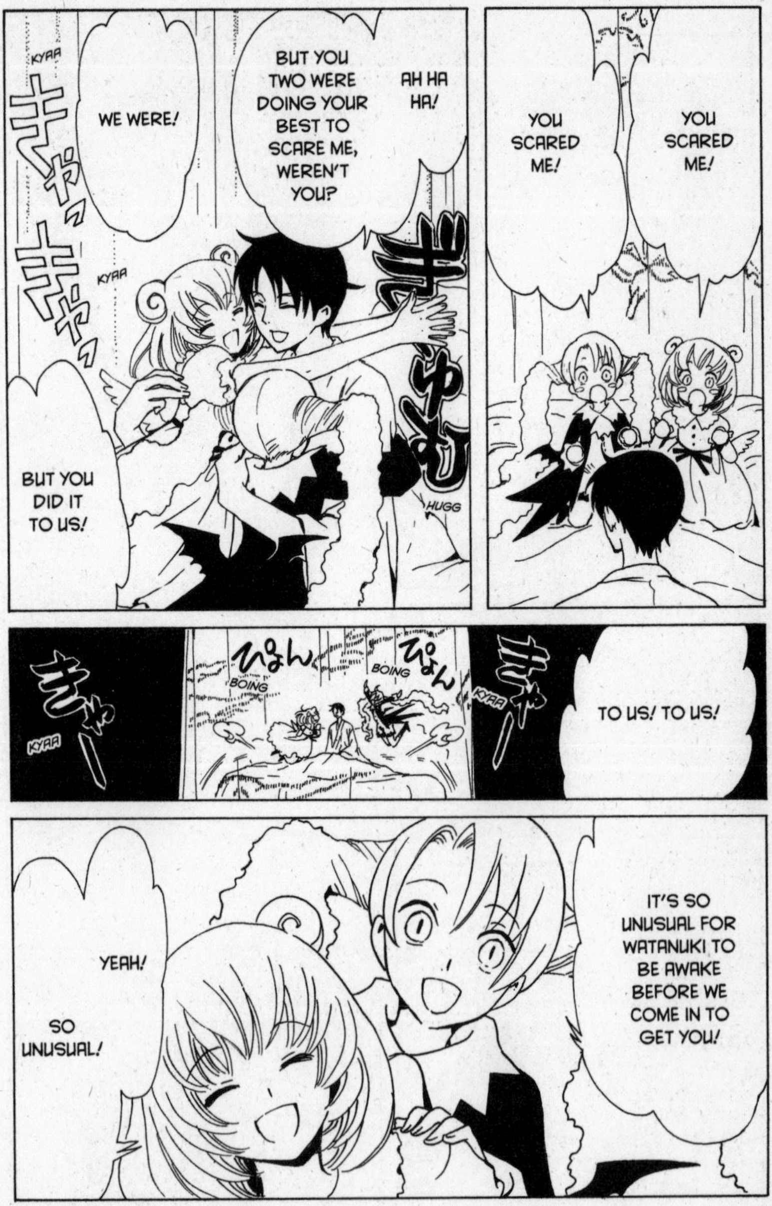
YOU SCARED ME!
YOU SCARED ME!
AH HA HA!
BUT YOU TWO WERE DOING YOUR BEST TO SCARE ME, WEREN'T YOU?
ぎゅむ
HUGG
WE WERE!
きゃっきゃっ
KYAA
KYAA
BUT YOU DID IT TO US!
TO US! TO US!
きゃー
KYAA
ぴょん
BOING
ぴょん
BOING
きゃー
KYAA
IT'S SO UNUSUAL FOR WATANUKI TO BE AWAKE BEFORE WE COME IN TO GET YOU!
YEAH!
SO UNUSUAL!

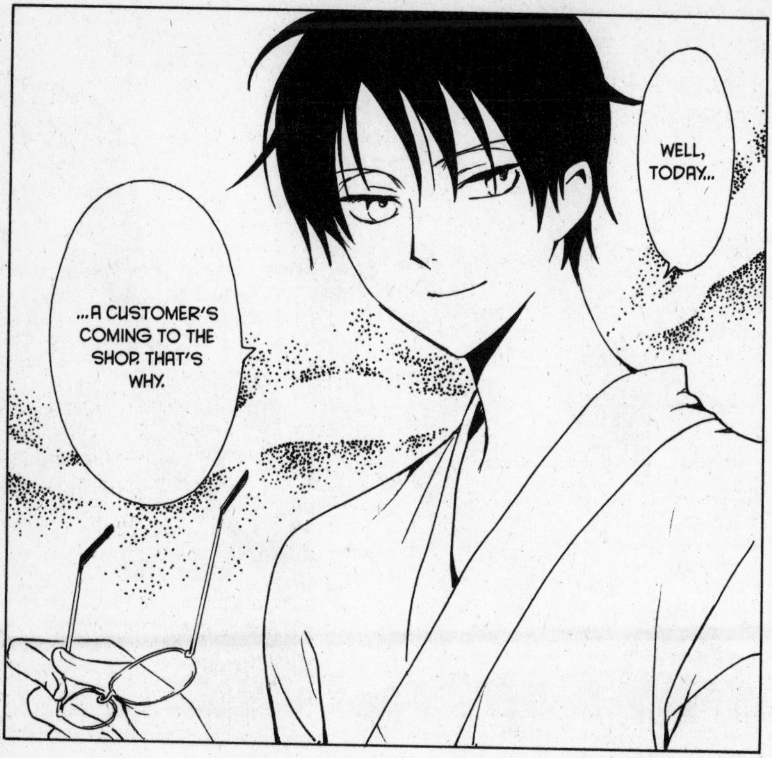
WELL, TODAY...
...A CUSTOMER'S COMING TO THE SHOP. THAT'S WHY.

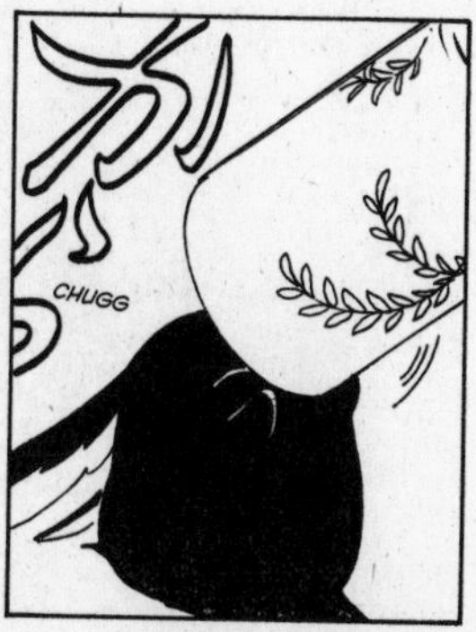
CHUGG

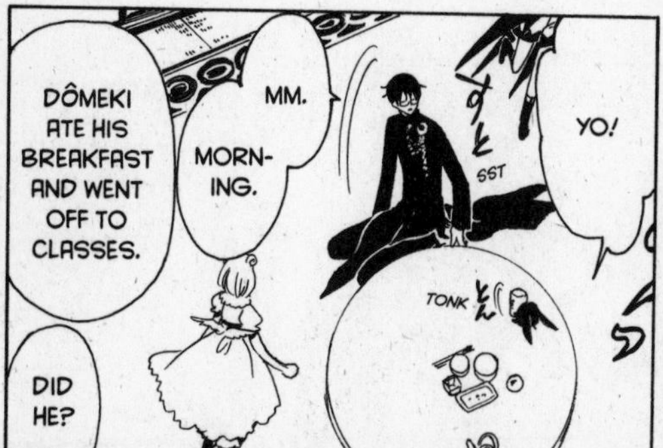
YO!
SST
MM.
MORNING.
DÔMEKI ATE HIS BREAKFAST AND WENT OFF TO CLASSES.
TONK
DID HE?

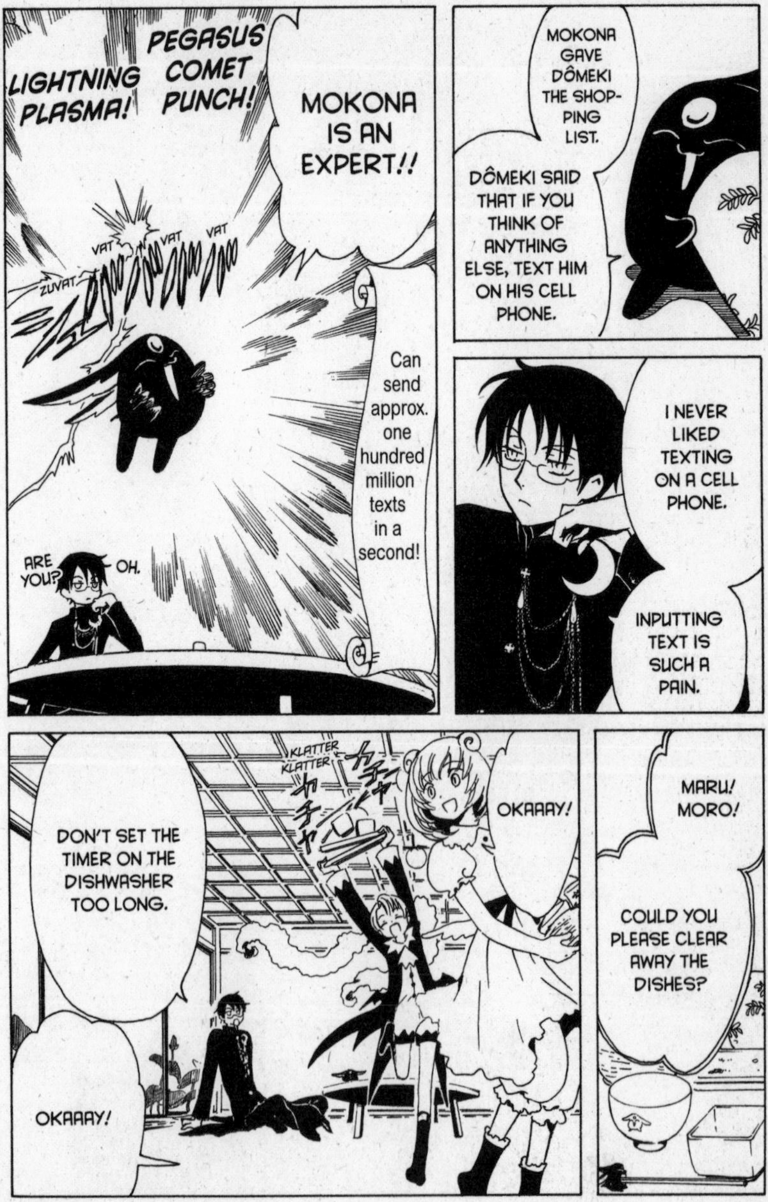
MOKONA GAVE DÔMEKI THE SHOP-PING LIST.
DÔMEKI SAID THAT IF YOU THINK OF ANYTHING ELSE, TEXT HIM ON HIS CELL PHONE.
I NEVER LIKED TEXTING ON A CELL PHONE.
INPUTTING TEXT IS SUCH A PAIN.
MOKONA IS AN EXPERT!!
PEGASUS COMET PUNCH!
LIGHTNING PLASMA!
VAT VAT VAT
ZUVAT
Can send approx. one hundred million texts in a second!
OH.
ARE YOU?
MARU! MORO!
COULD YOU PLEASE CLEAR AWAY THE DISHES?
OKAAAY!
KLATTER KLATTER
DON'T SET THE TIMER ON THE DISHWASHER TOO LONG.
OKAAAY!

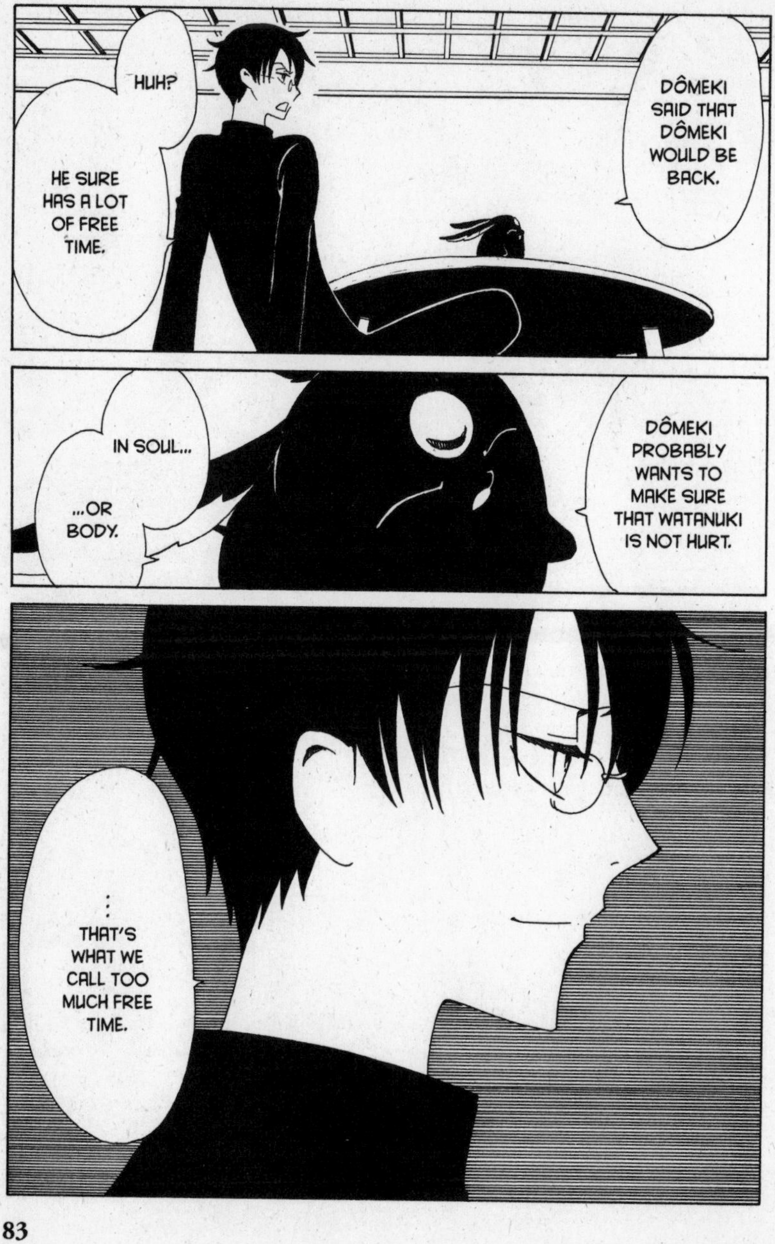
DÔMEKI SAID THAT DÔMEKI WOULD BE BACK.
HUH?
HE SURE HAS A LOT OF FREE TIME.
DÔMEKI PROBABLY WANTS TO MAKE SURE THAT WATANUKI IS NOT HURT.
IN SOUL...
...OR BODY.
... THAT'S WHAT WE CALL TOO MUCH FREE TIME.

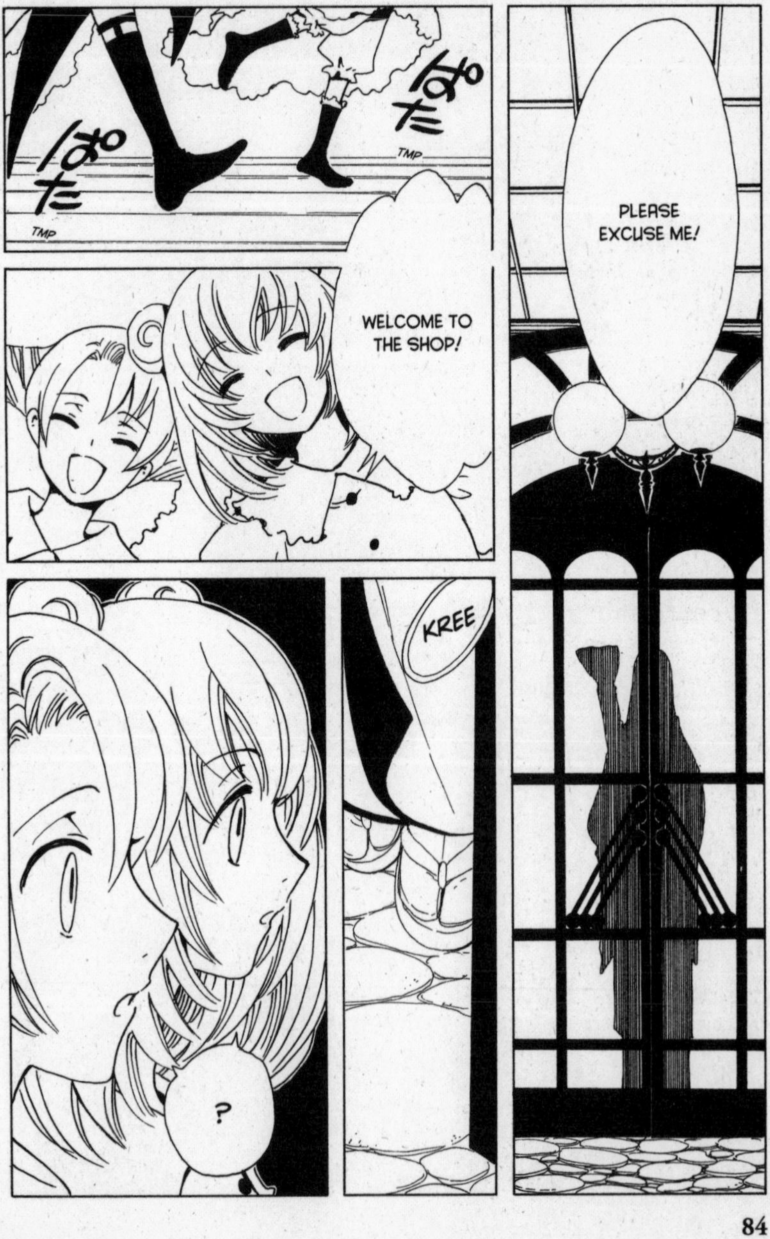
PLEASE EXCUSE ME!
ぱた
TMP
ぱた
TMP
WELCOME TO THE SHOP!
KREE
?

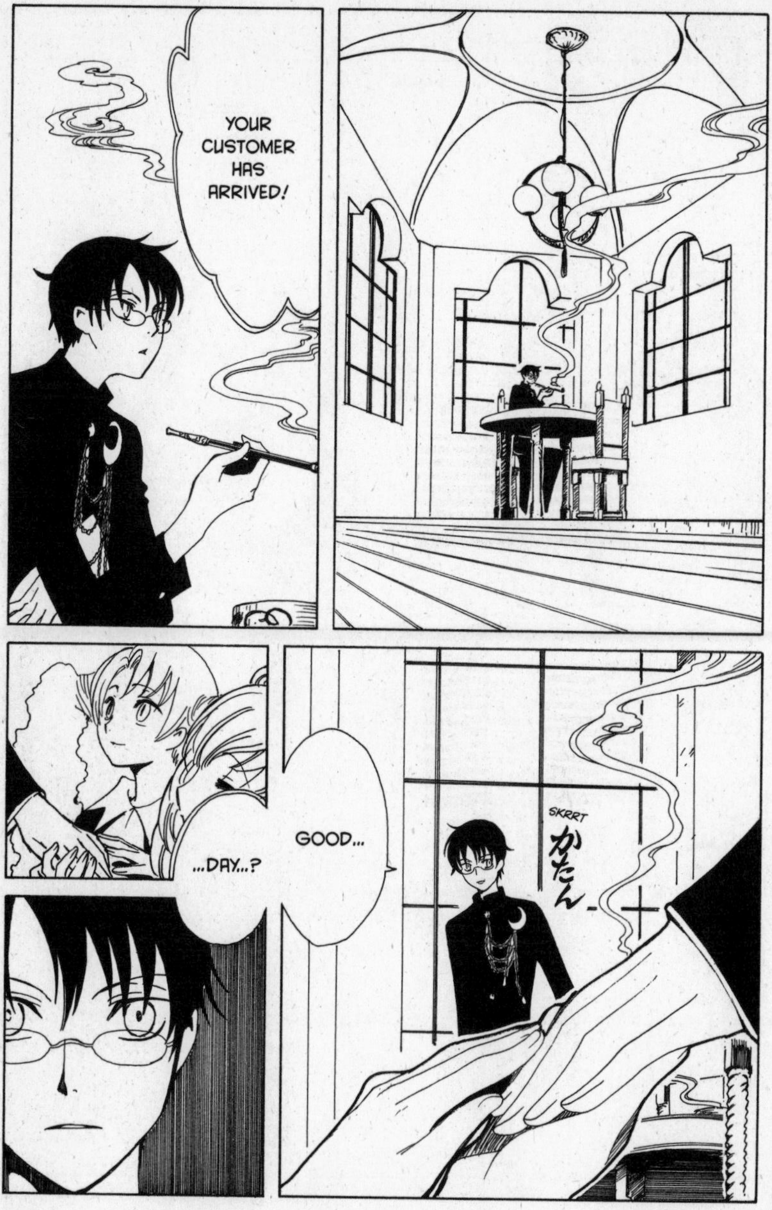
YOUR CUSTOMER HAS ARRIVED!
SKRRT
かたん
GOOD...
...DAY...?

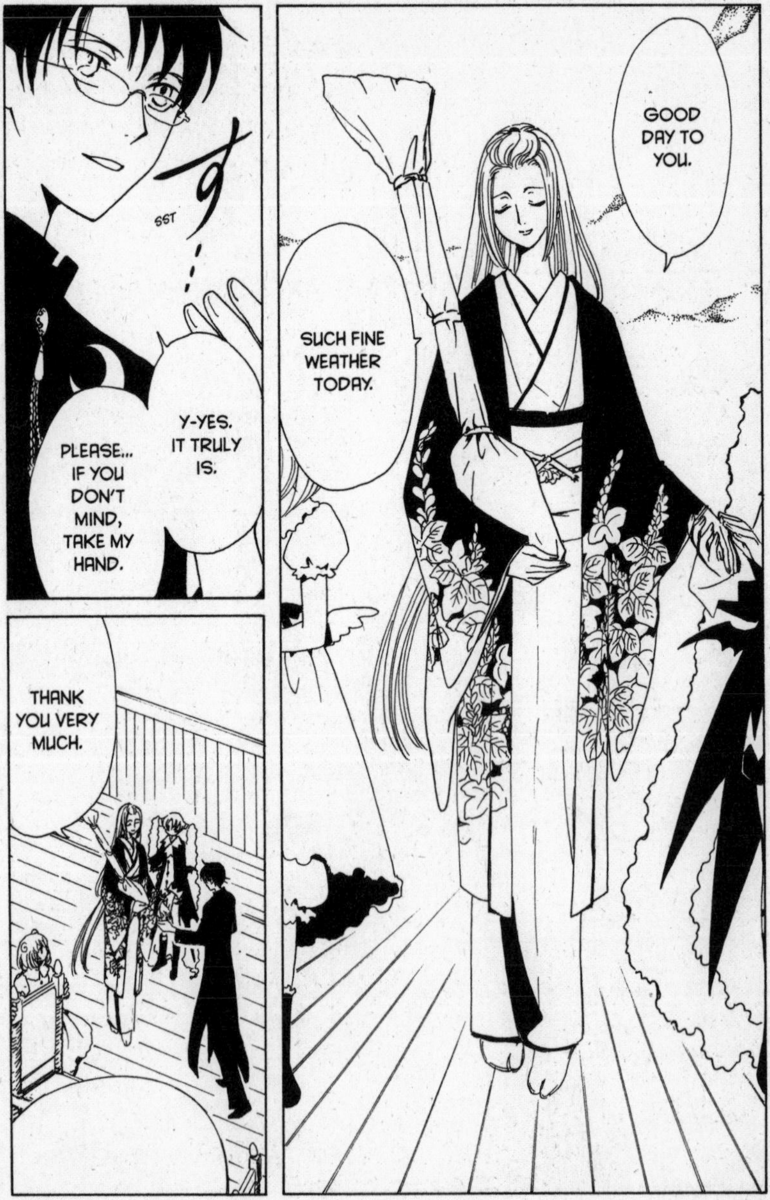
GOOD DAY TO YOU.
SUCH FINE WEATHER TODAY.
Y-YES. IT TRULY IS.
SST
PLEASE... IF YOU DON'T MIND, TAKE MY HAND.
THANK YOU VERY MUCH.

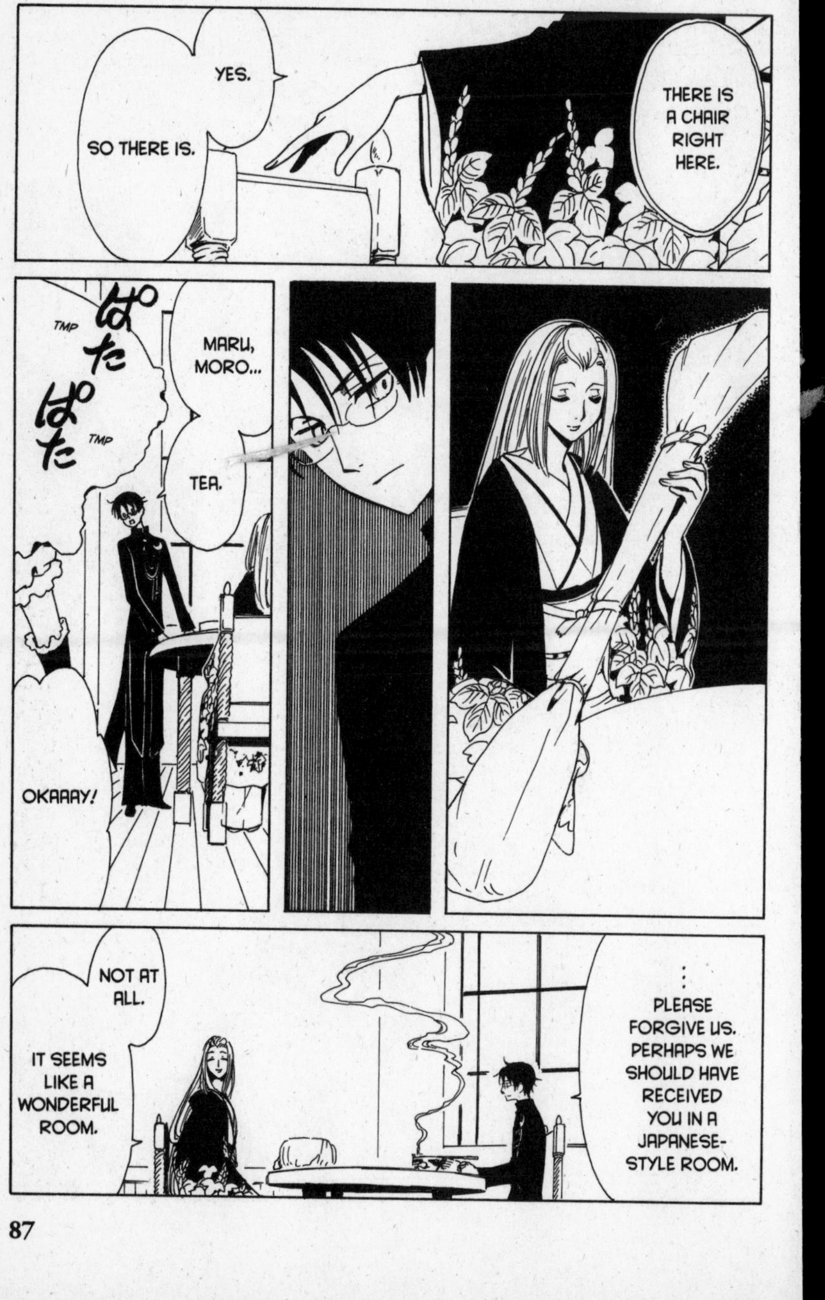
THERE IS A CHAIR RIGHT HERE.
YES.
SO THERE IS.
MARU, MORO...
TEA.
ぱたぱた
TMP
TMP
OKAAAY!
...
PLEASE FORGIVE US. PERHAPS WE SHOULD HAVE RECEIVED YOU IN A JAPANESE-STYLE ROOM.
NOT AT ALL.
IT SEEMS LIKE A WONDERFUL ROOM.

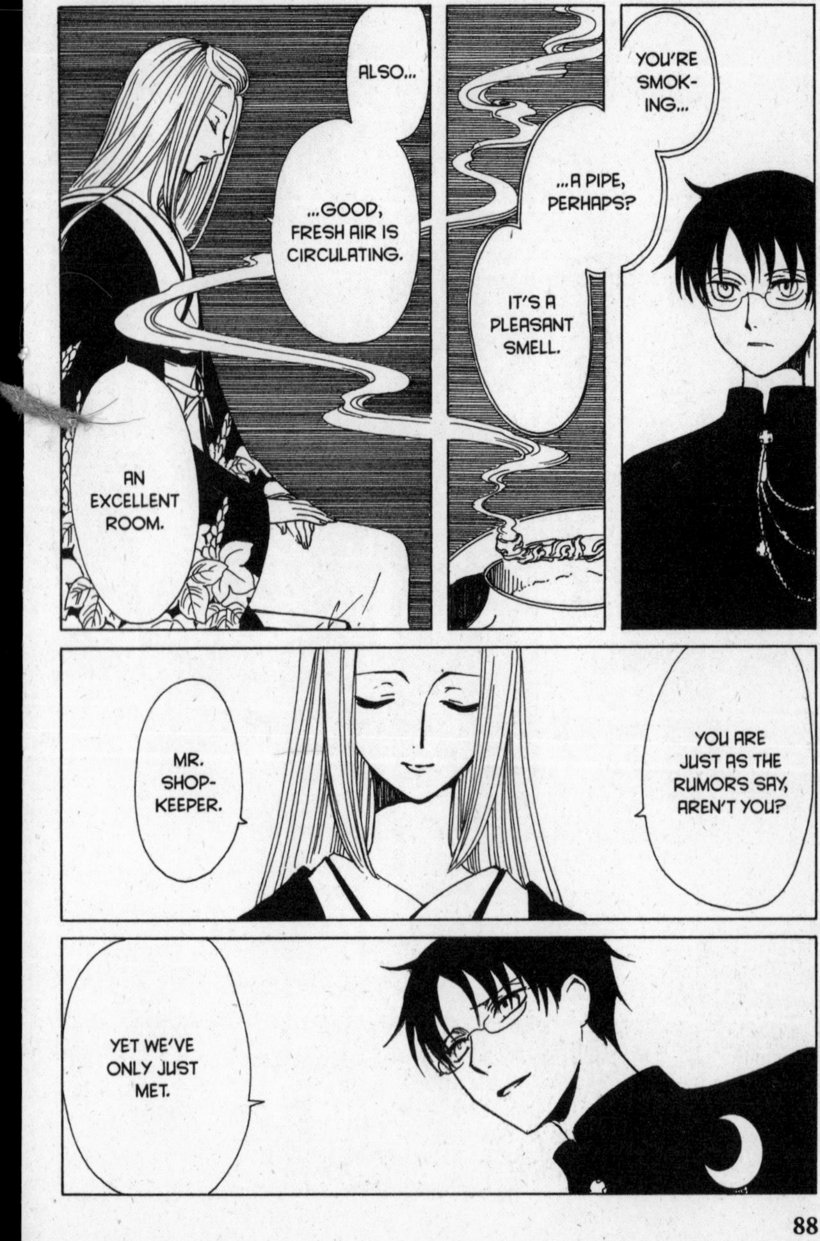
YOU'RE SMOKING...
...A PIPE, PERHAPS?
IT'S A PLEASANT SMELL.
ALSO...
...GOOD, FRESH AIR IS CIRCULATING.
AN EXCELLENT ROOM.
YOU ARE JUST AS THE RUMORS SAY, AREN'T YOU?
MR. SHOPKEEPER.
YET WE'VE ONLY JUST MET.

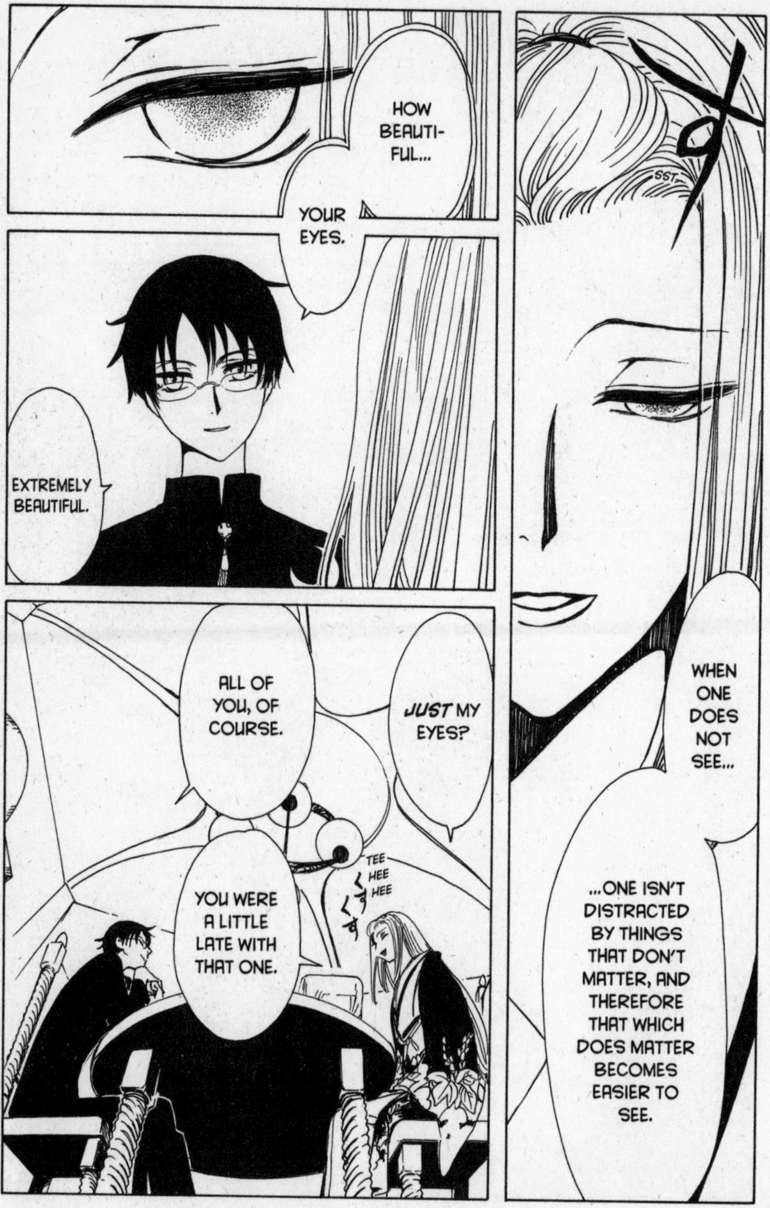
SST
WHEN ONE DOES NOT SEE...
...ONE ISN'T DISTRACTED BY THINGS THAT DON'T MATTER, AND THEREFORE THAT WHICH DOES MATTER BECOMES EASIER TO SEE.
HOW BEAUTI-FUL...
YOUR EYES.
EXTREMELY BEAUTIFUL.
JUST MY EYES?
ALL OF YOU, OF COURSE.
TEE HEE HEE
くすくす
YOU WERE A LITTLE LATE WITH THAT ONE.

FLAFF

SHALL WE DISCUSS WHY I INTRUDED ON YOUR SHOP TODAY?

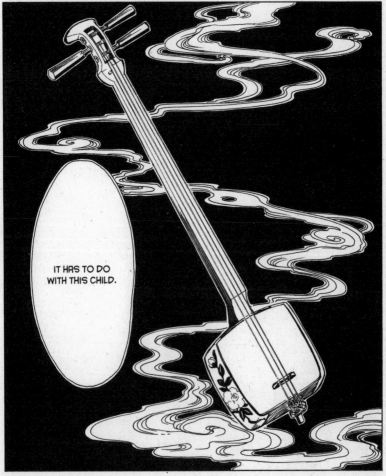

IT HAS TO DO WITH THIS CHILD.

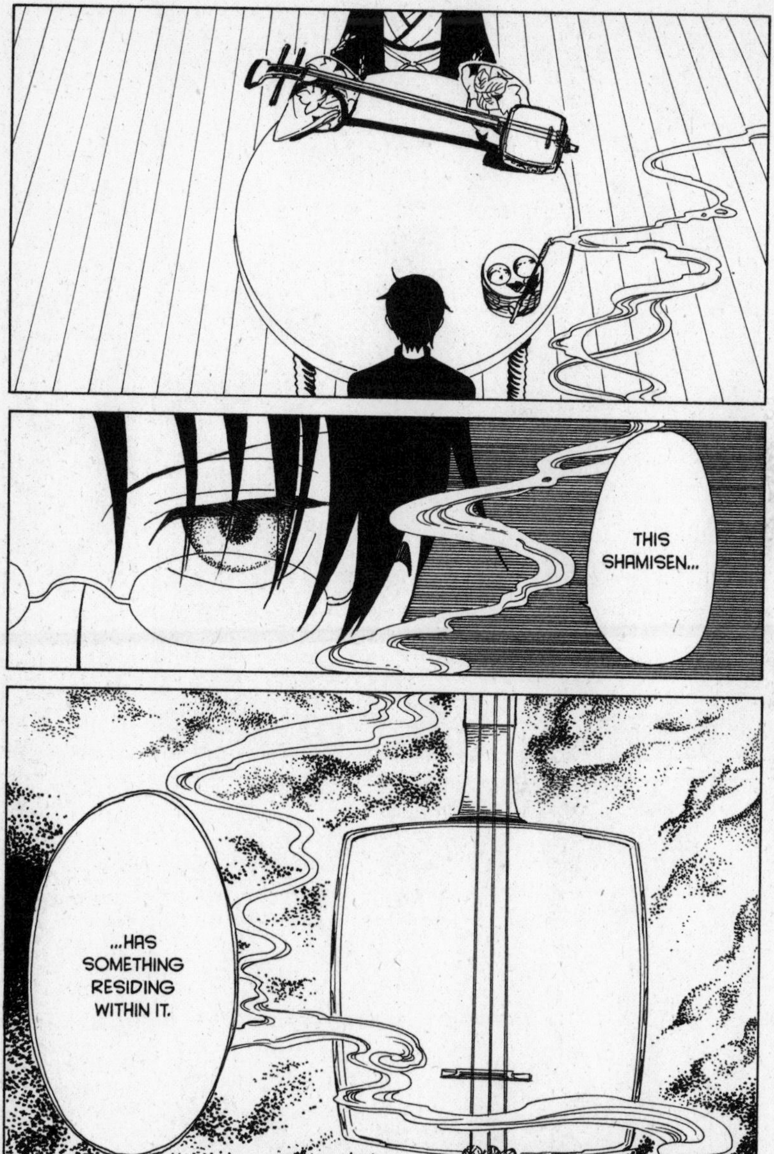
THIS SHAMISEN...
...HAS SOMETHING RESIDING WITHIN IT.

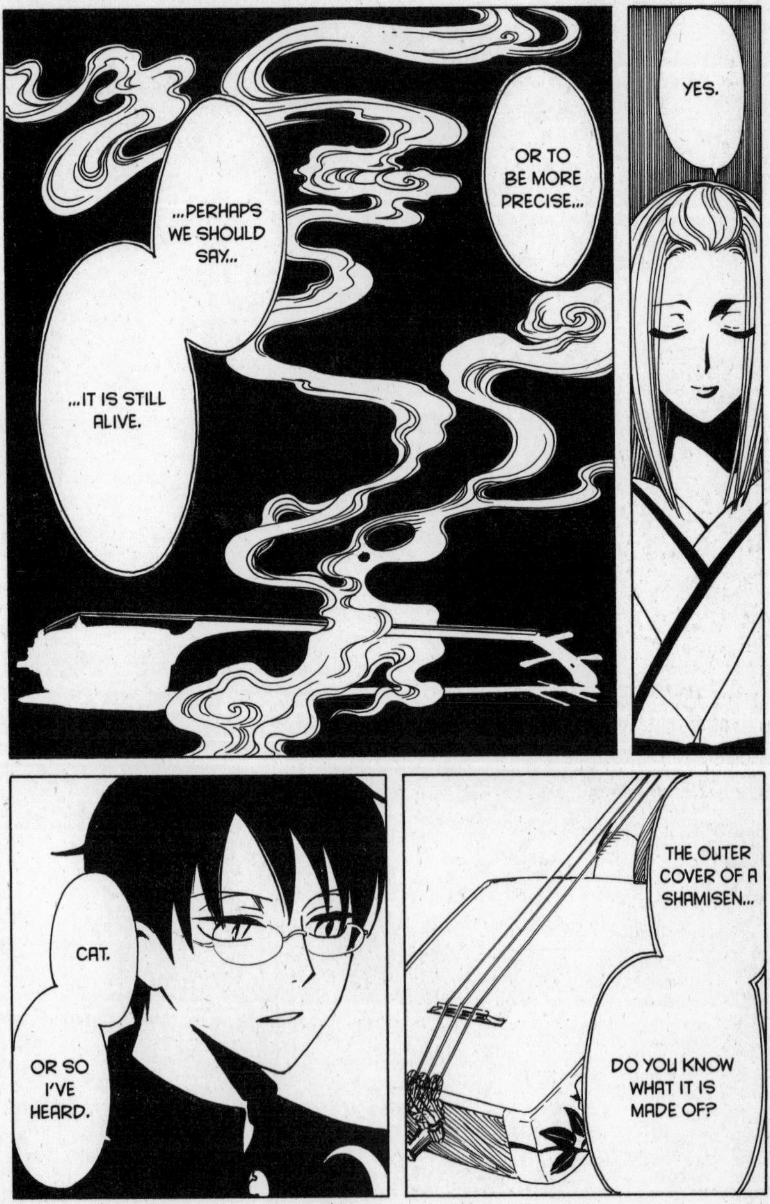
YES.
OR TO BE MORE PRECISE...
...PERHAPS WE SHOULD SAY...
...IT IS STILL ALIVE.
THE OUTER COVER OF A SHAMISEN...
DO YOU KNOW WHAT IT IS MADE OF?
CAT.
OR SO I'VE HEARD.

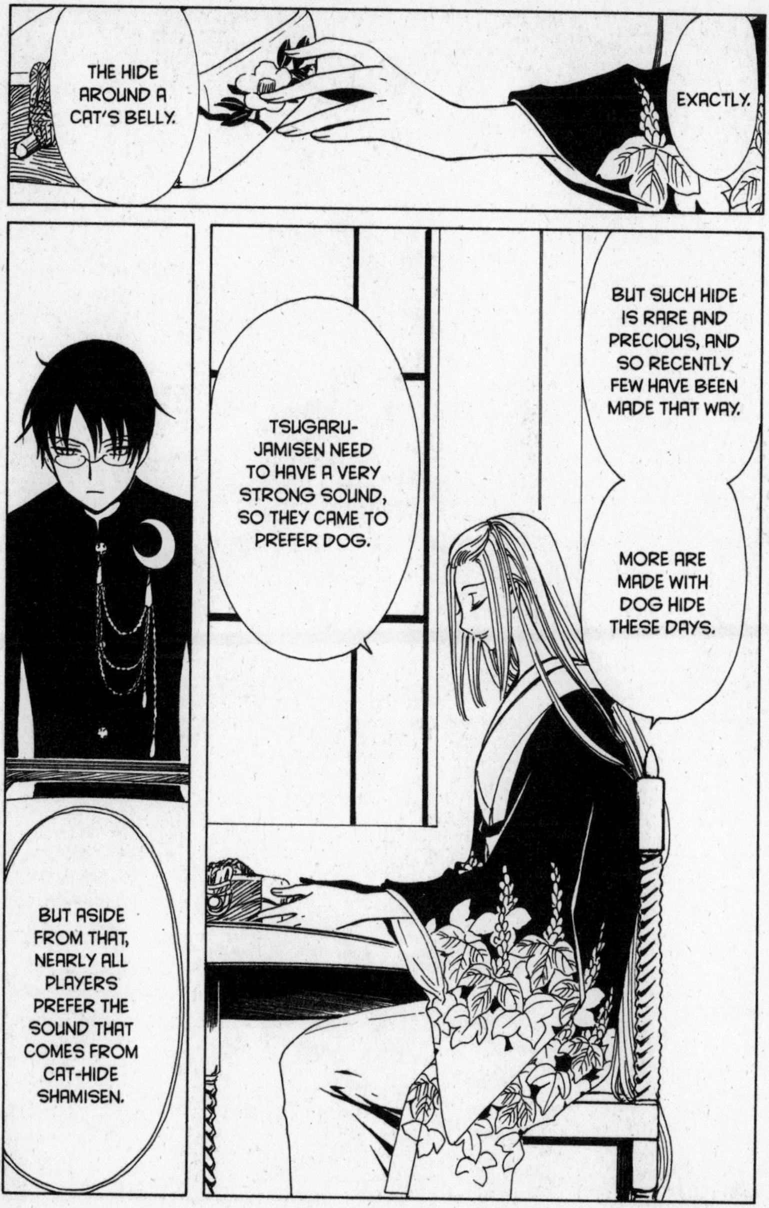
EXACTLY.
THE HIDE AROUND A CAT'S BELLY.
BUT SUCH HIDE IS RARE AND PRECIOUS, AND SO RECENTLY FEW HAVE BEEN MADE THAT WAY.
MORE ARE MADE WITH DOG HIDE THESE DAYS.
TSUGARU-JAMISEN NEED TO HAVE A VERY STRONG SOUND, SO THEY CAME TO PREFER DOG.
BUT ASIDE FROM THAT, NEARLY ALL PLAYERS PREFER THE SOUND THAT COMES FROM CAT-HIDE SHAMISEN.

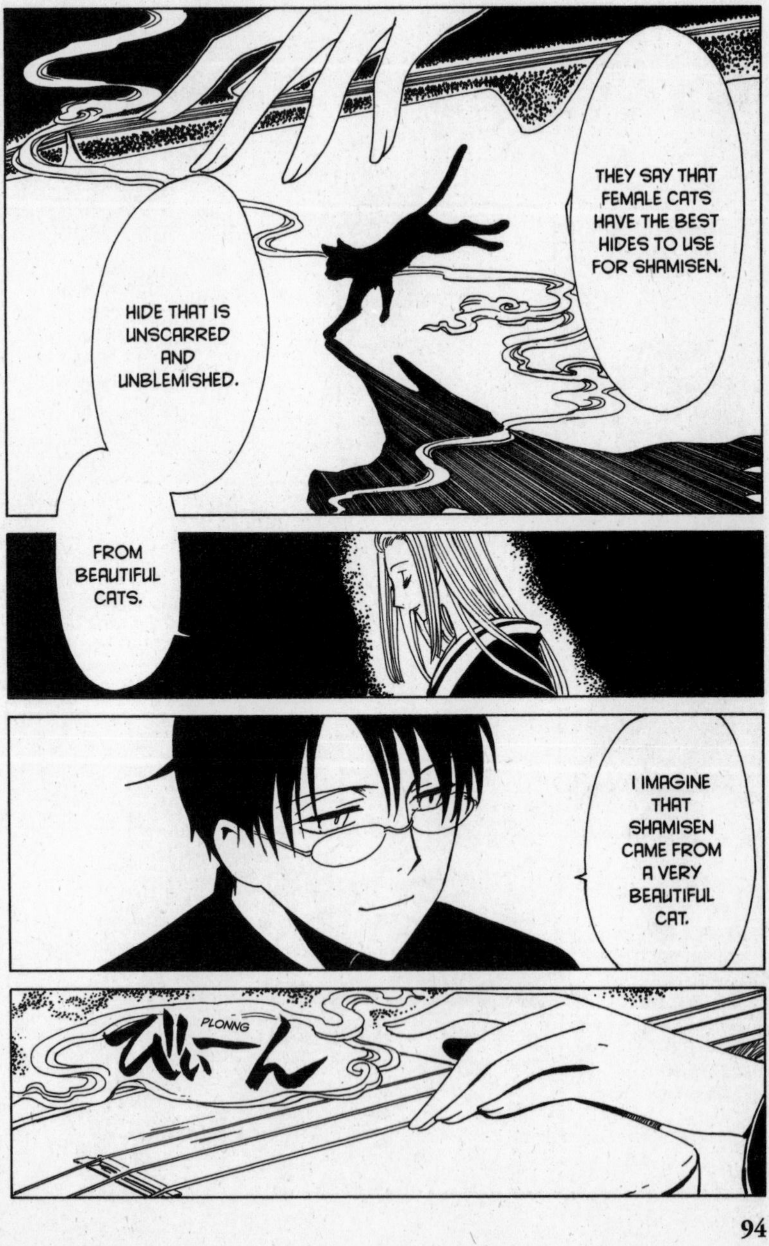
THEY SAY THAT FEMALE CATS HAVE THE BEST HIDES TO USE FOR SHAMISEN.
HIDE THAT IS UNSCARRED AND UNBLEMISHED.
FROM BEAUTIFUL CATS.
I IMAGINE THAT SHAMISEN CAME FROM A VERY BEAUTIFUL CAT.
PLONNG

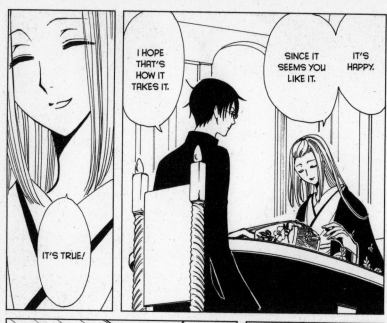

IT'S HAPPY.
SINCE IT SEEMS YOU LIKE IT.
I HOPE THAT'S HOW IT TAKES IT.
IT'S TRUE!
IT'S BEEN A WONDERFUL CHILD, ALWAYS GIVING OFF A VERY LOVELY SOUND.
BUT ABOUT TEN DAYS AGO, IT DECIDED TO BECOME SILENT.
AND SINCE IT RESPONDED TO ME THIS TIME...
...I MUST ASSUME THAT BRINGING IT TO THIS SHOP WAS THE CORRECT THING TO DO.

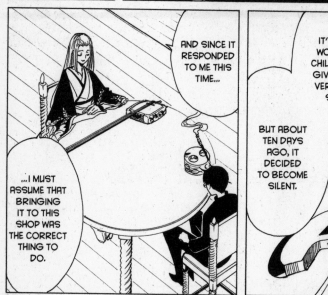

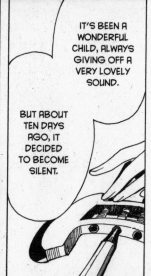

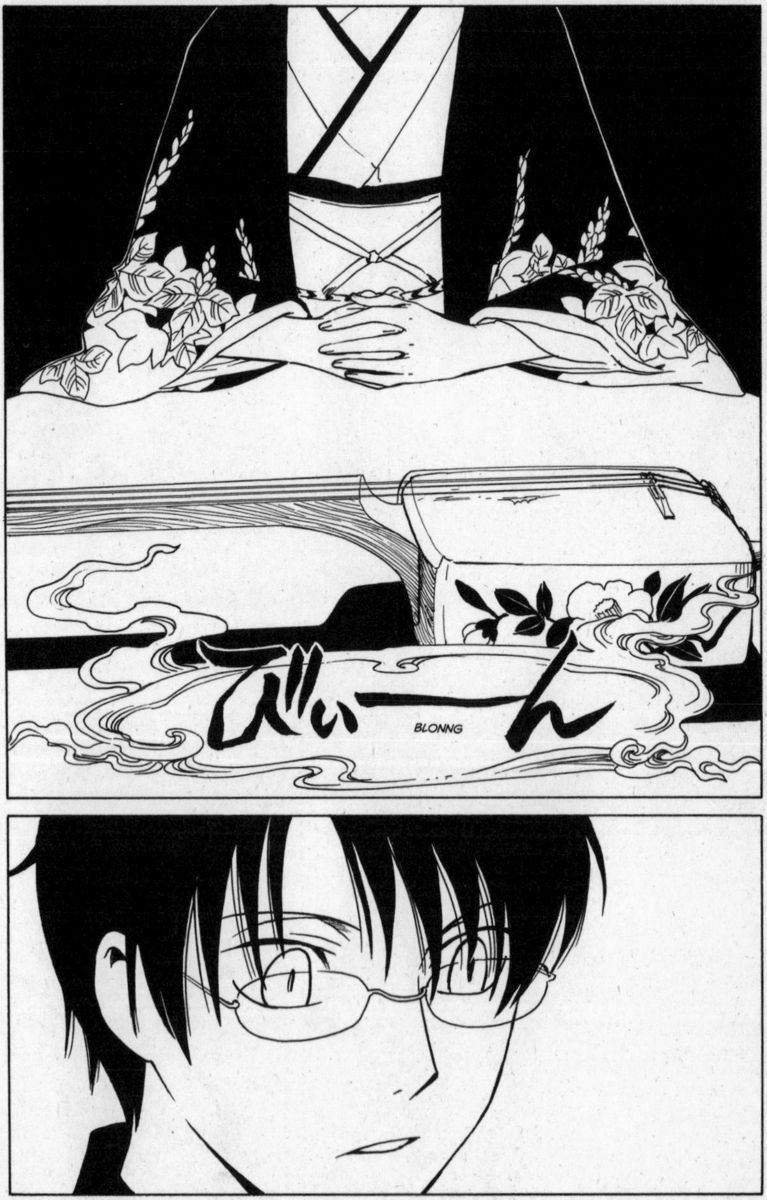
びぃーーん
BLONNG

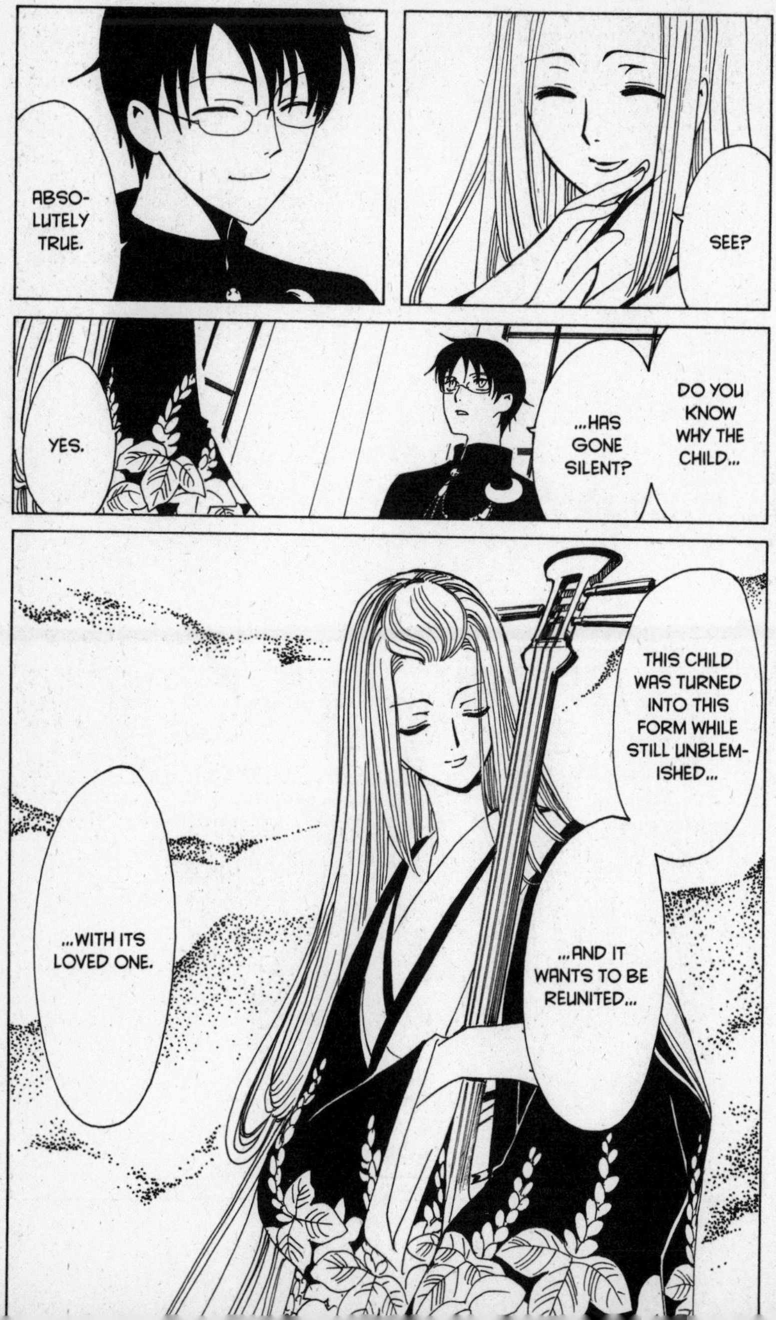
SEE?
ABSO-LUTELY TRUE.
DO YOU KNOW WHY THE CHILD...
...HAS GONE SILENT?
YES.
THIS CHILD WAS TURNED INTO THIS FORM WHILE STILL UNBLEM-ISHED...
...AND IT WANTS TO BE REUNITED...
...WITH ITS LOVED ONE.

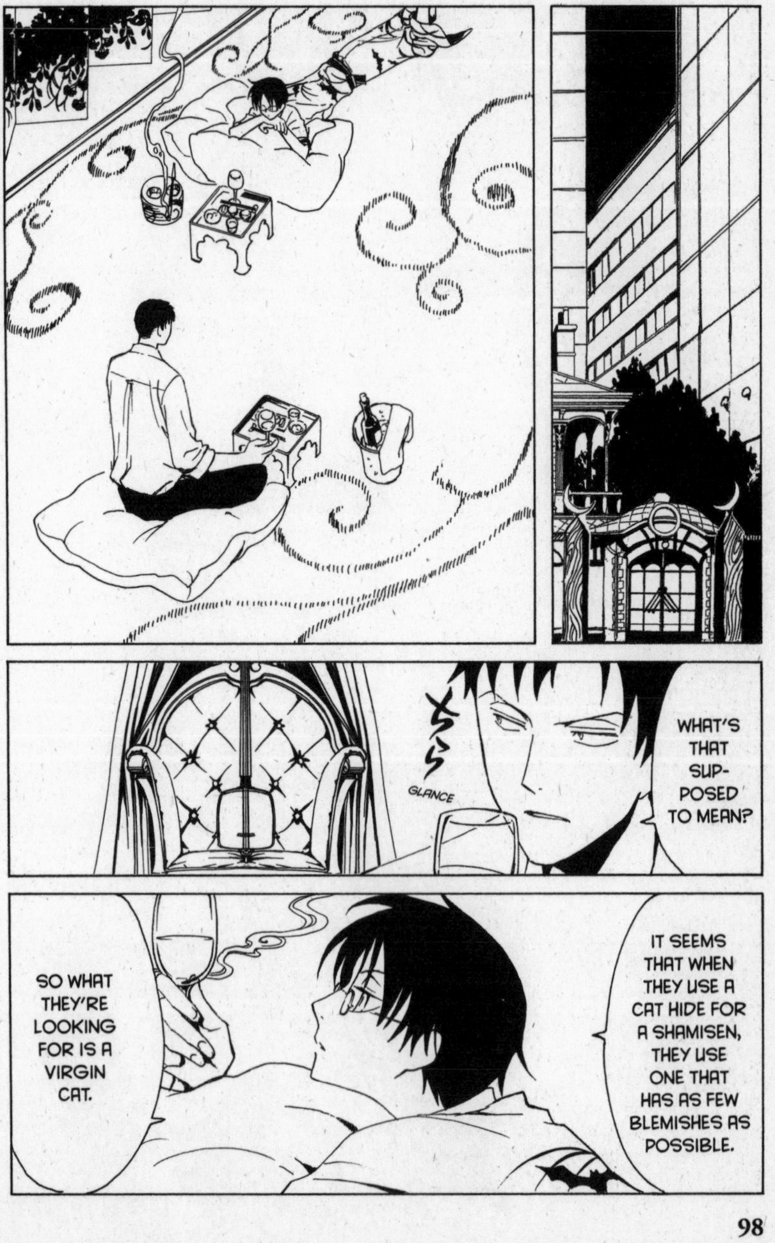
ちら
GLANCE
WHAT'S THAT SUP-POSED TO MEAN?
IT SEEMS THAT WHEN THEY USE A CAT HIDE FOR A SHAMISEN, THEY USE ONE THAT HAS AS FEW BLEMISHES AS POSSIBLE.
SO WHAT THEY'RE LOOKING FOR IS A VIRGIN CAT.

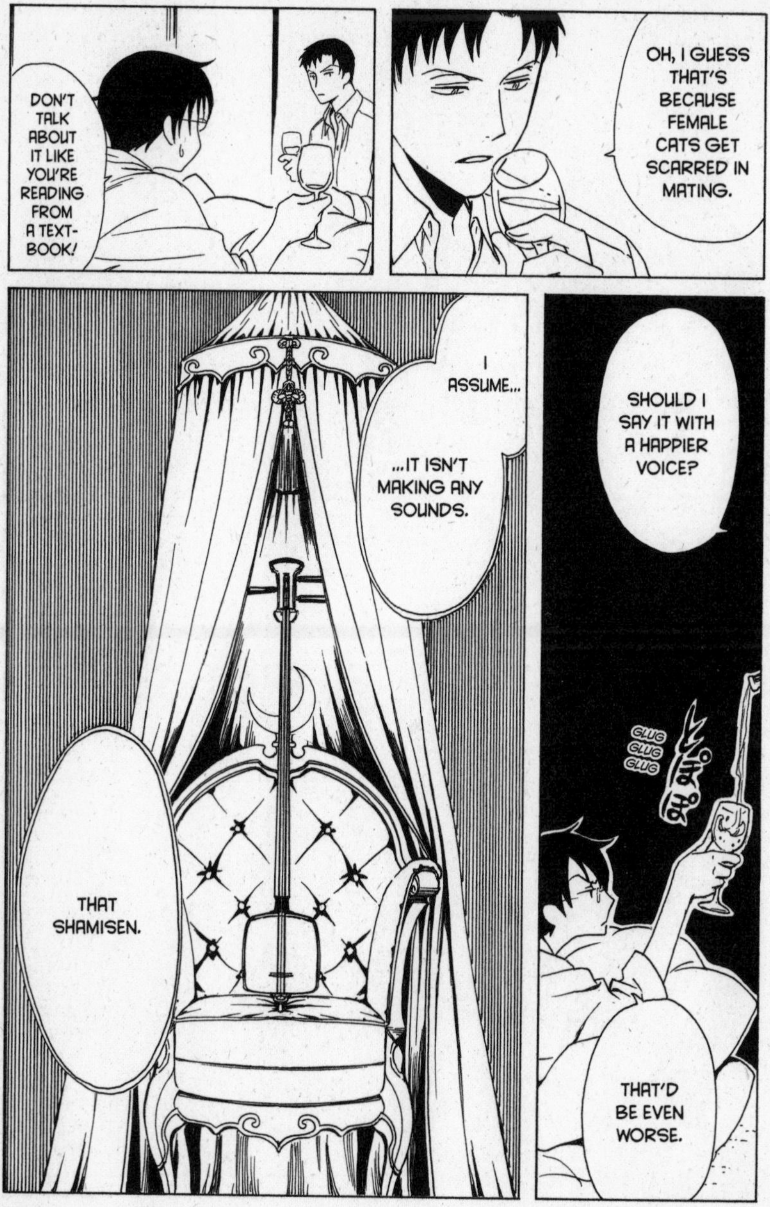
OH, I GUESS THAT'S BECAUSE FEMALE CATS GET SCARRED IN MATING.
DON'T TALK ABOUT IT LIKE YOU'RE READING FROM A TEXT-BOOK!
SHOULD I SAY IT WITH A HAPPIER VOICE?
GLUG GLUG GLUG
THAT'D BE EVEN WORSE.
I ASSUME...
...IT ISN'T MAKING ANY SOUNDS.
THAT SHAMISEN.

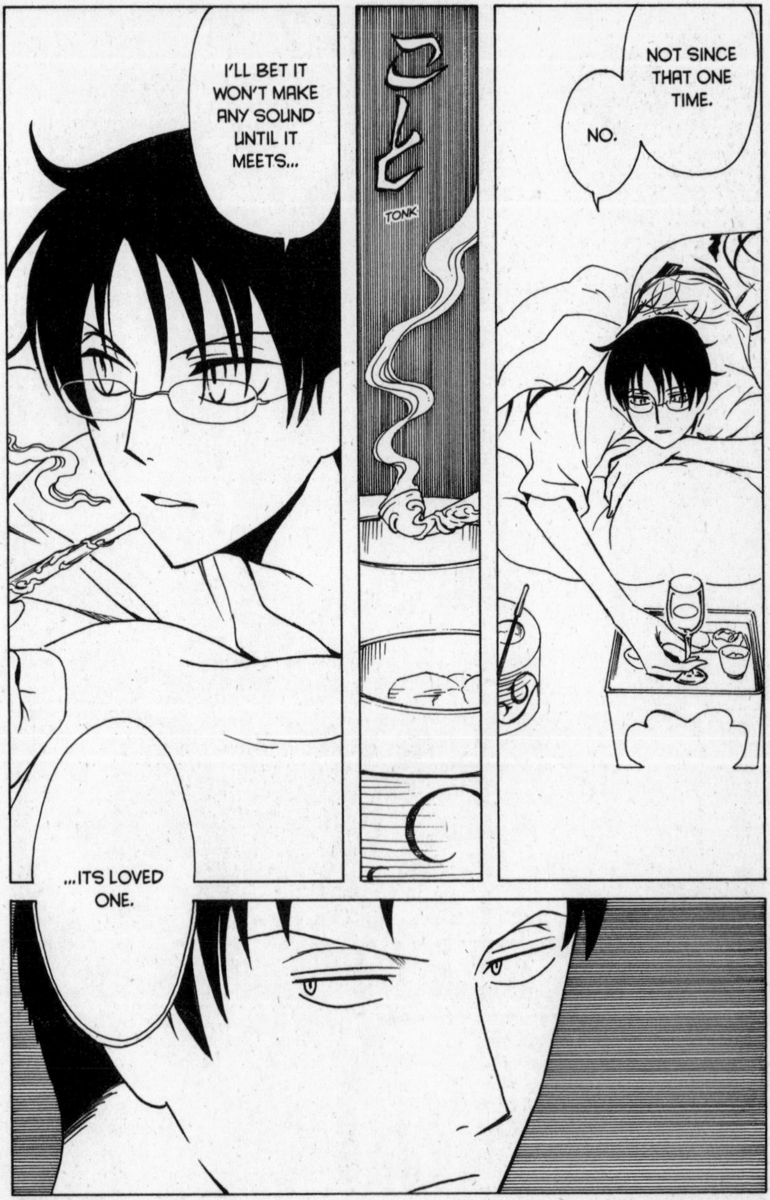
NOT SINCE THAT ONE TIME.
NO.
TONK
I'LL BET IT WON'T MAKE ANY SOUND UNTIL IT MEETS...
...ITS LOVED ONE.

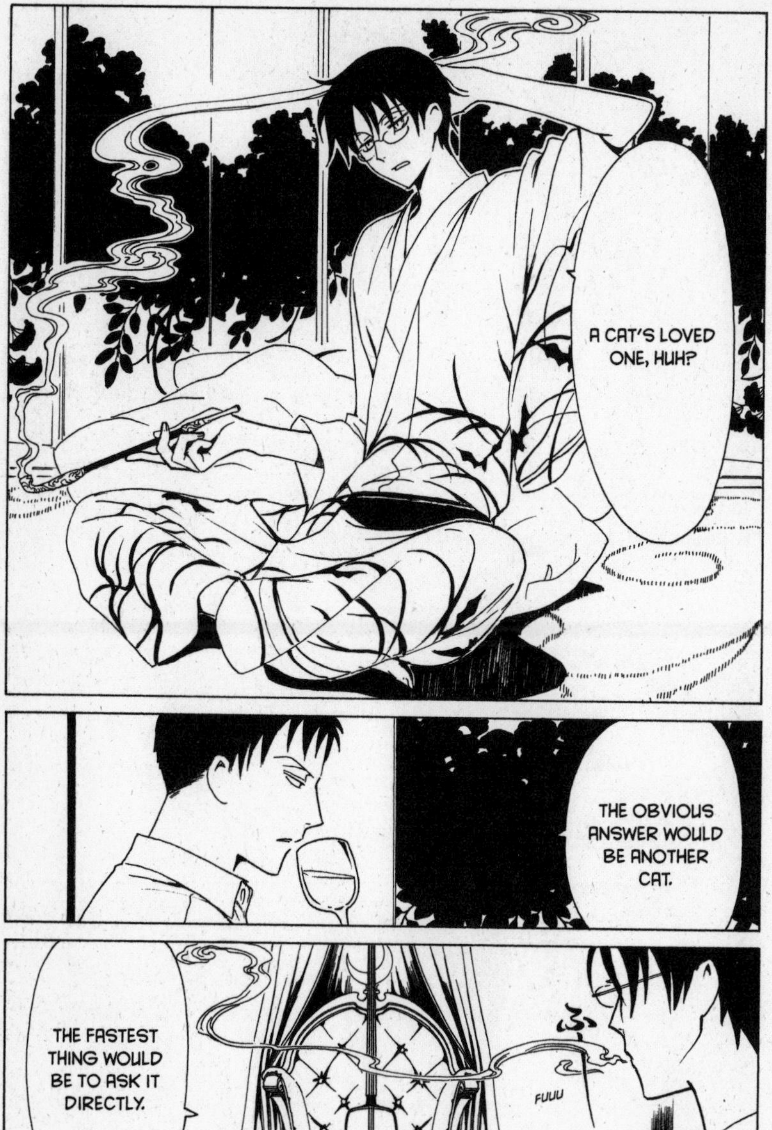
A CAT'S LOVED ONE, HUH?
THE OBVIOUS ANSWER WOULD BE ANOTHER CAT.
ふー
FUUU
...
THE FASTEST THING WOULD BE TO ASK IT DIRECTLY.

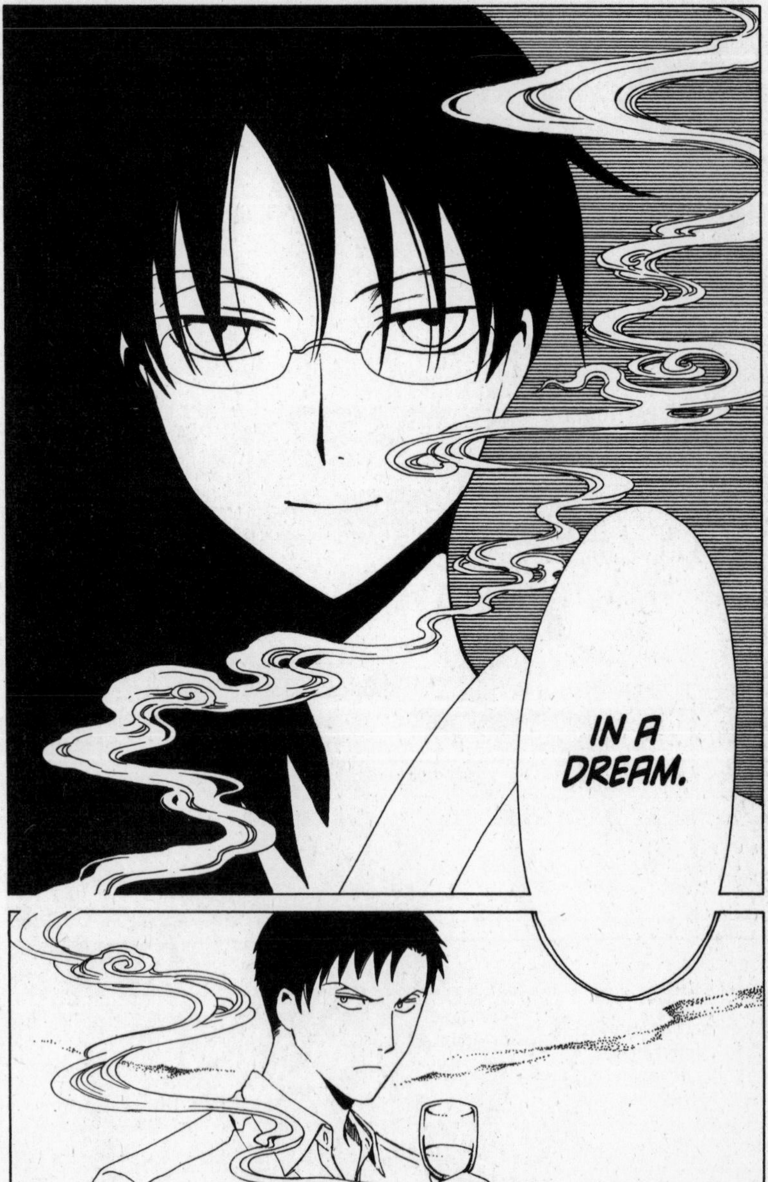
IN A DREAM.

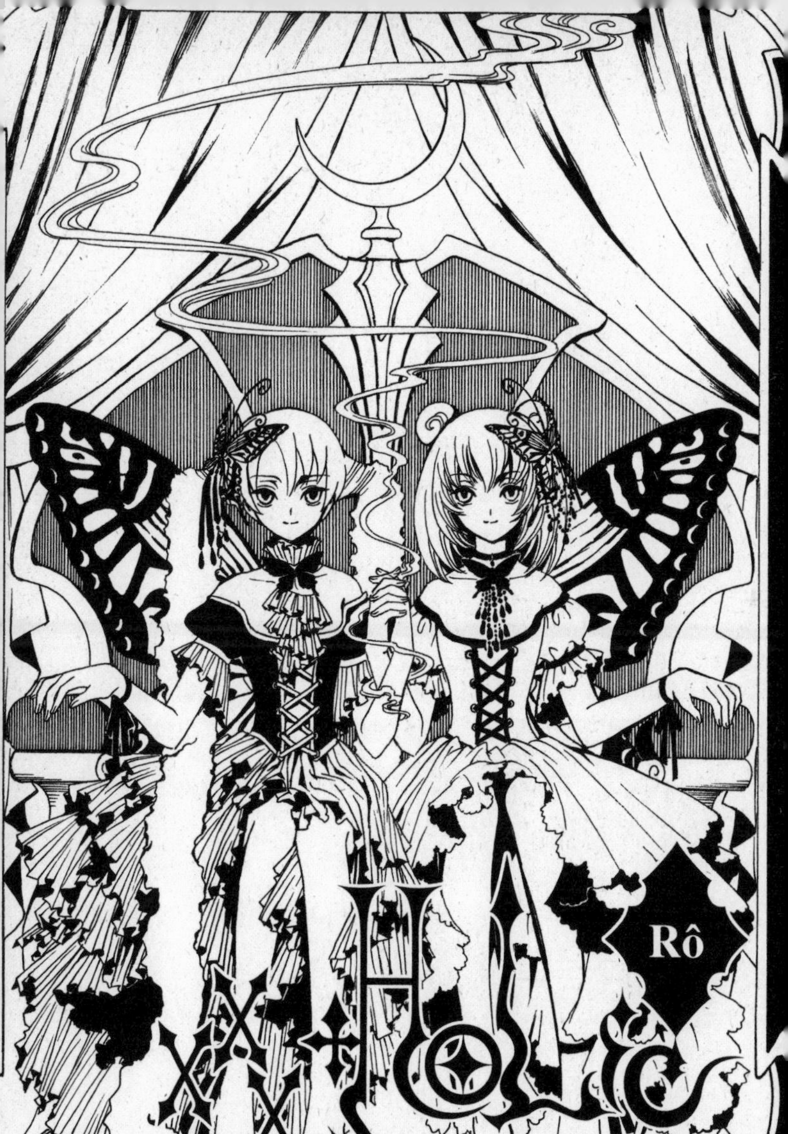
xxxHOLiC
Rô
〜×××ホリック・ロウ〜

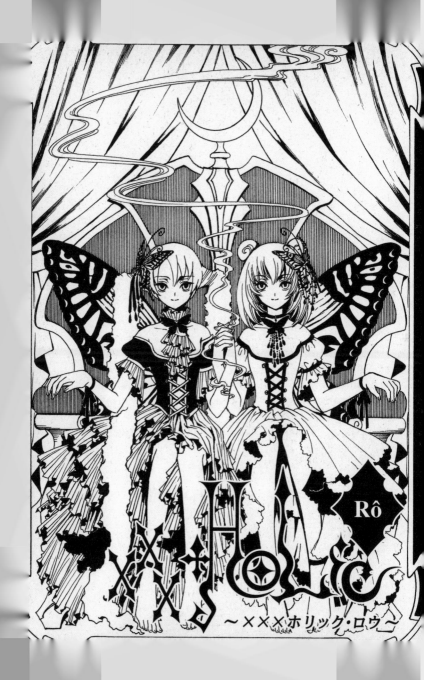

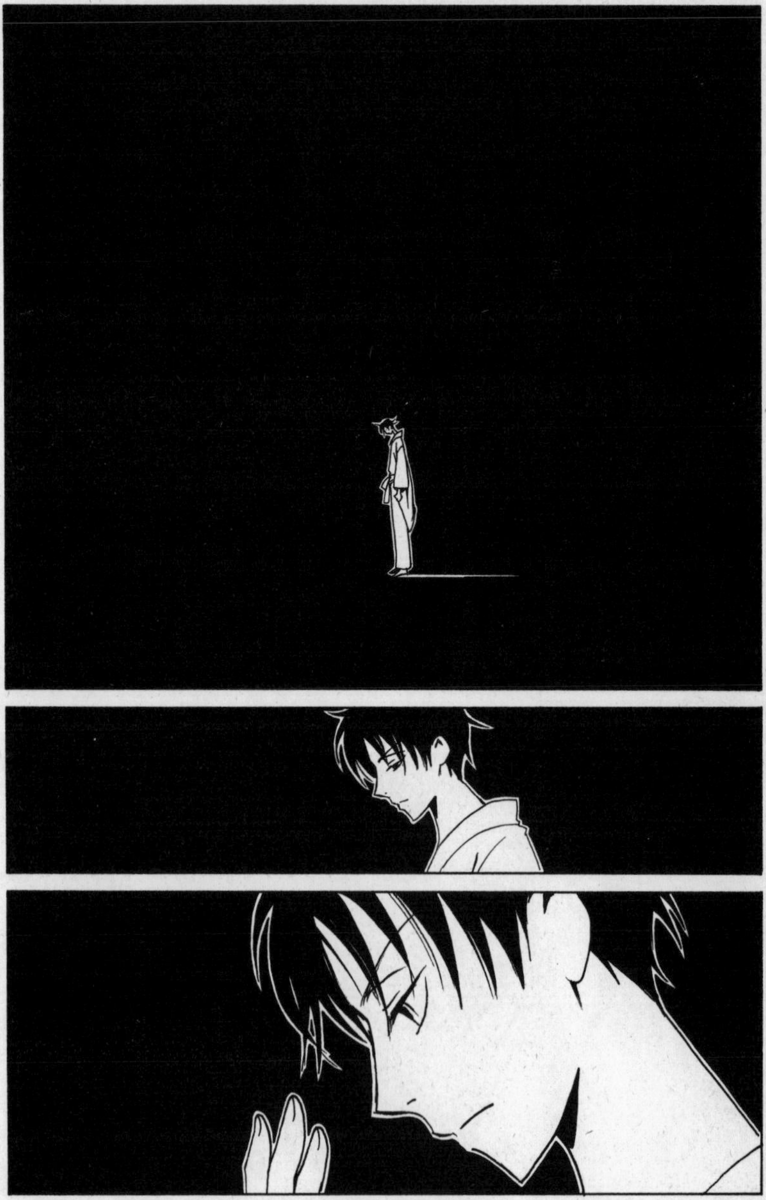

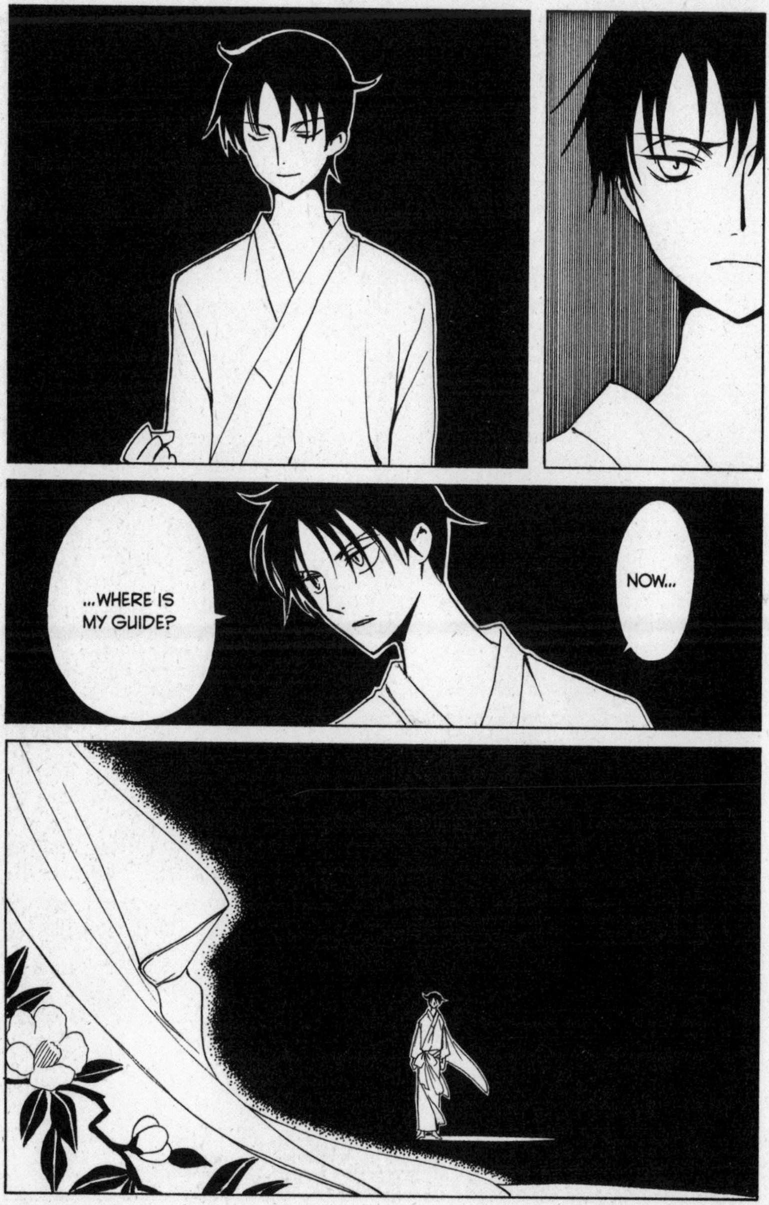
NOW...
...WHERE IS MY GUIDE?

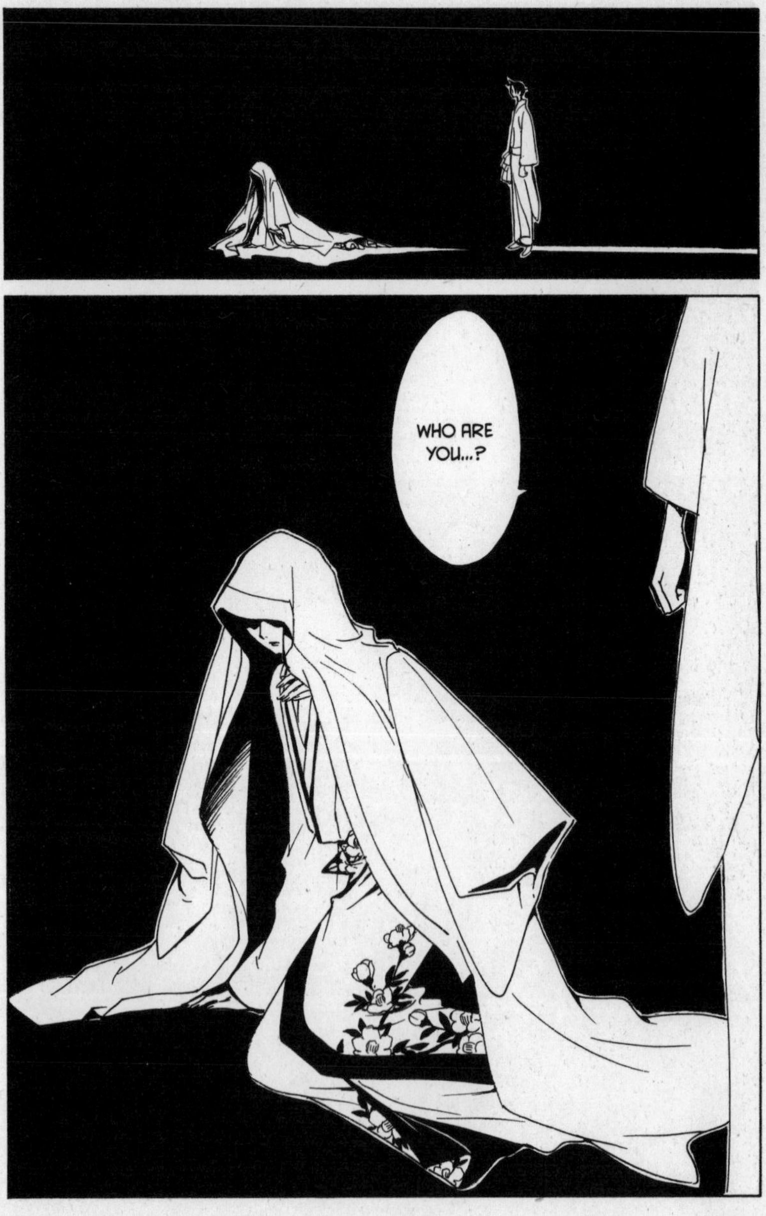
WHO ARE YOU...?

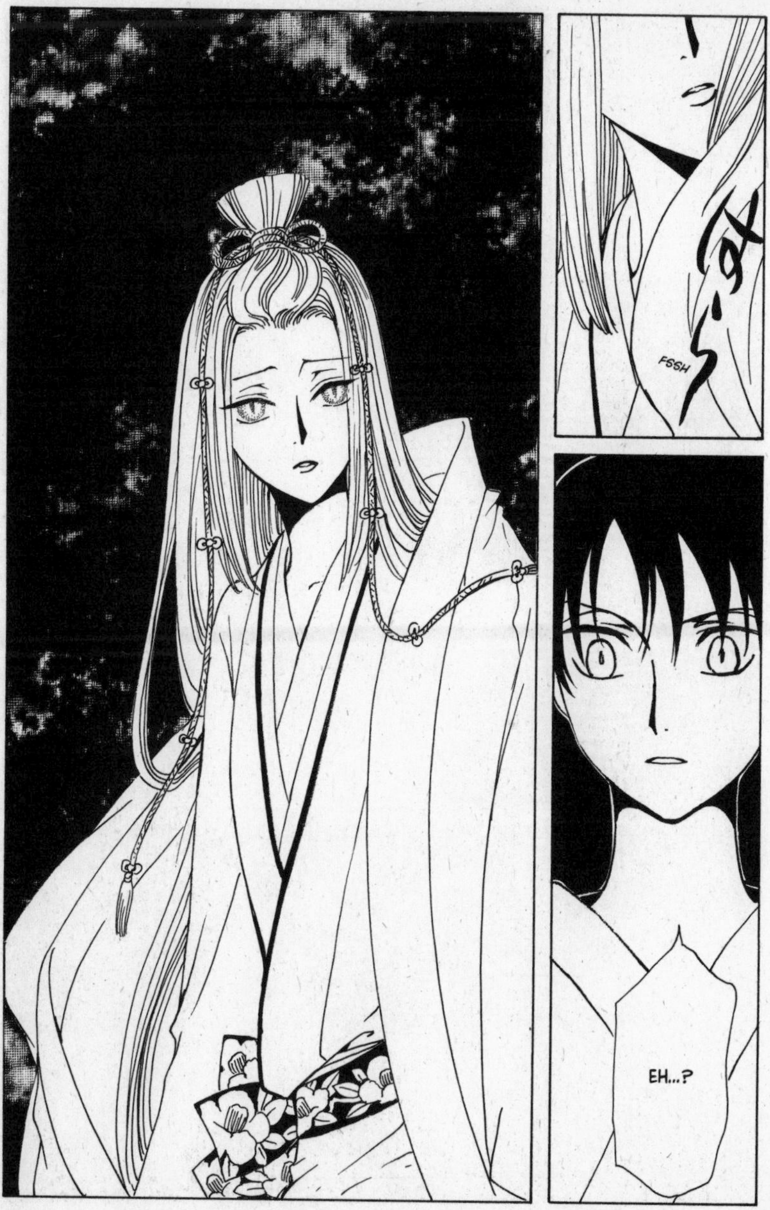
FSSH
EH...?

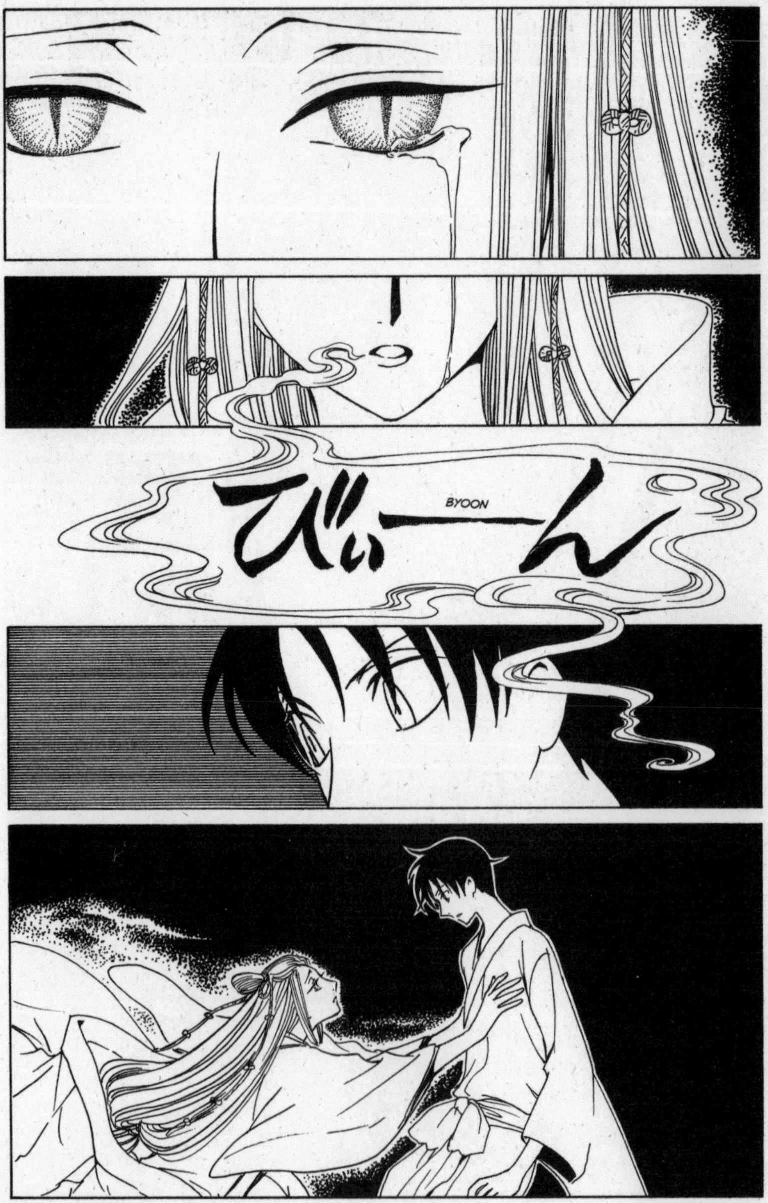
びぃーん
BYOON

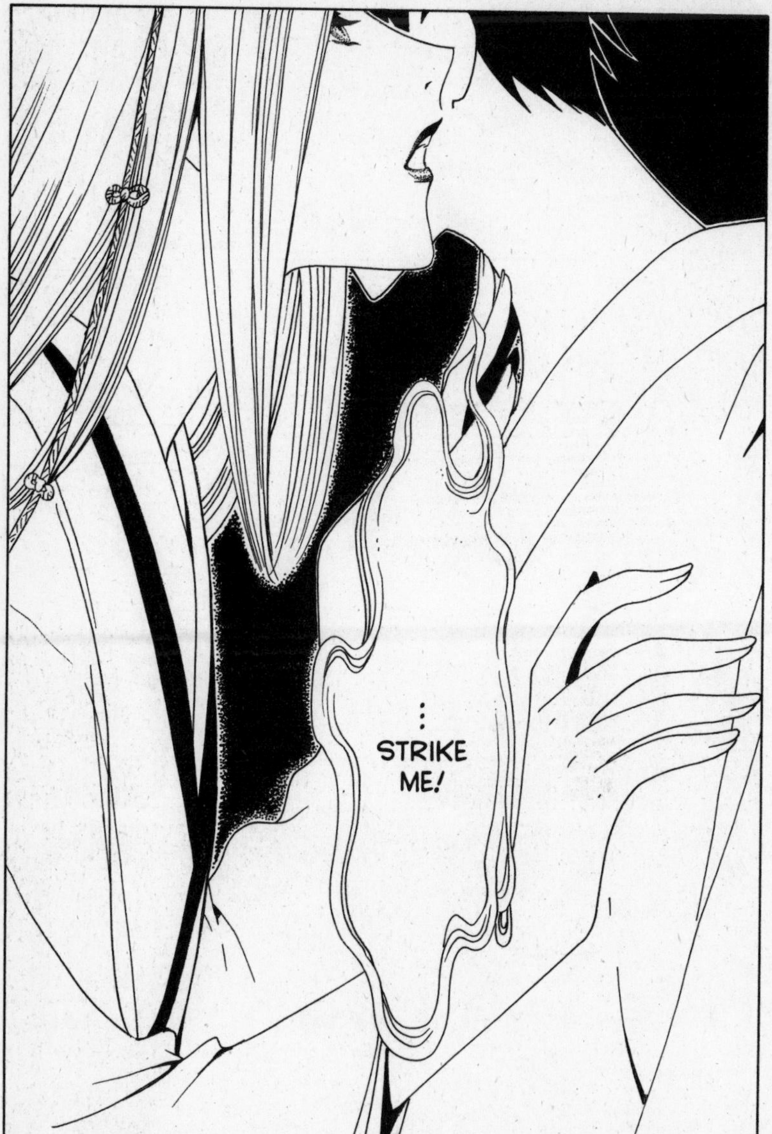
...STRIKE ME!

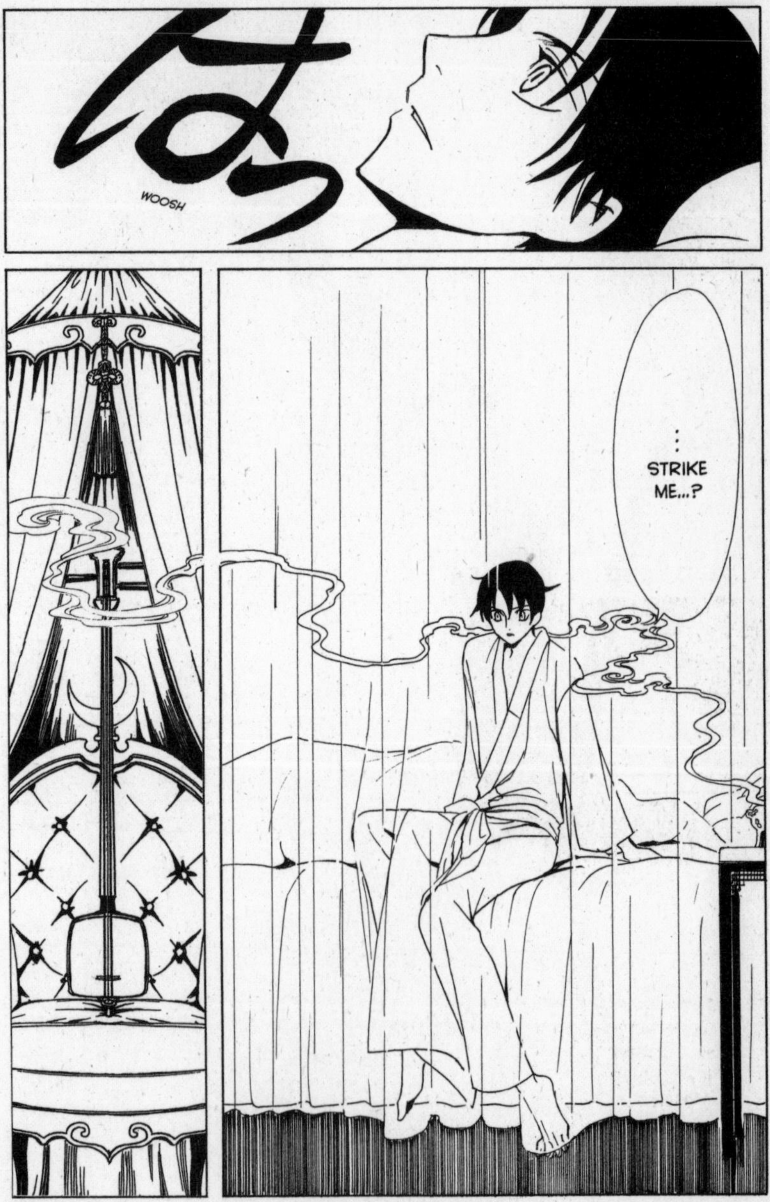
はっ
WOOSH
...
STRIKE ME...?

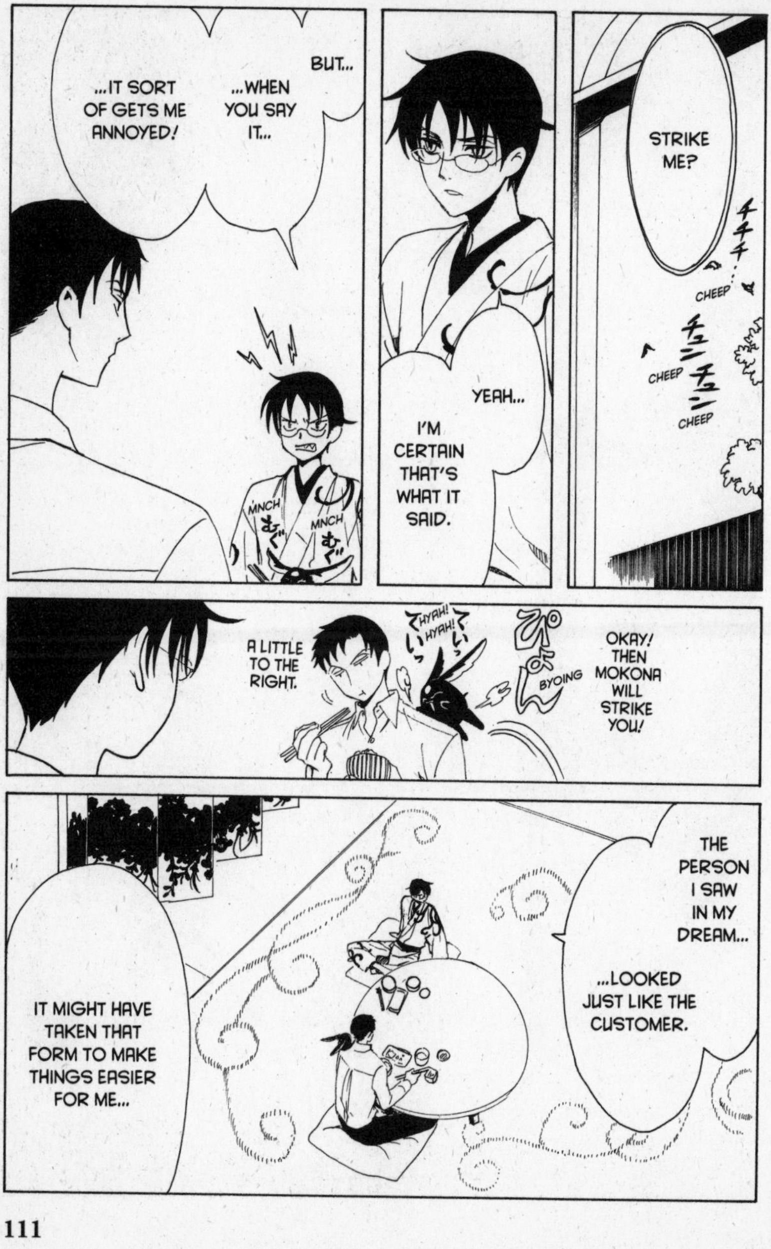
STRIKE ME?
チチチ
CHEEP
チュン
CHEEP
チュン
CHEEP
YEAH...
I'M CERTAIN THAT'S WHAT IT SAID.
BUT...
...WHEN YOU SAY IT...
...IT SORT OF GETS ME ANNOYED!
MNCH
むぐ
MNCH
むぐ
OKAY! THEN MOKONA WILL STRIKE YOU!
ぴょん
BYOING
てぃっ
HYAH!
てぃっ
HYAH!
A LITTLE TO THE RIGHT.
THE PERSON I SAW IN MY DREAM...
...LOOKED JUST LIKE THE CUSTOMER.
IT MIGHT HAVE TAKEN THAT FORM TO MAKE THINGS EASIER FOR ME...

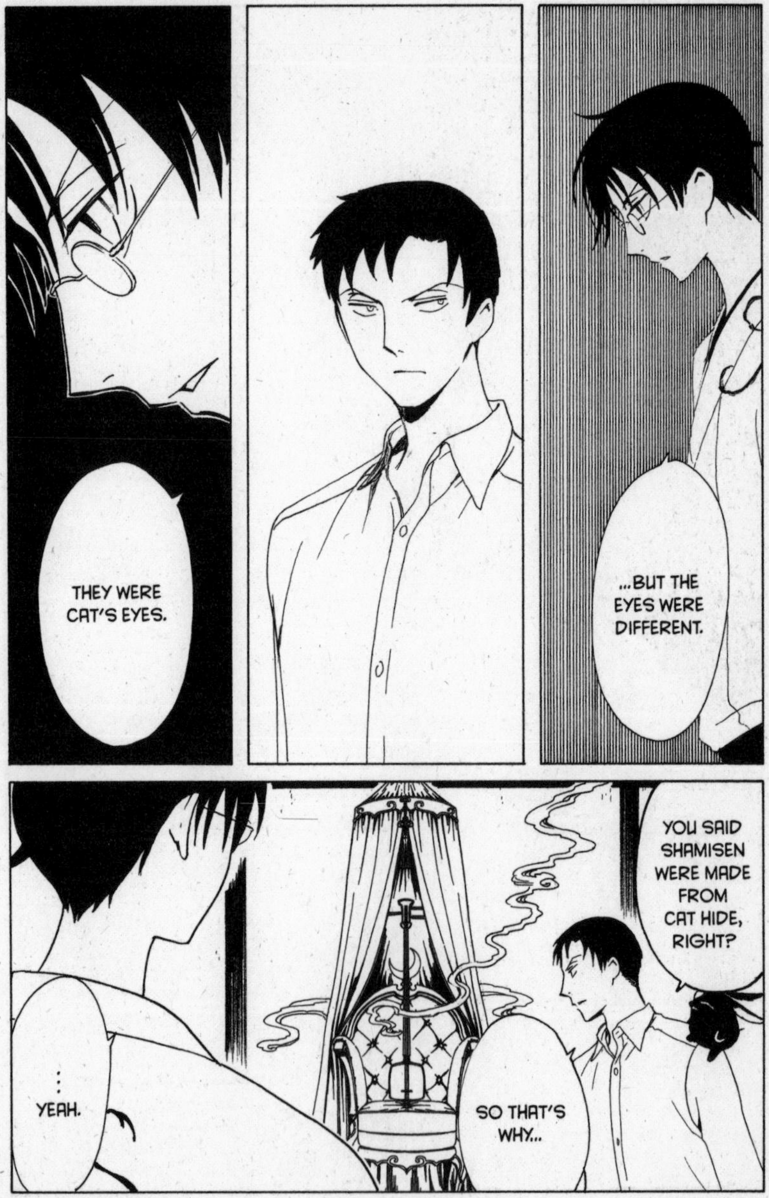
...BUT THE EYES WERE DIFFERENT.
THEY WERE CAT'S EYES.
YOU SAID SHAMISEN WERE MADE FROM CAT HIDE, RIGHT?
SO THAT'S WHY...
... YEAH.

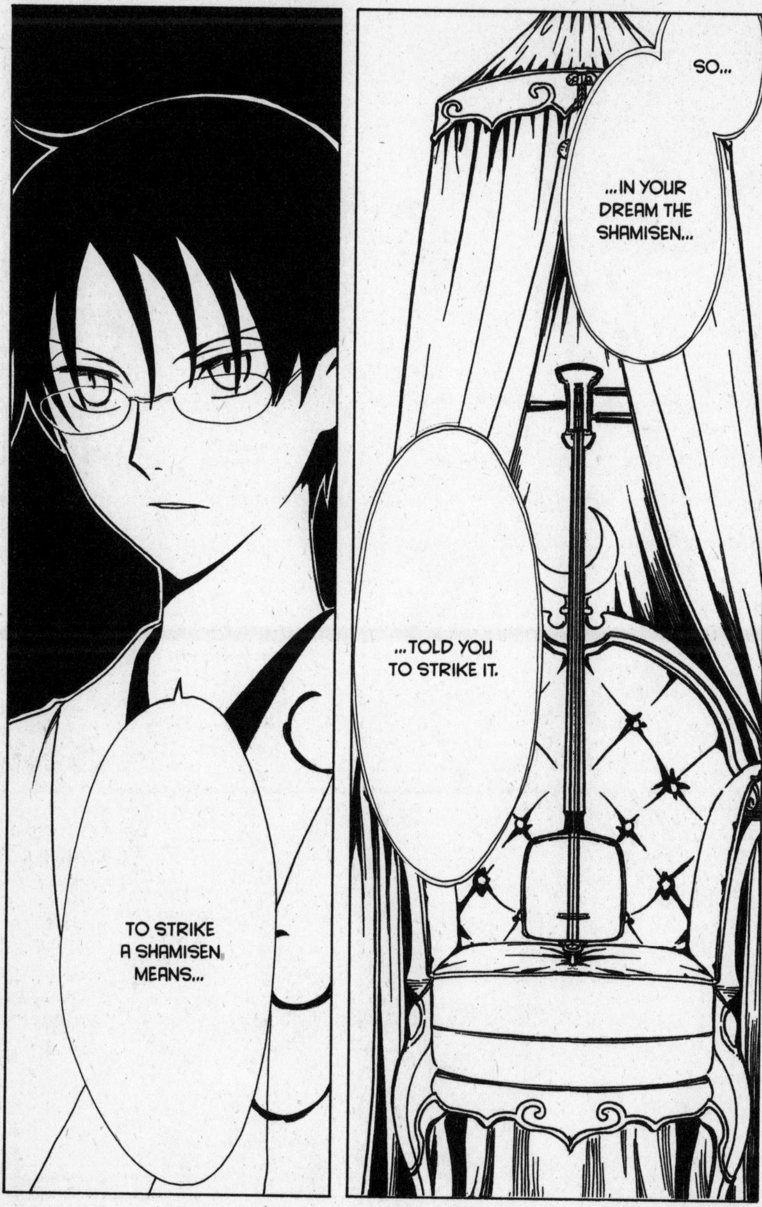
SO...
...IN YOUR DREAM THE SHAMISEN...
...TOLD YOU TO STRIKE IT.
TO STRIKE A SHAMISEN MEANS...

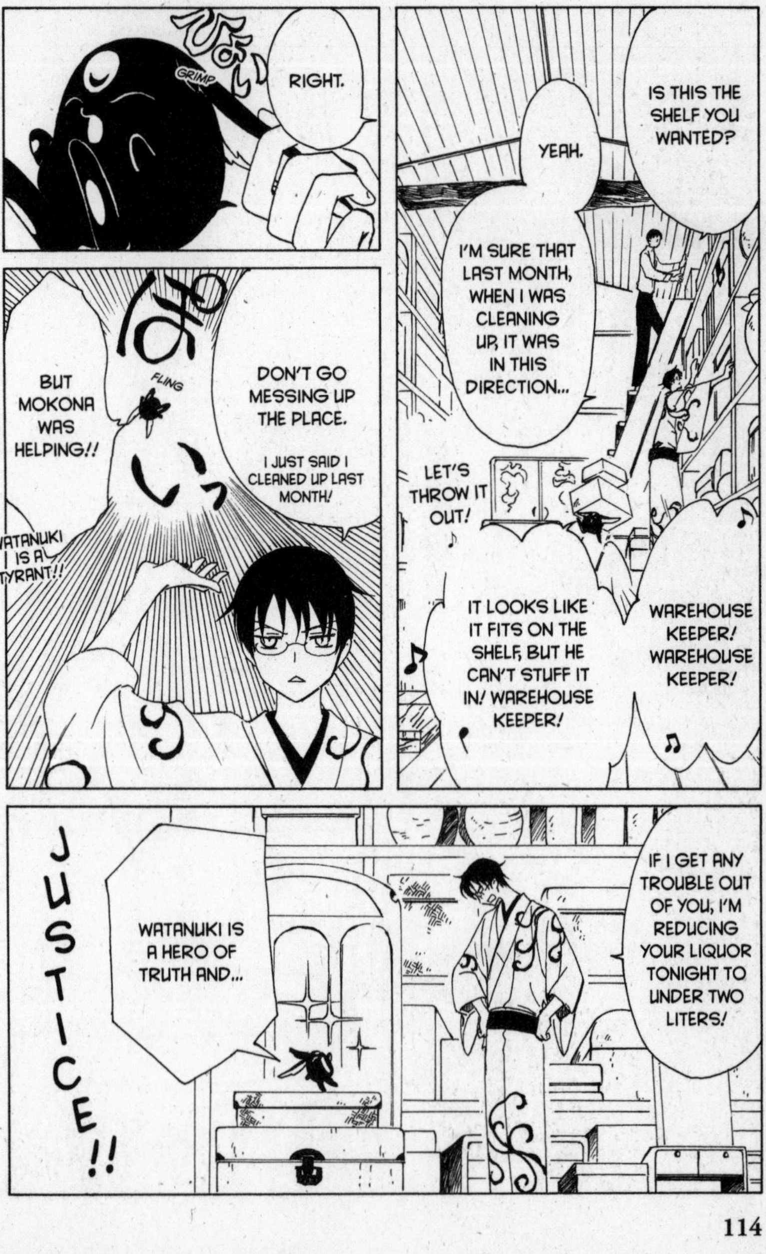
IS THIS THE SHELF YOU WANTED?
YEAH.
I'M SURE THAT LAST MONTH, WHEN I WAS CLEANING UP, IT WAS IN THIS DIRECTION...
LET'S THROW IT OUT! ♪
WAREHOUSE KEEPER! WAREHOUSE KEEPER! ♪
IT LOOKS LIKE IT FITS ON THE SHELF, BUT HE CAN'T STUFF IT IN! WAREHOUSE KEEPER! ♪
GRIMP
RIGHT.
DON'T GO MESSING UP THE PLACE.
I JUST SAID I CLEANED UP LAST MONTH!
ぽいっ
FLING
BUT MOKONA WAS HELPING!!
WATANUKI IS A TYRANT!!
IF I GET ANY TROUBLE OUT OF YOU, I'M REDUCING YOUR LIQUOR TONIGHT TO UNDER TWO LITERS!
WATANUKI IS A HERO OF TRUTH AND...
JUSTICE!!

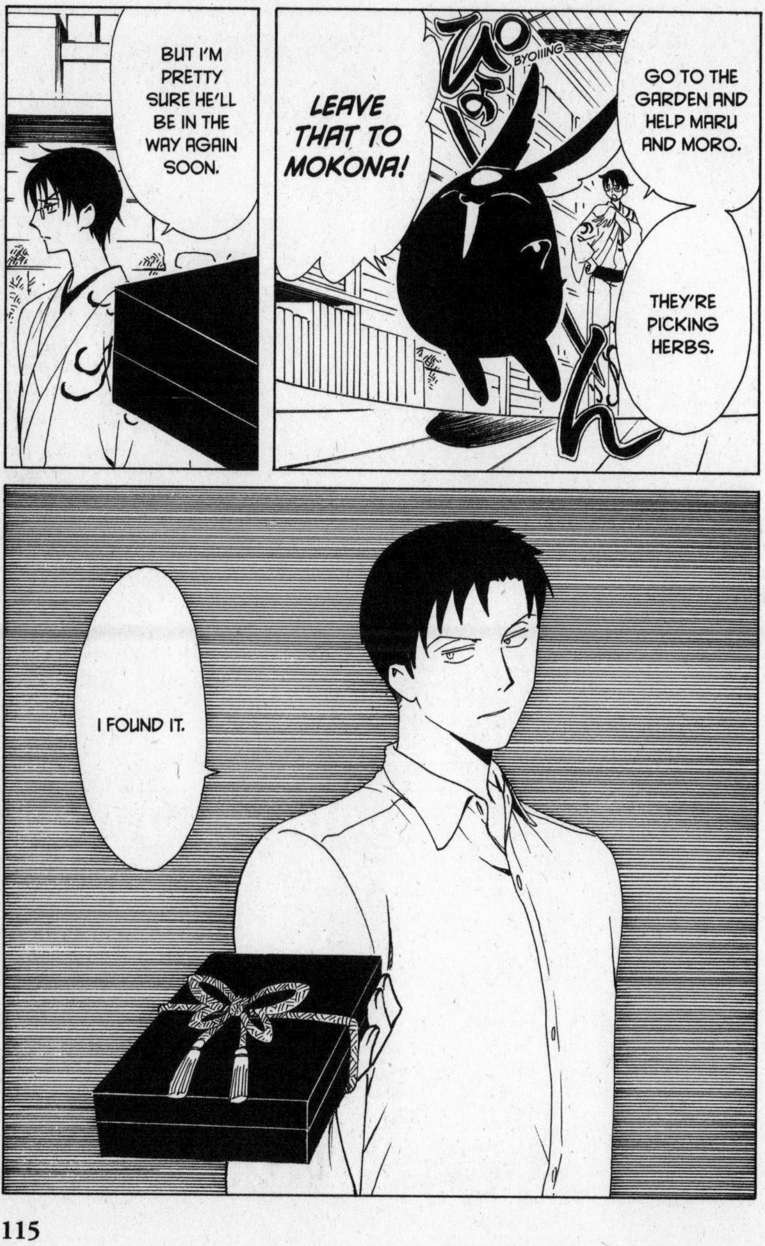
GO TO THE GARDEN AND HELP MARU AND MORO.
THEY'RE PICKING HERBS.
BYOIIING
LEAVE THAT TO MOKONA!
BUT I'M PRETTY SURE HE'LL BE IN THE WAY AGAIN SOON.
I FOUND IT.

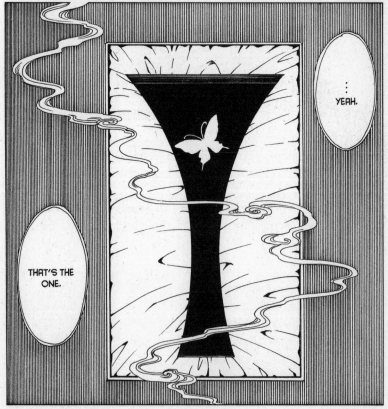

YEAH.

THAT'S THE
ONE.

116

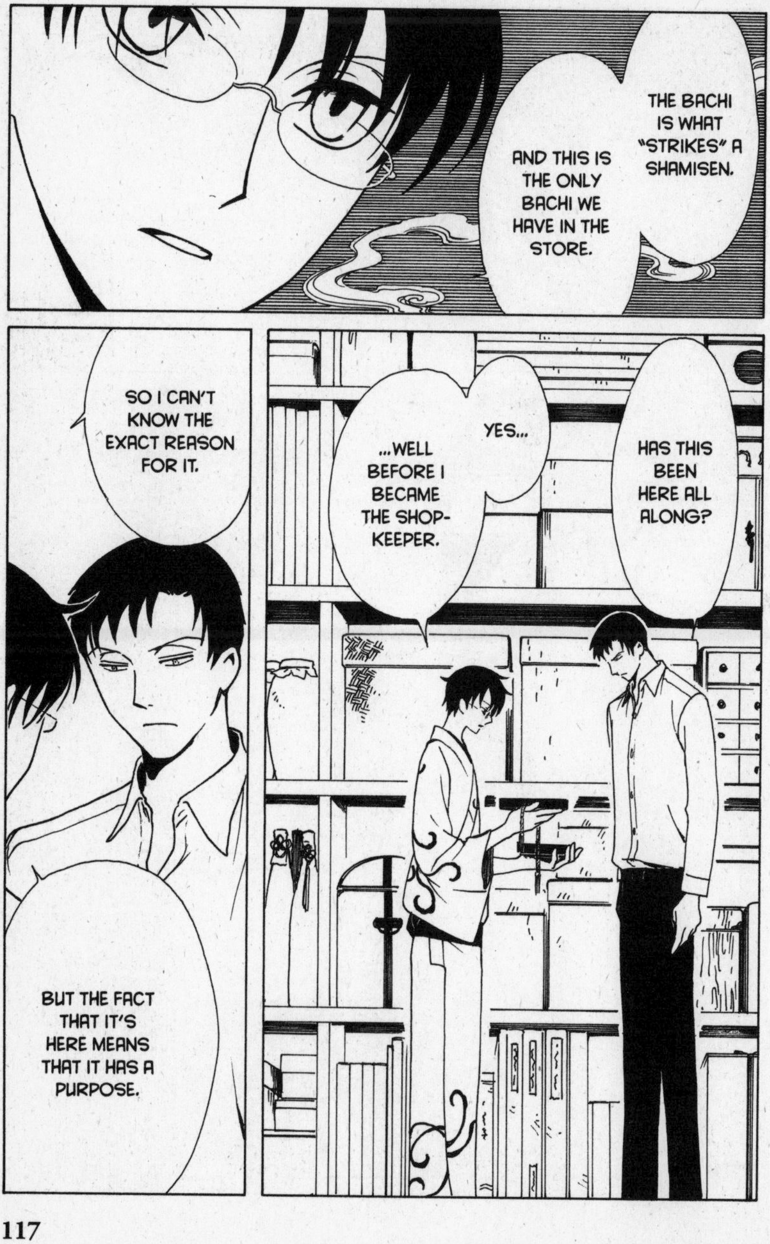
THE BACHI IS WHAT "STRIKES" A SHAMISEN.
AND THIS IS THE ONLY BACHI WE HAVE IN THE STORE.
HAS THIS BEEN HERE ALL ALONG?
YES...
...WELL BEFORE I BECAME THE SHOP-KEEPER.
SO I CAN'T KNOW THE EXACT REASON FOR IT.
BUT THE FACT THAT IT'S HERE MEANS THAT IT HAS A PURPOSE.

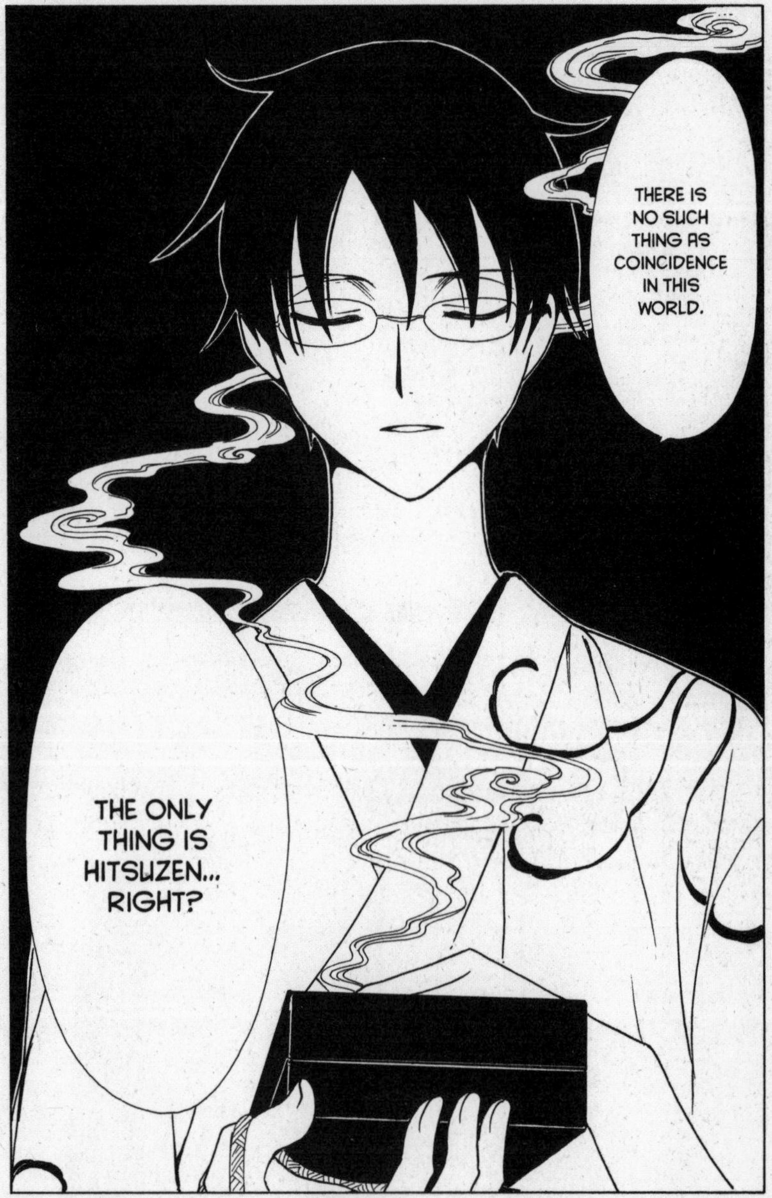
THERE IS NO SUCH THING AS COINCIDENCE IN THIS WORLD.
THE ONLY THING IS HITSUZEN... RIGHT?

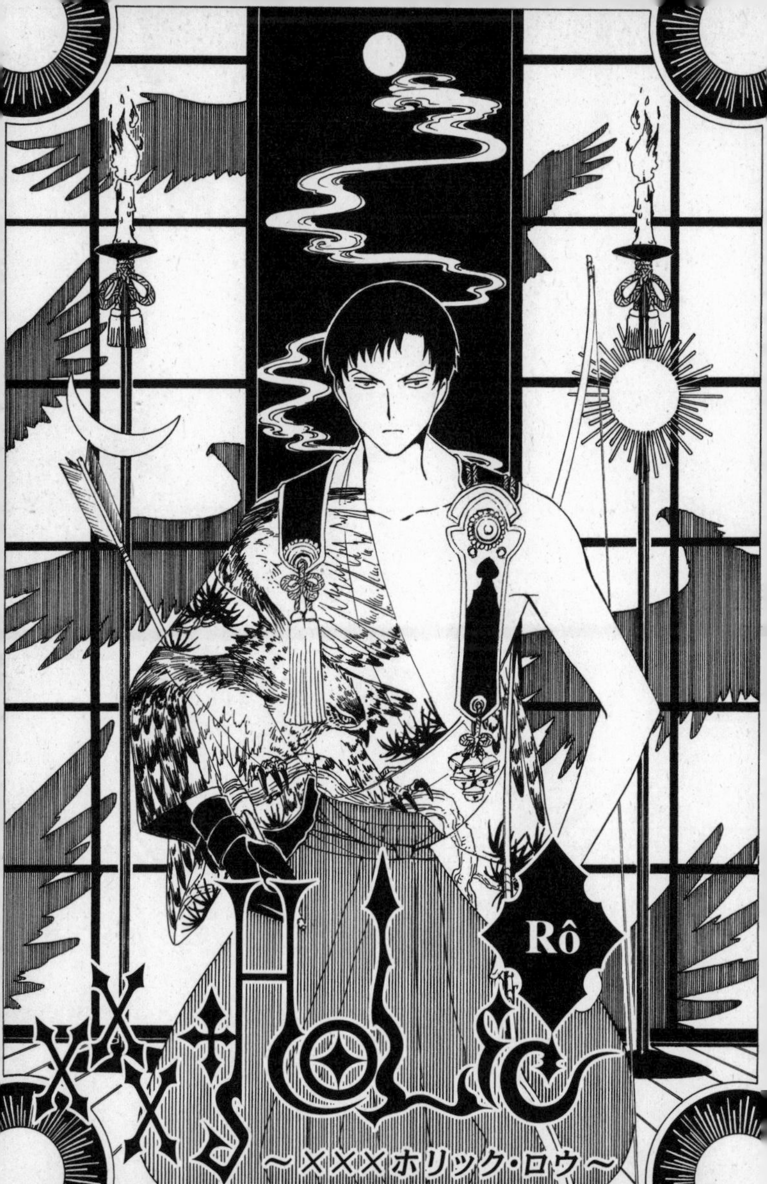
xxxHOLiC
Rô
～×××ホリック・ロウ～

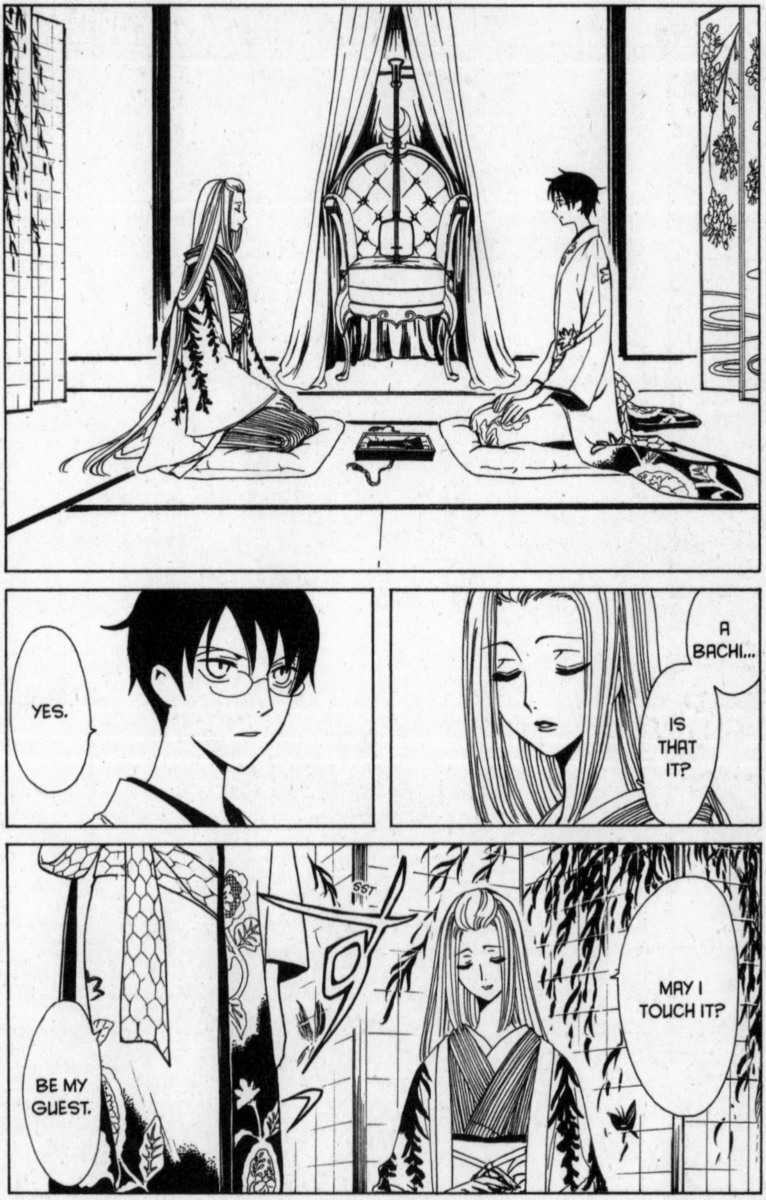
A BACHI...
IS THAT IT?
YES.
MAY I TOUCH IT?
SST
BE MY GUEST.

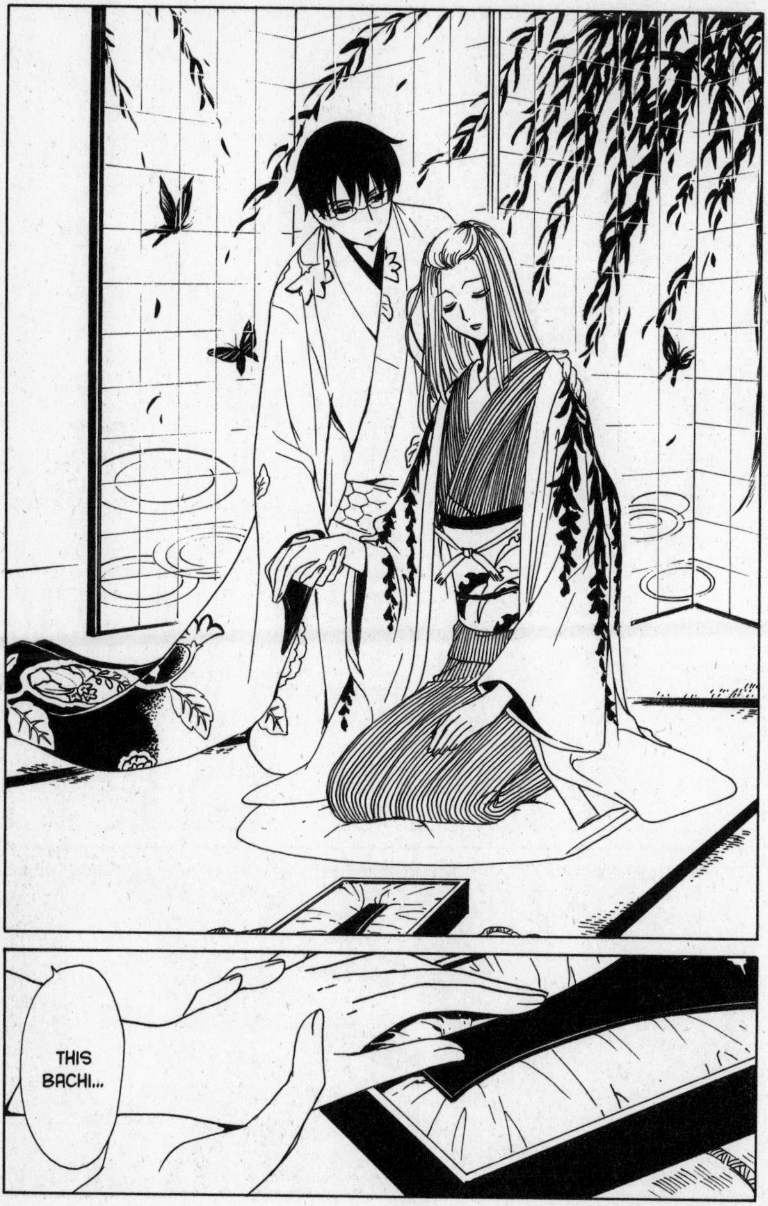
THIS BACHI...

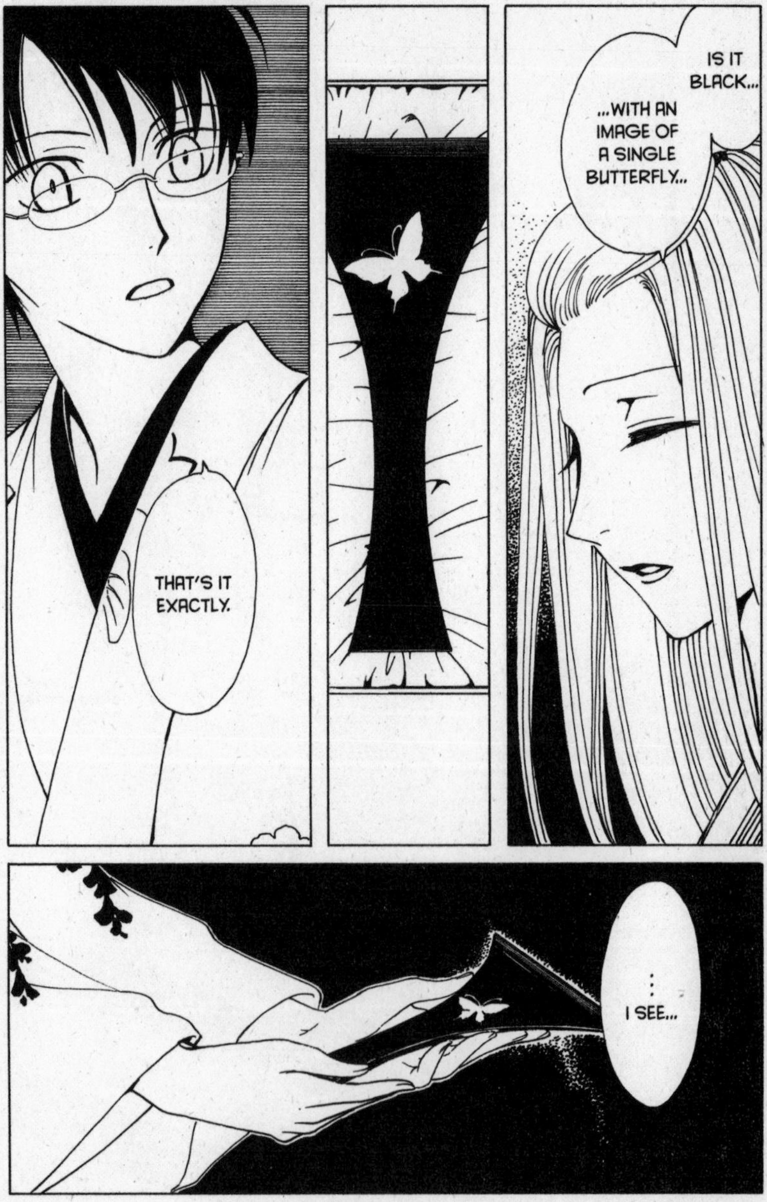
IS IT BLACK...
...WITH AN IMAGE OF A SINGLE BUTTERFLY...
THAT'S IT EXACTLY.
... I SEE...

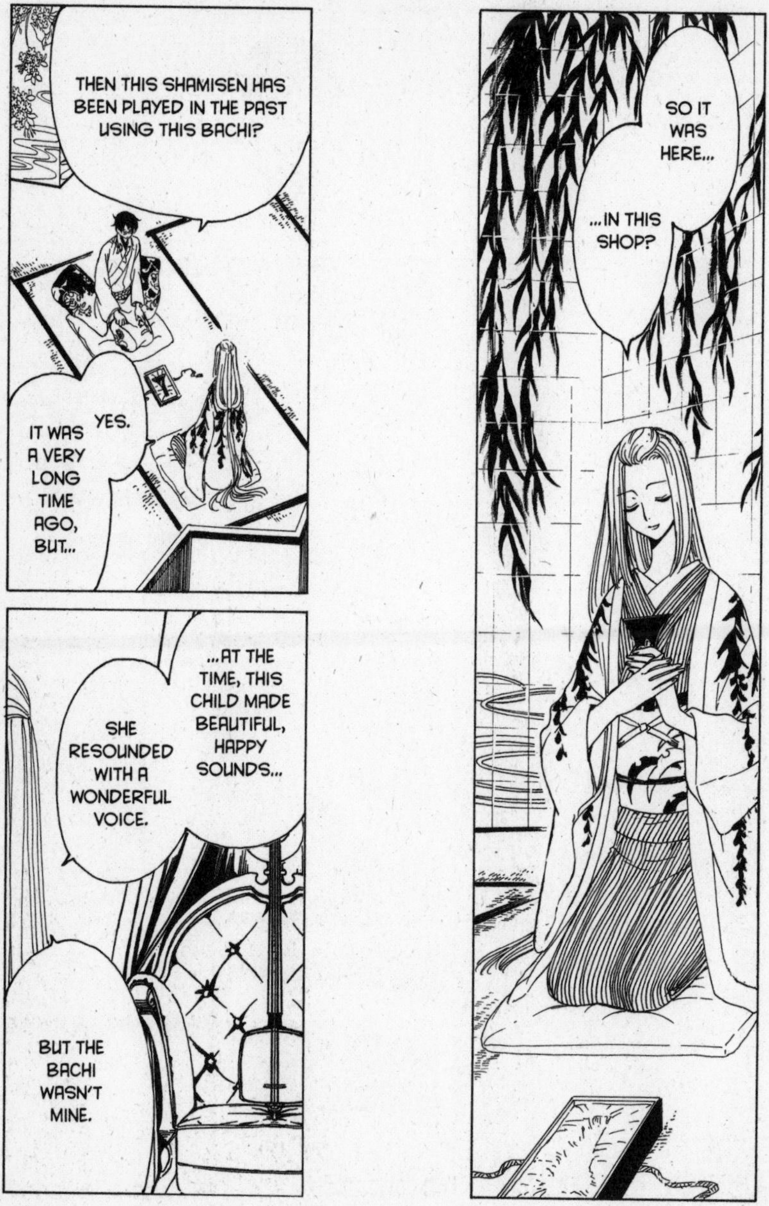
SO IT WAS HERE...
...IN THIS SHOP?
THEN THIS SHAMISEN HAS BEEN PLAYED IN THE PAST USING THIS BACHI?
YES.
IT WAS A VERY LONG TIME AGO, BUT...
...AT THE TIME, THIS CHILD MADE BEAUTIFUL, HAPPY SOUNDS...
SHE RESOUNDED WITH A WONDERFUL VOICE.
BUT THE BACHI WASN'T MINE.

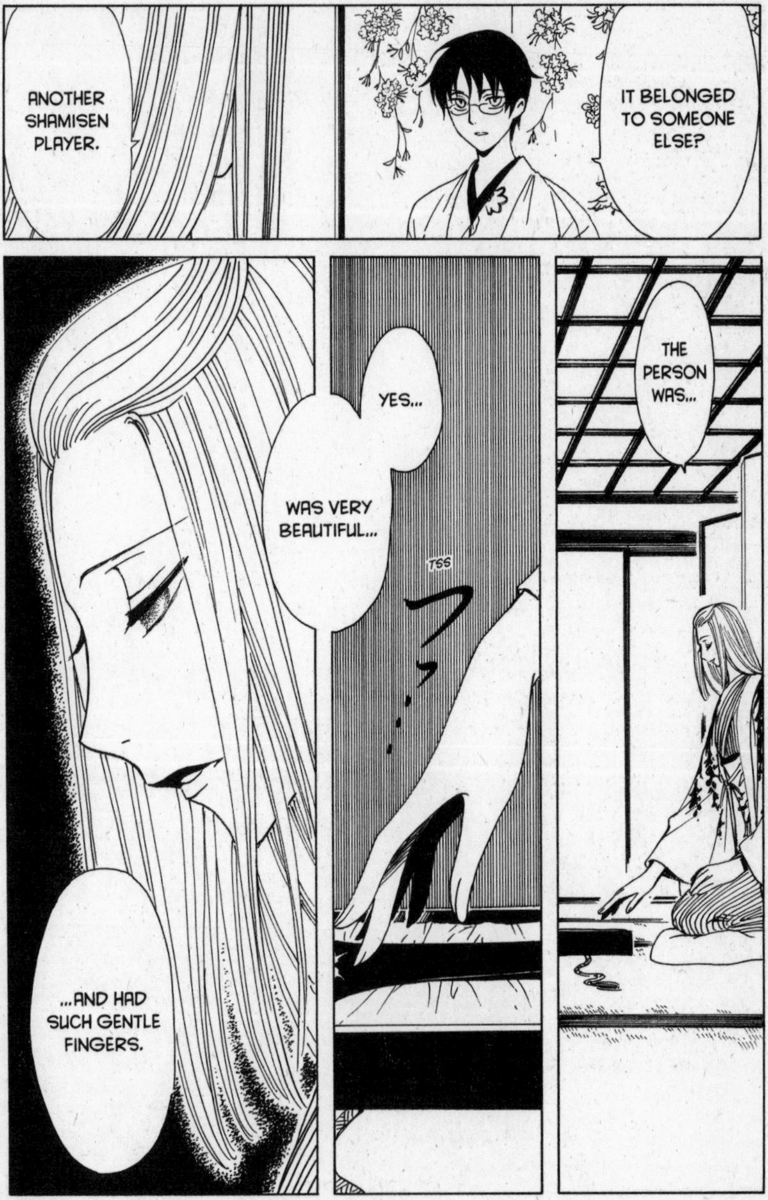
IT BELONGED TO SOMEONE ELSE?
ANOTHER SHAMISEN PLAYER.
THE PERSON WAS...
YES...
WAS VERY BEAUTIFUL...
TSS
...AND HAD SUCH GENTLE FINGERS.

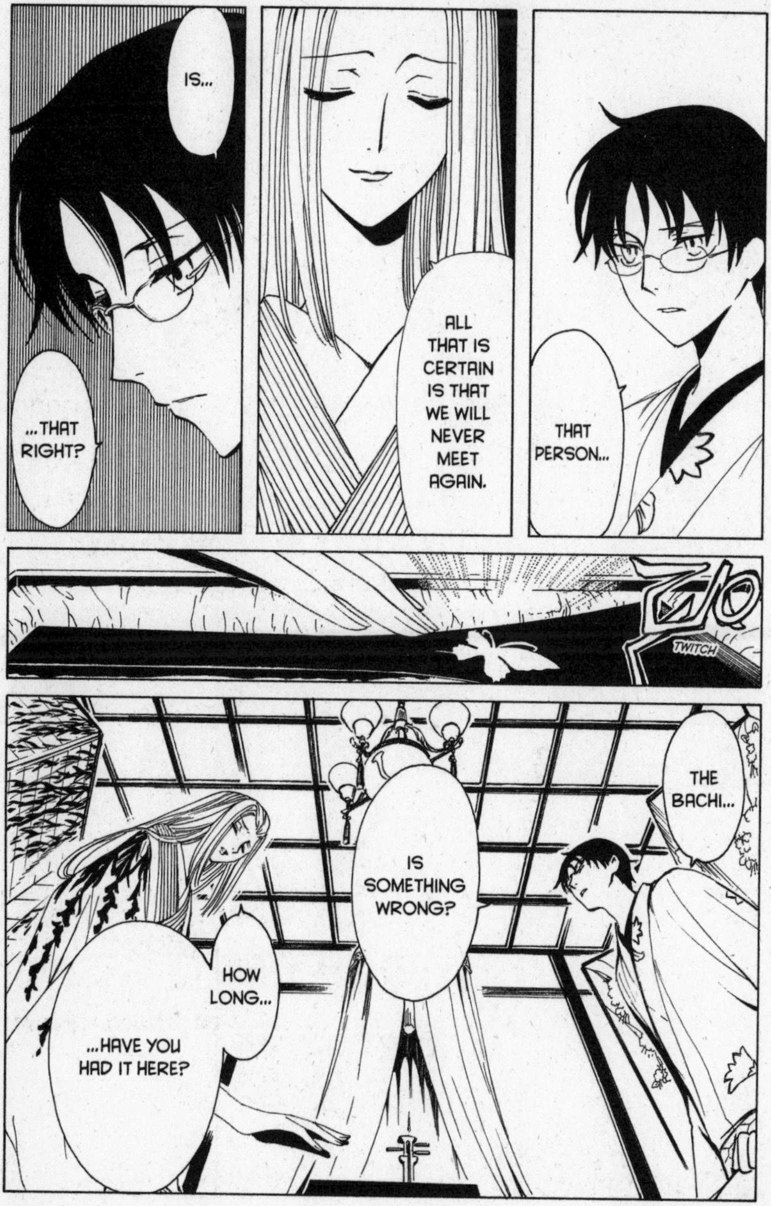
THAT PERSON...
ALL THAT IS CERTAIN IS THAT WE WILL NEVER MEET AGAIN.
IS...
...THAT RIGHT?
TWITCH
THE BACHI...
IS SOMETHING WRONG?
HOW LONG...
...HAVE YOU HAD IT HERE?

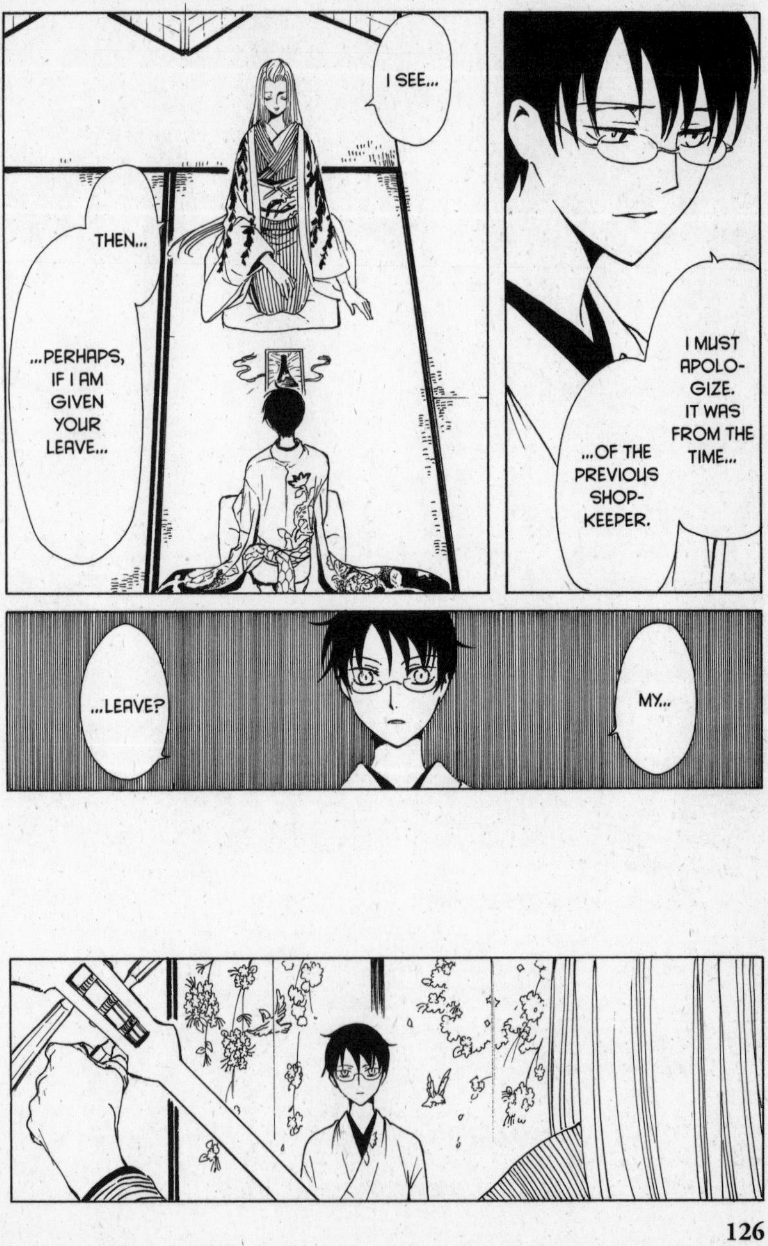
I MUST APOLO-GIZE. IT WAS FROM THE TIME...
...OF THE PREVIOUS SHOP-KEEPER.
I SEE...
THEN...
...PERHAPS, IF I AM GIVEN YOUR LEAVE...
MY...
...LEAVE?

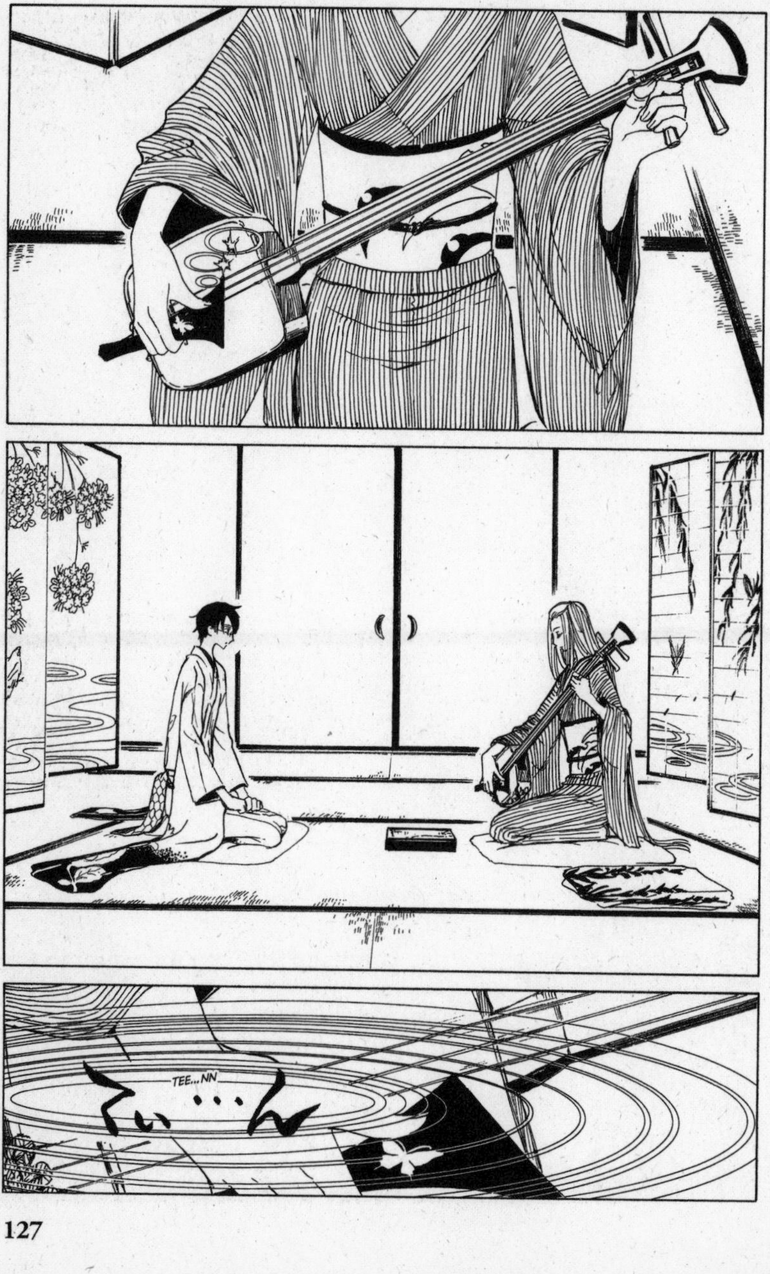
てぃ…ん
TEE...NN

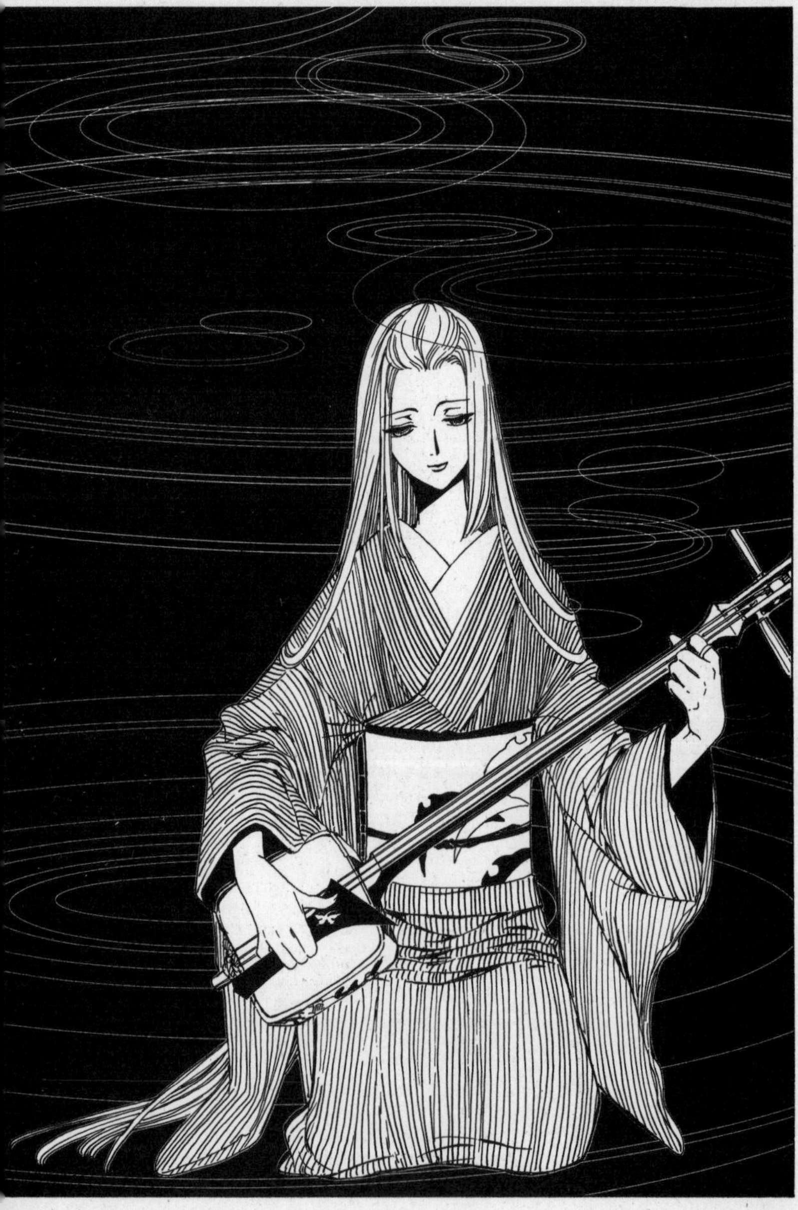

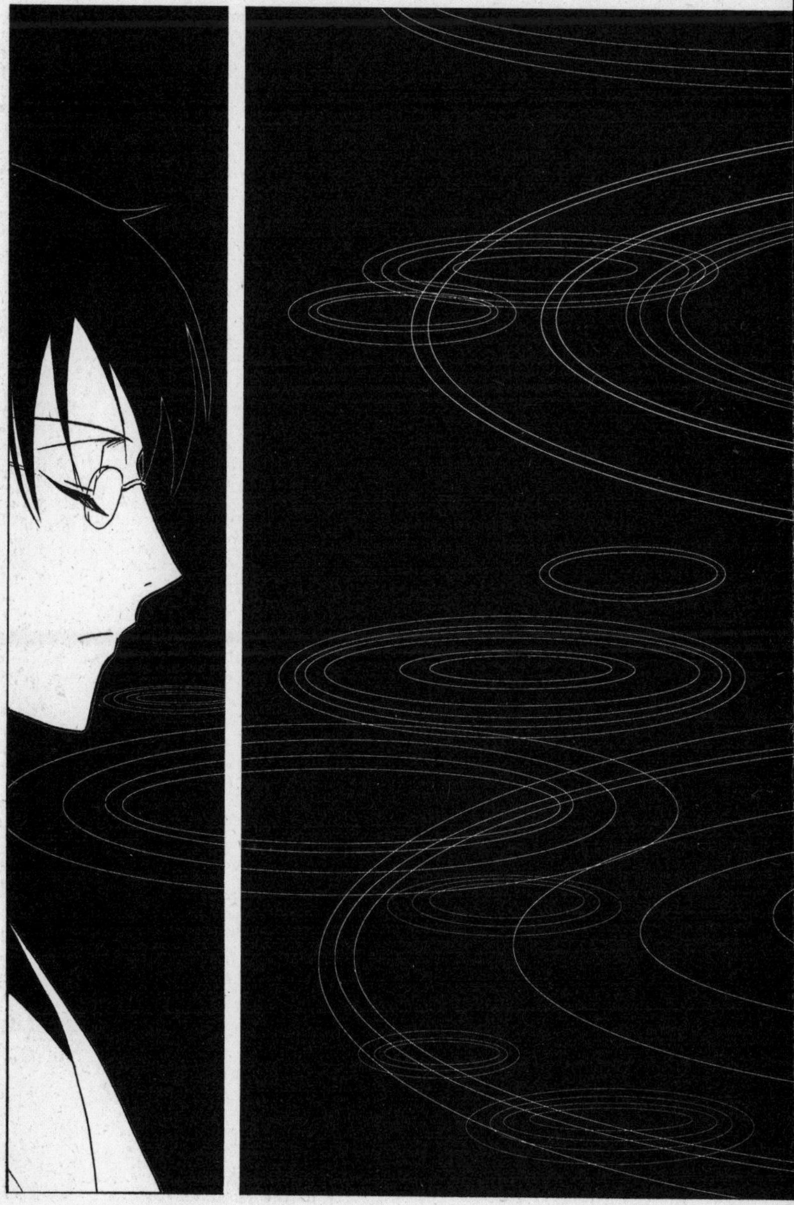

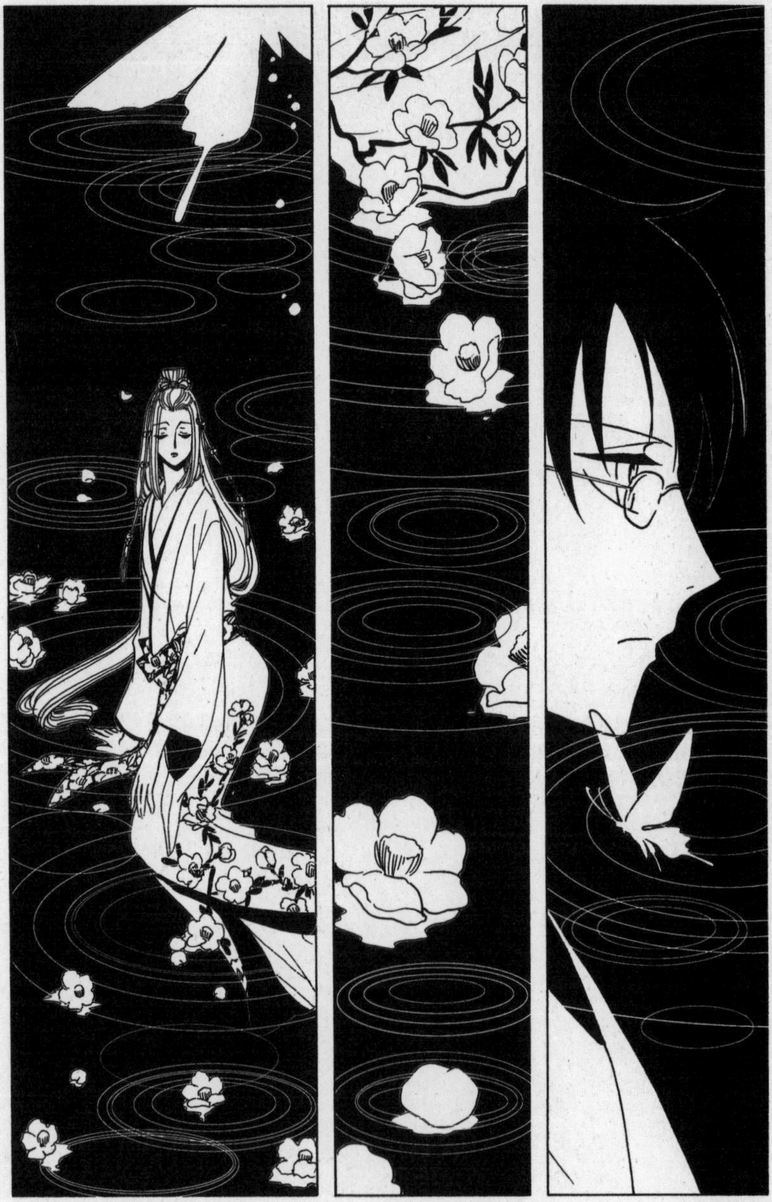

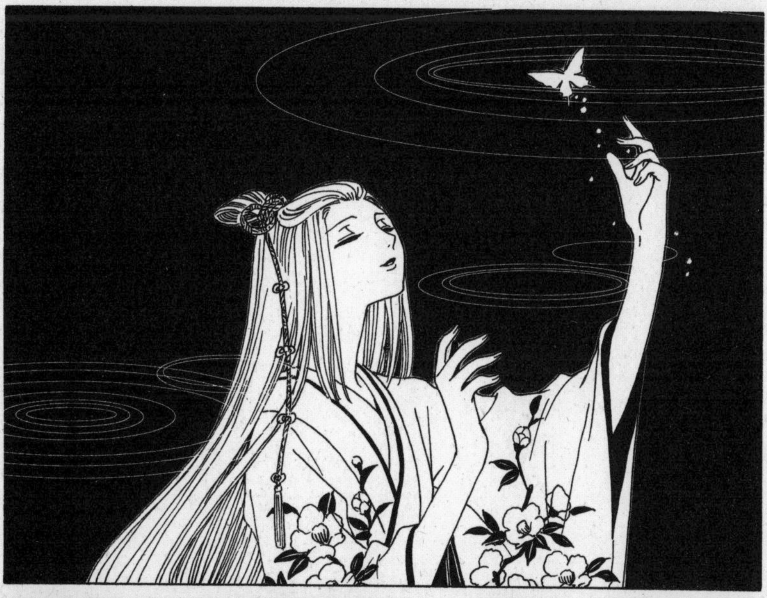
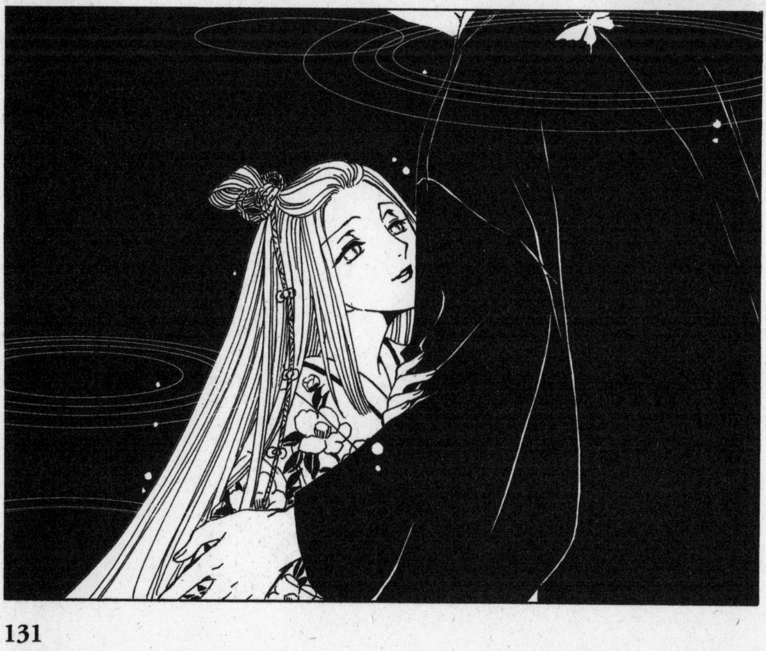

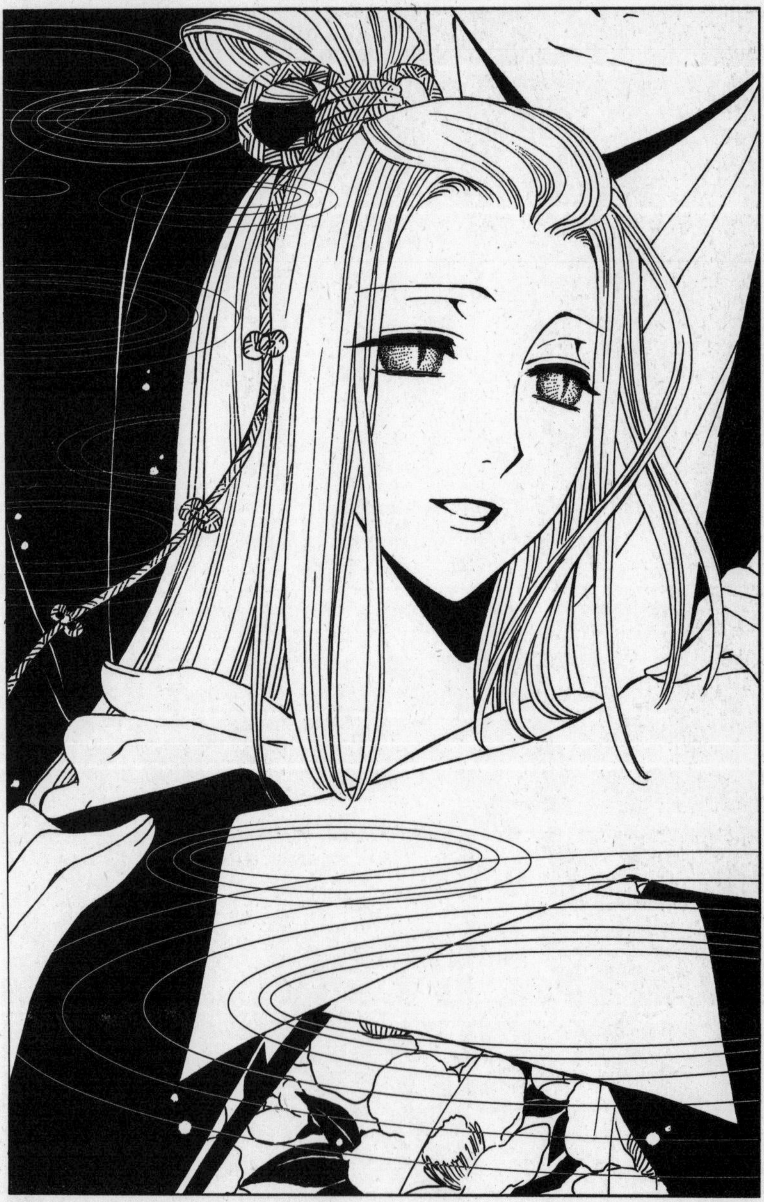

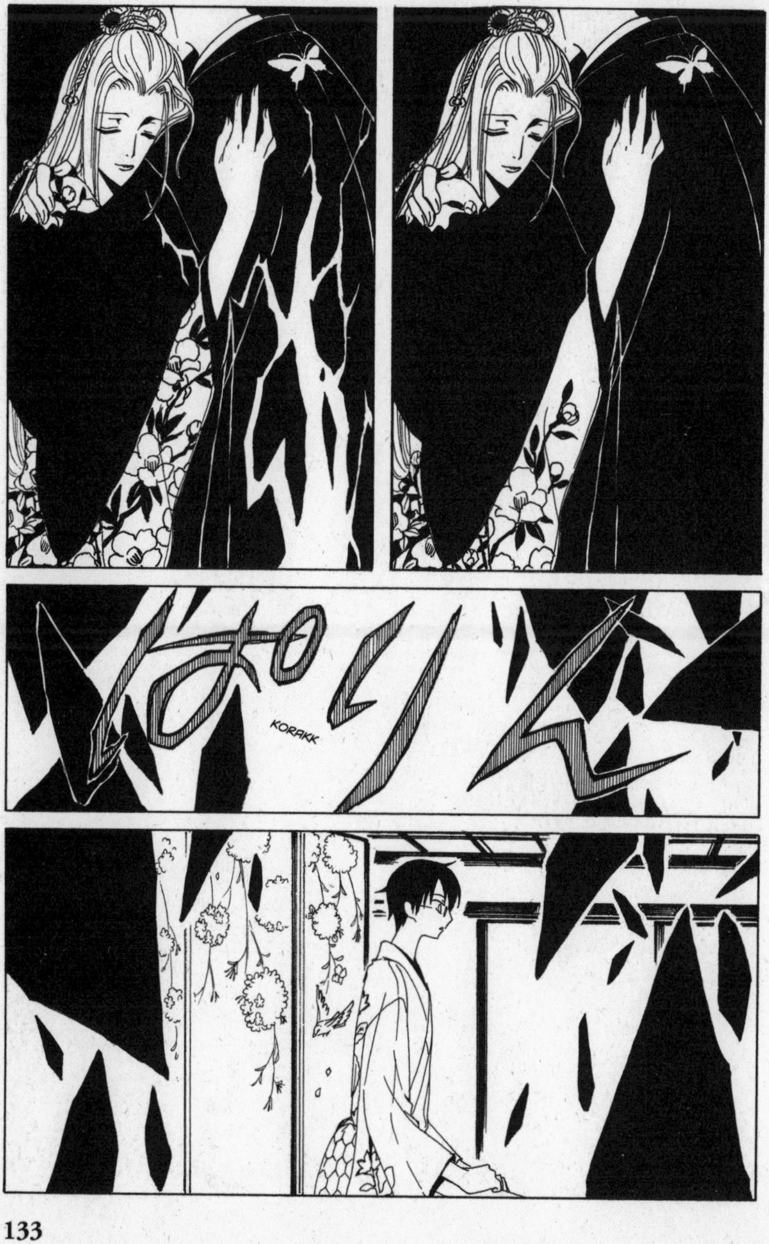
KORAKK

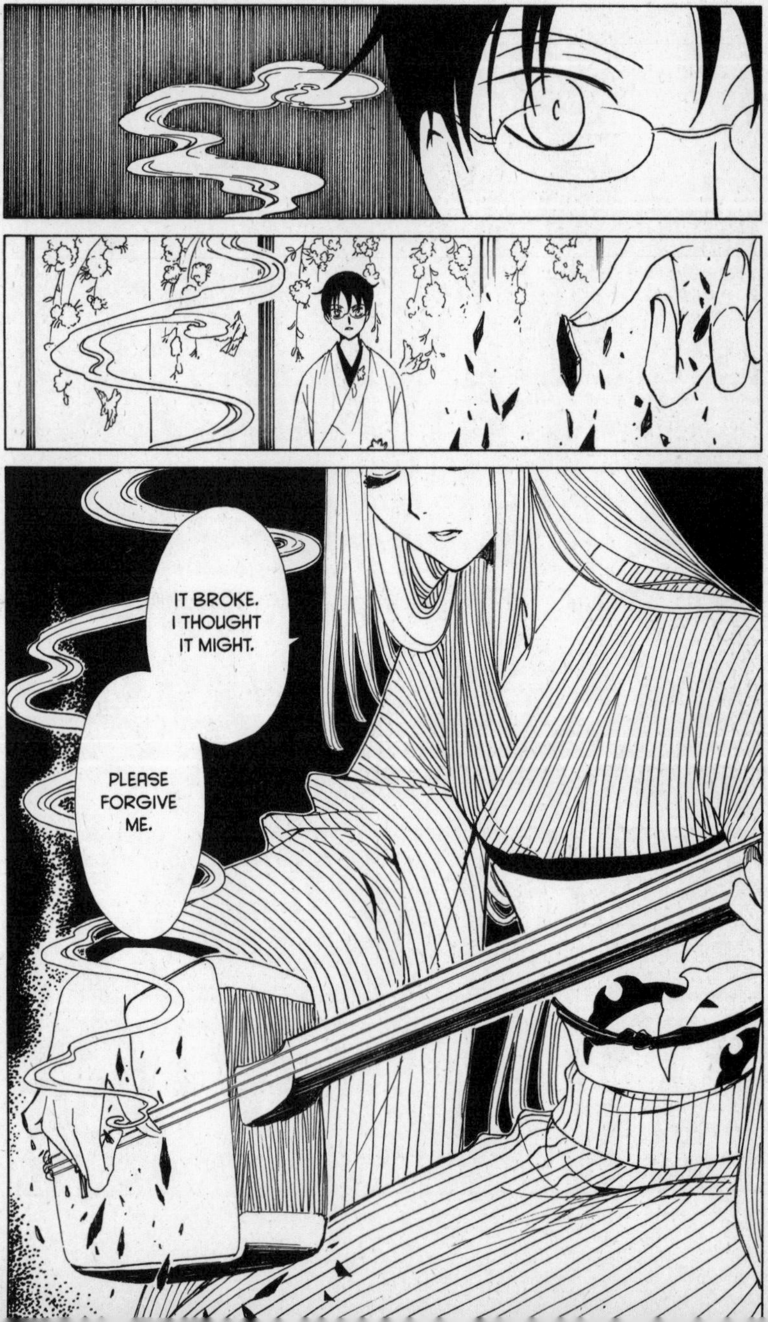
IT BROKE. I THOUGHT IT MIGHT.
PLEASE FORGIVE ME.

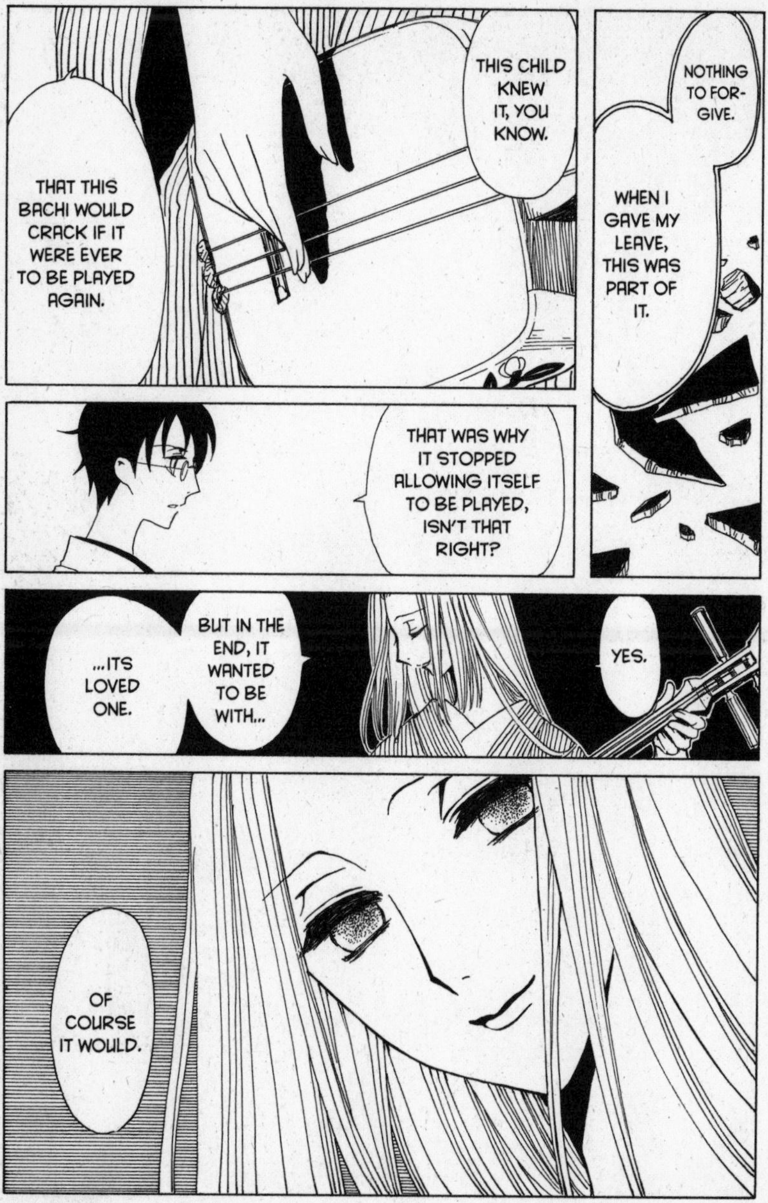
NOTHING TO FOR-GIVE.
WHEN I GAVE MY LEAVE, THIS WAS PART OF IT.
THIS CHILD KNEW IT, YOU KNOW.
THAT THIS BACHI WOULD CRACK IF IT WERE EVER TO BE PLAYED AGAIN.
THAT WAS WHY IT STOPPED ALLOWING ITSELF TO BE PLAYED, ISN'T THAT RIGHT?
YES.
BUT IN THE END, IT WANTED TO BE WITH...
...ITS LOVED ONE.
OF COURSE IT WOULD.

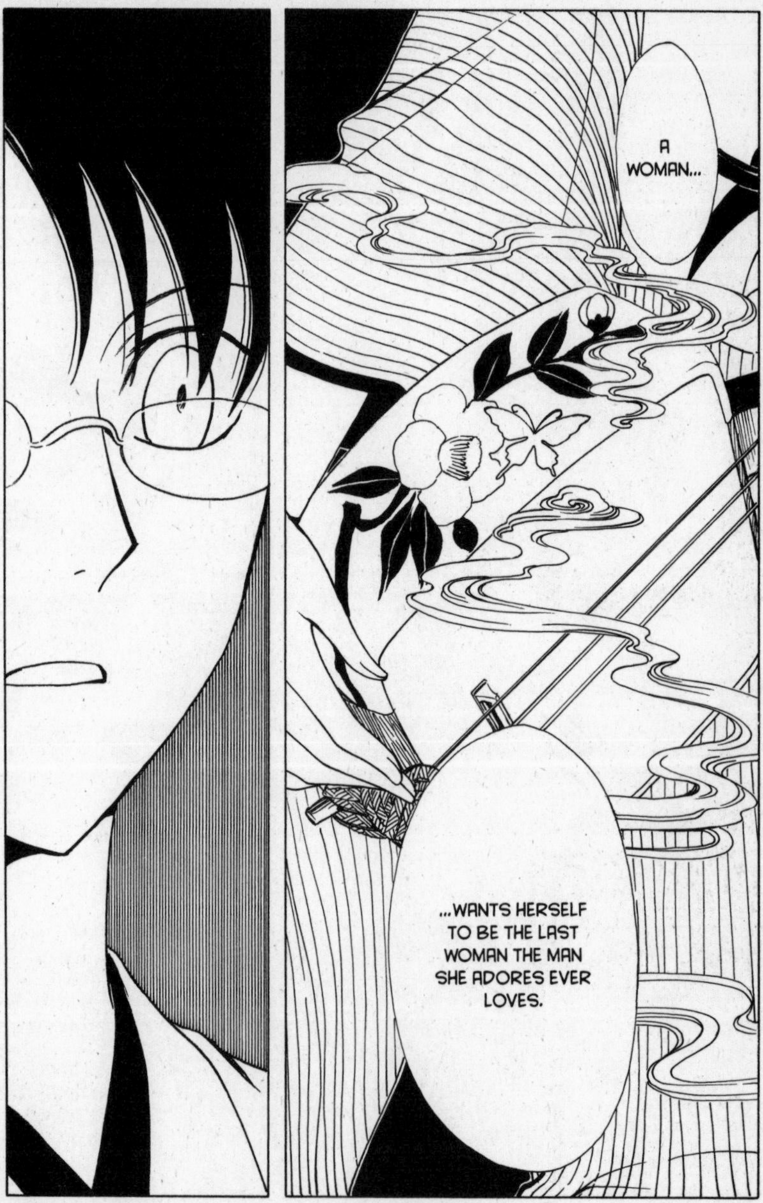
A WOMAN...
...WANTS HERSELF TO BE THE LAST WOMAN THE MAN SHE ADORES EVER LOVES.

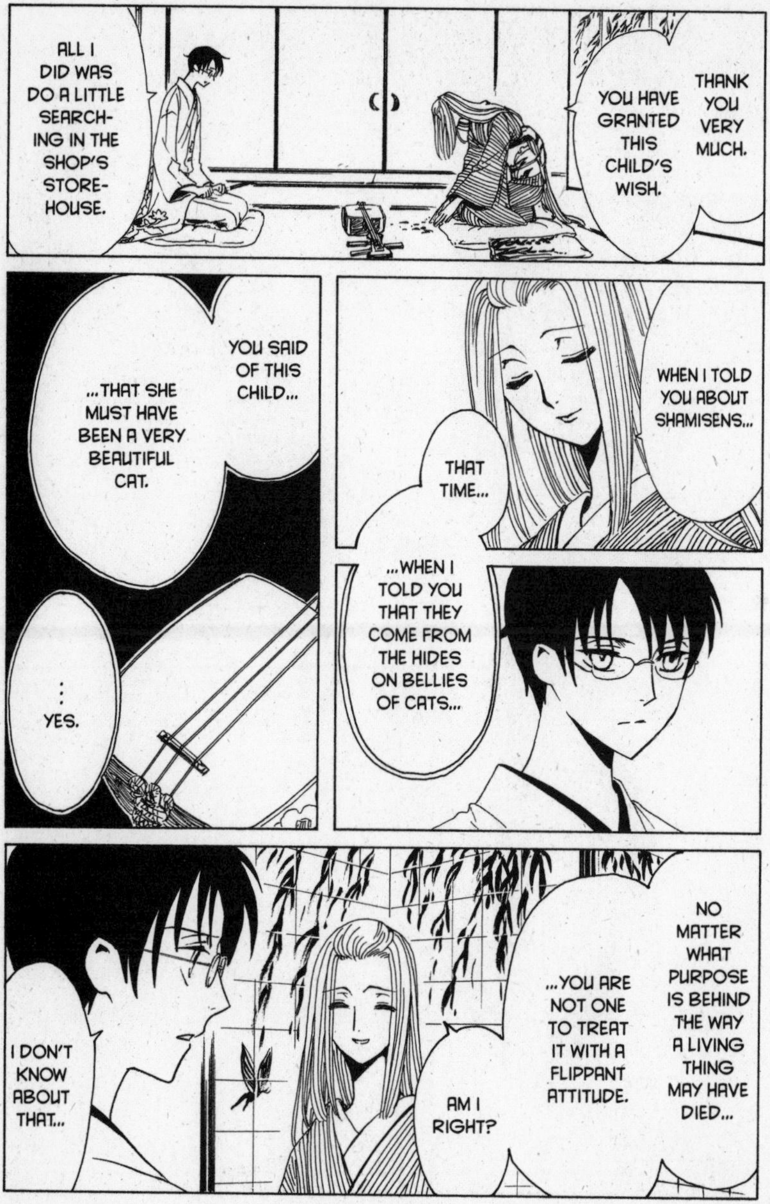
THANK YOU VERY MUCH.
YOU HAVE GRANTED THIS CHILD'S WISH.
ALL I DID WAS DO A LITTLE SEARCHING IN THE SHOP'S STOREHOUSE.
WHEN I TOLD YOU ABOUT SHAMISENS...
THAT TIME...
...WHEN I TOLD YOU THAT THEY COME FROM THE HIDES ON BELLIES OF CATS...
YOU SAID OF THIS CHILD...
...THAT SHE MUST HAVE BEEN A VERY BEAUTIFUL CAT.
... YES.
NO MATTER WHAT PURPOSE IS BEHIND THE WAY A LIVING THING MAY HAVE DIED...
...YOU ARE NOT ONE TO TREAT IT WITH A FLIPPANT ATTITUDE.
AM I RIGHT?
I DON'T KNOW ABOUT THAT...

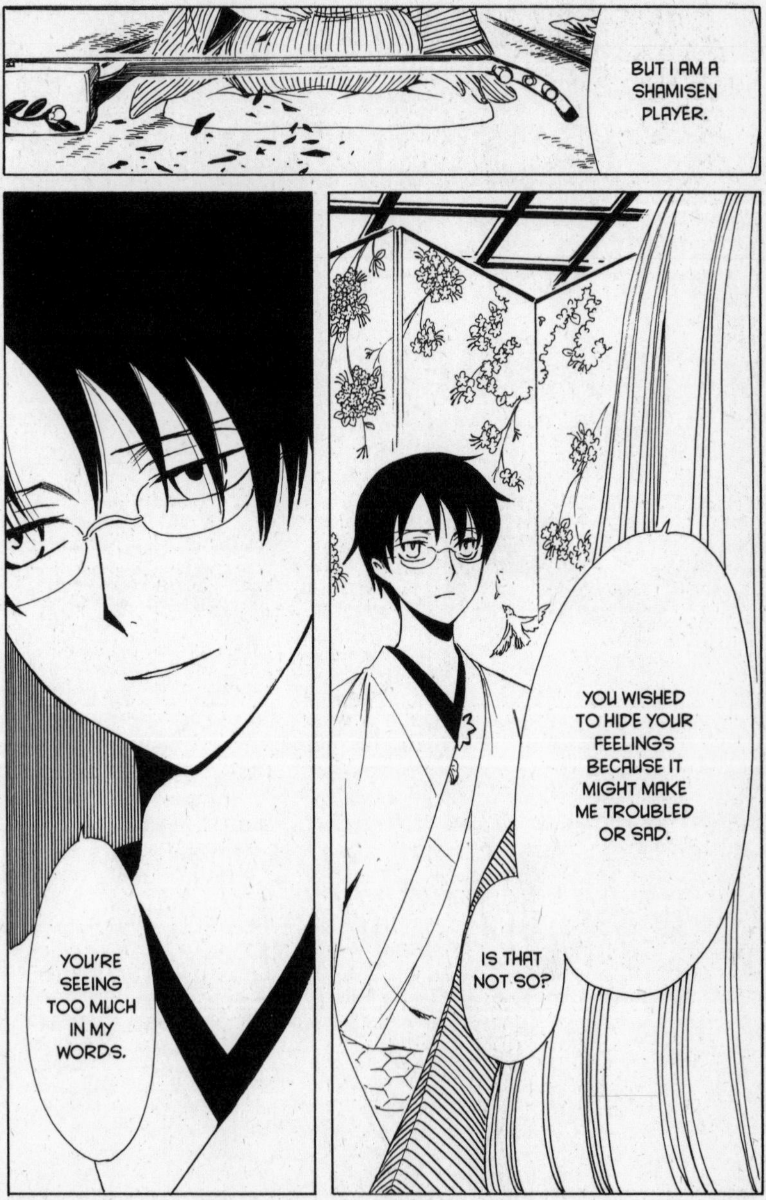
BUT I AM A SHAMISEN PLAYER.
YOU WISHED TO HIDE YOUR FEELINGS BECAUSE IT MIGHT MAKE ME TROUBLED OR SAD.
IS THAT NOT SO?
YOU'RE SEEING TOO MUCH IN MY WORDS.

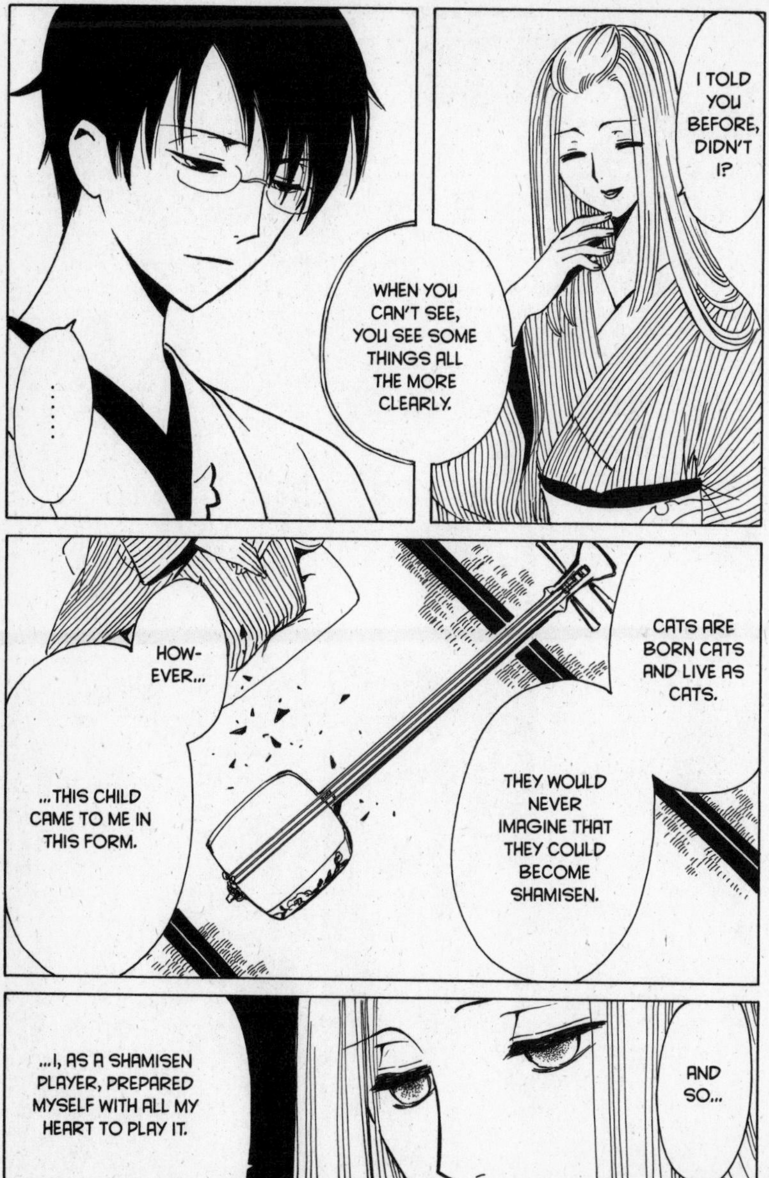
I TOLD YOU BEFORE, DIDN'T I?
WHEN YOU CAN'T SEE, YOU SEE SOME THINGS ALL THE MORE CLEARLY.
......
CATS ARE BORN CATS AND LIVE AS CATS.
THEY WOULD NEVER IMAGINE THAT THEY COULD BECOME SHAMISEN.
HOW-EVER...
...THIS CHILD CAME TO ME IN THIS FORM.
AND SO...
...I, AS A SHAMISEN PLAYER, PREPARED MYSELF WITH ALL MY HEART TO PLAY IT.

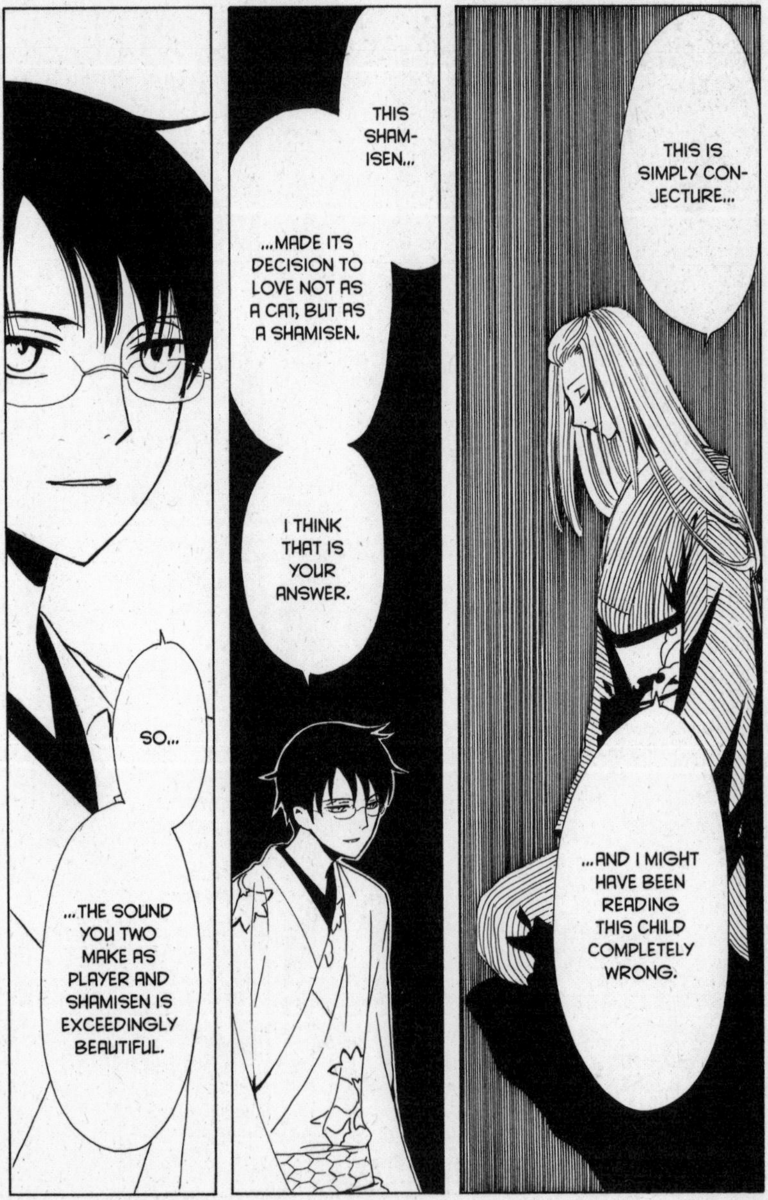
THIS IS SIMPLY CONJECTURE...
...AND I MIGHT HAVE BEEN READING THIS CHILD COMPLETELY WRONG.
THIS SHAMISEN...
...MADE ITS DECISION TO LOVE NOT AS A CAT, BUT AS A SHAMISEN.
I THINK THAT IS YOUR ANSWER.
SO...
...THE SOUND YOU TWO MAKE AS PLAYER AND SHAMISEN IS EXCEEDINGLY BEAUTIFUL.

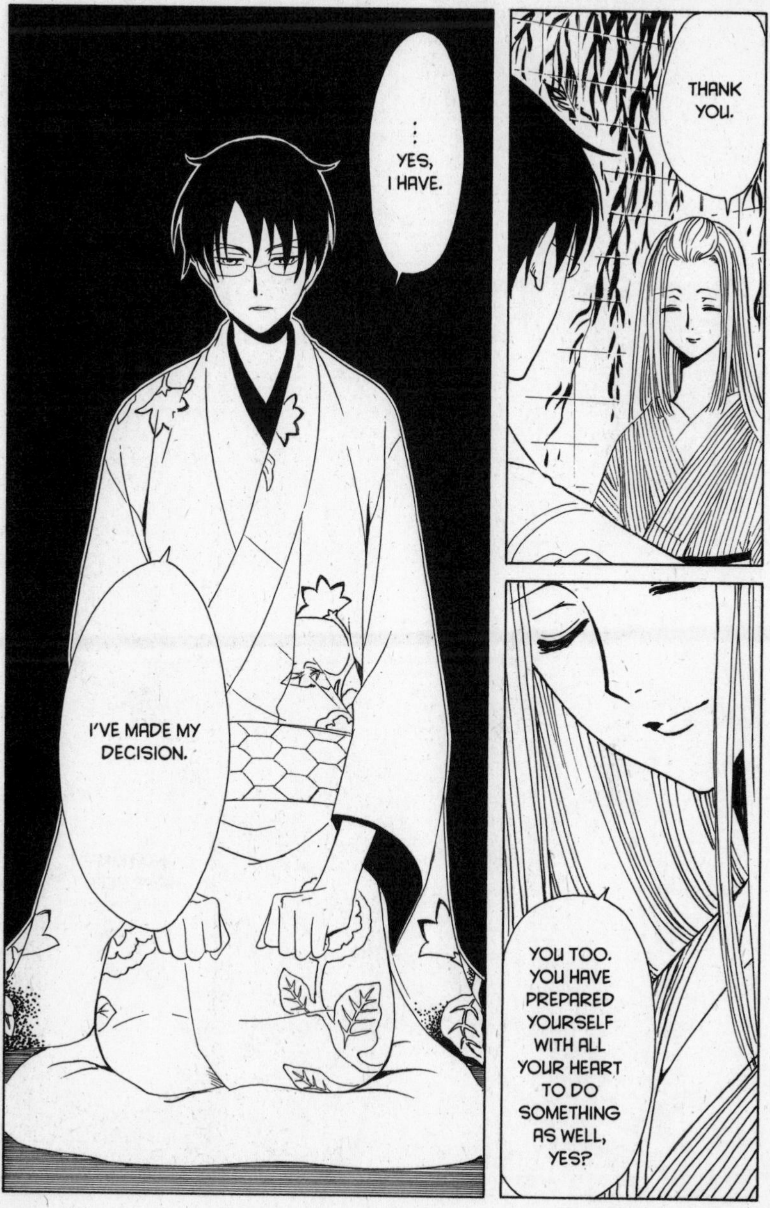
THANK YOU.
YOU TOO. YOU HAVE PREPARED YOURSELF WITH ALL YOUR HEART TO DO SOMETHING AS WELL, YES?
... YES, I HAVE.
I'VE MADE MY DECISION.

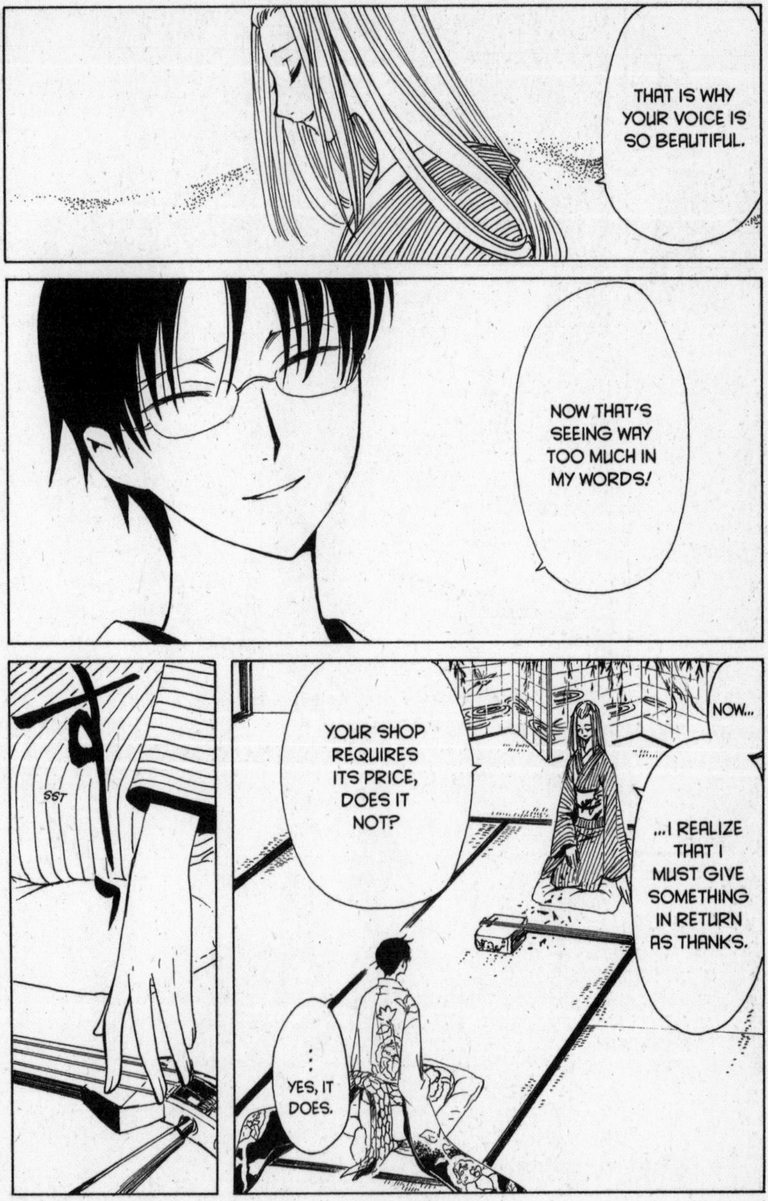
THAT IS WHY YOUR VOICE IS SO BEAUTIFUL.
NOW THAT'S SEEING WAY TOO MUCH IN MY WORDS!
NOW...
...I REALIZE THAT I MUST GIVE SOMETHING IN RETURN AS THANKS.
YOUR SHOP REQUIRES ITS PRICE, DOES IT NOT?
... YES, IT DOES.
SST

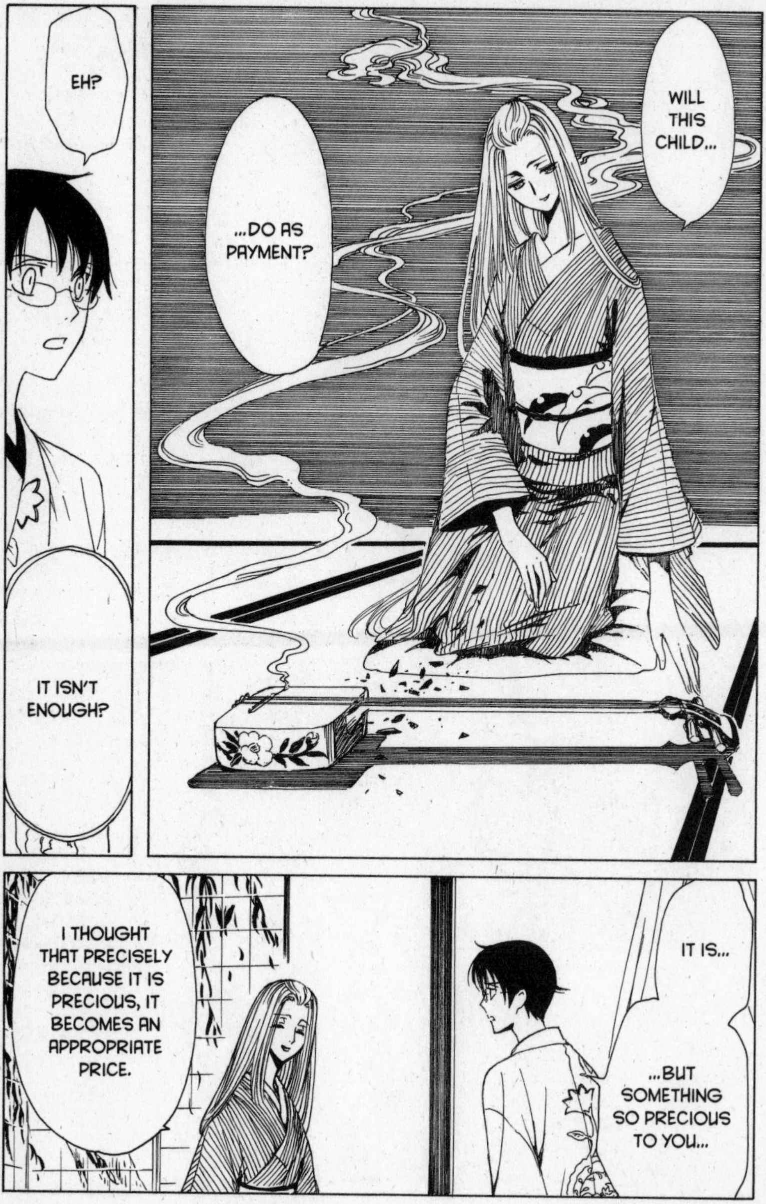
WILL THIS CHILD...
...DO AS PAYMENT?
EH?
IT ISN'T ENOUGH?
IT IS...
...BUT SOMETHING SO PRECIOUS TO YOU...
I THOUGHT THAT PRECISELY BECAUSE IT IS PRECIOUS, IT BECOMES AN APPROPRIATE PRICE.

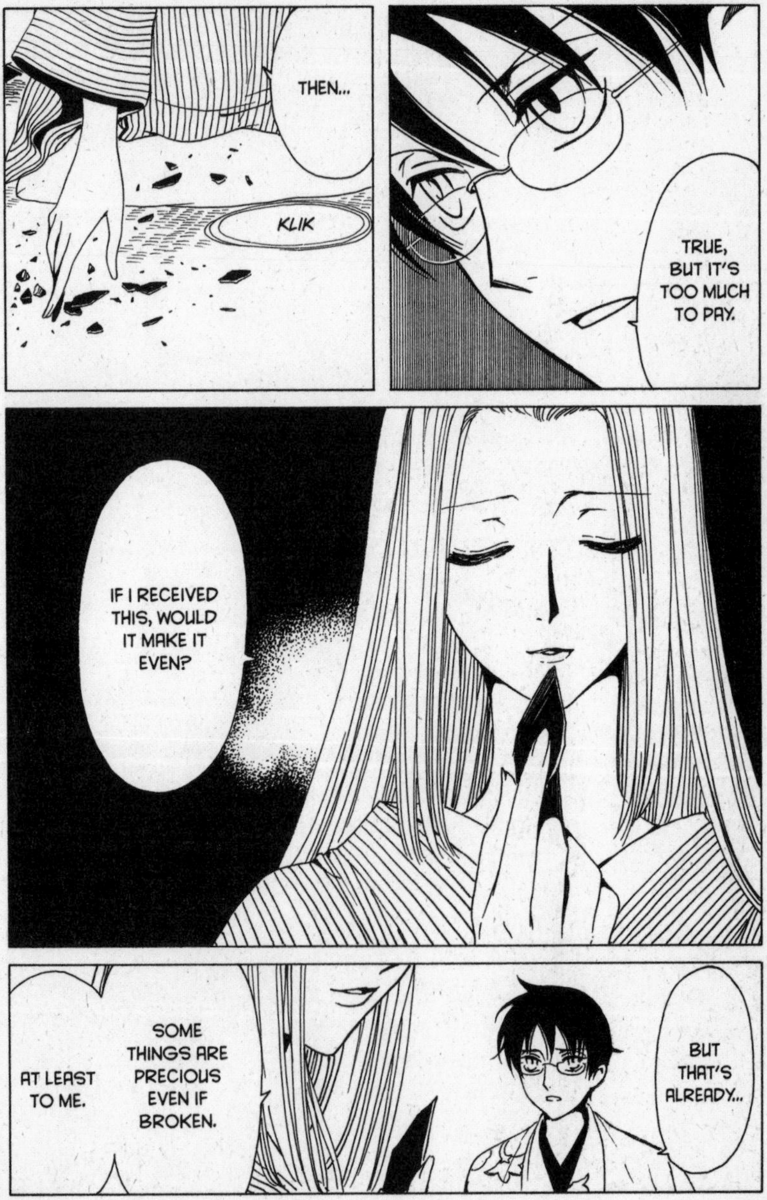
TRUE, BUT IT'S TOO MUCH TO PAY.
THEN...
KLIK
IF I RECEIVED THIS, WOULD IT MAKE IT EVEN?
BUT THAT'S ALREADY...
SOME THINGS ARE PRECIOUS EVEN IF BROKEN.
AT LEAST TO ME.

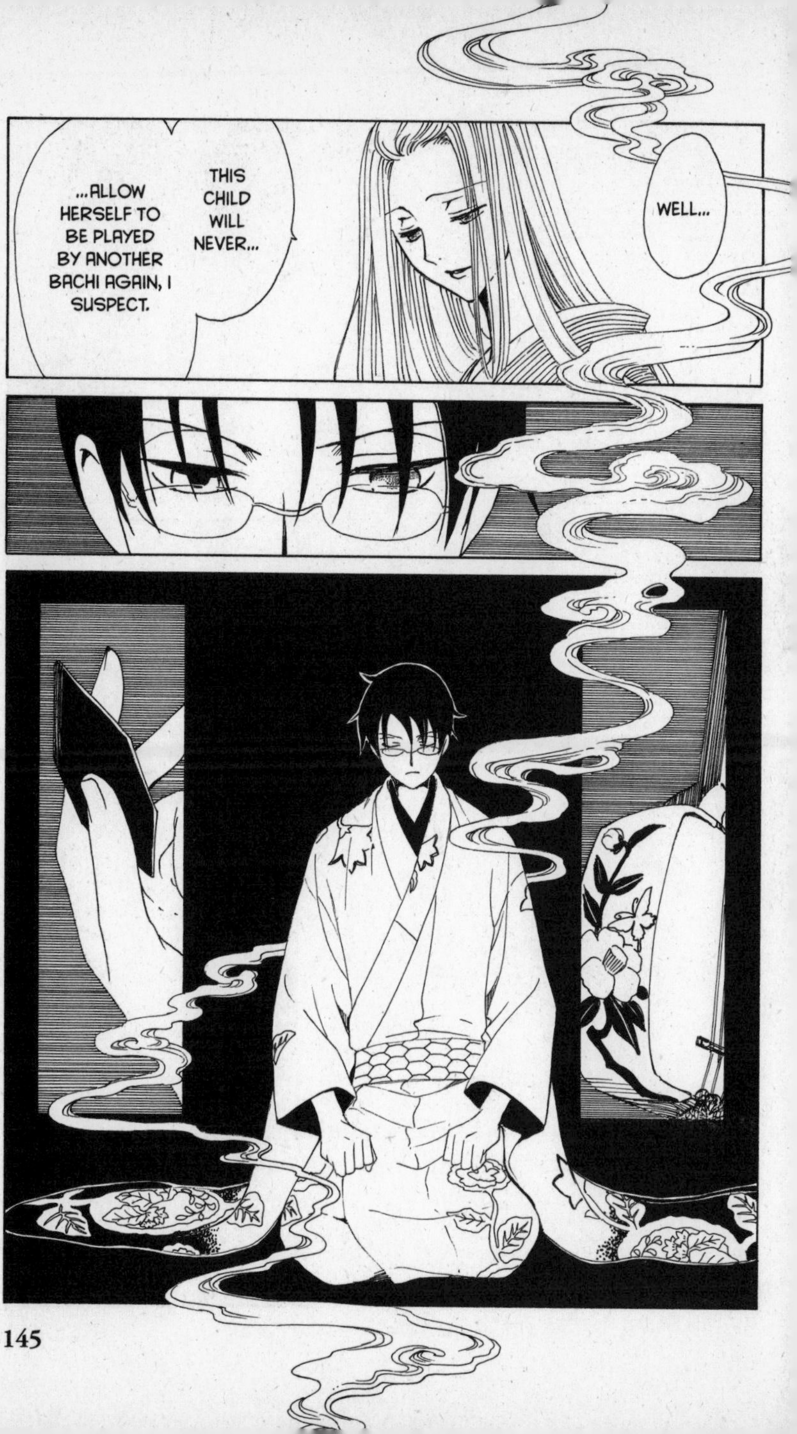
WELL...
THIS CHILD WILL NEVER...
...ALLOW HERSELF TO BE PLAYED BY ANOTHER BACHI AGAIN, I SUSPECT.

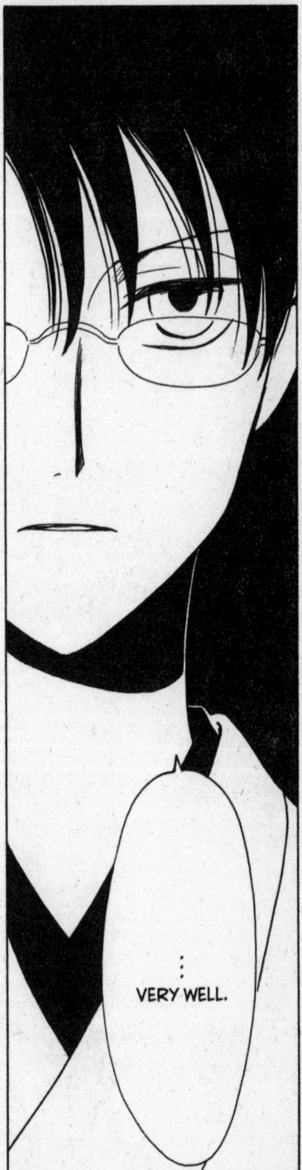
...VERY WELL.

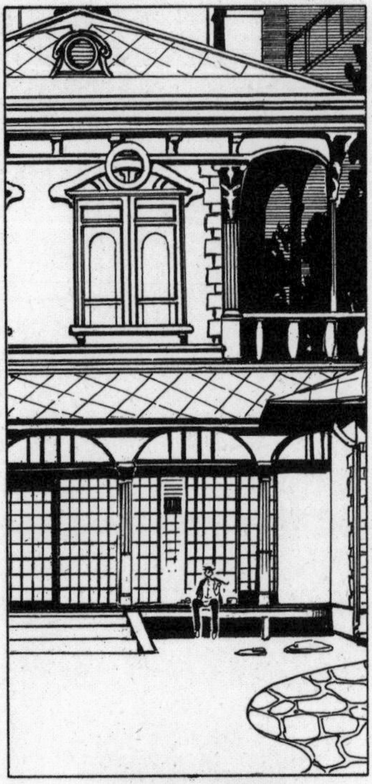

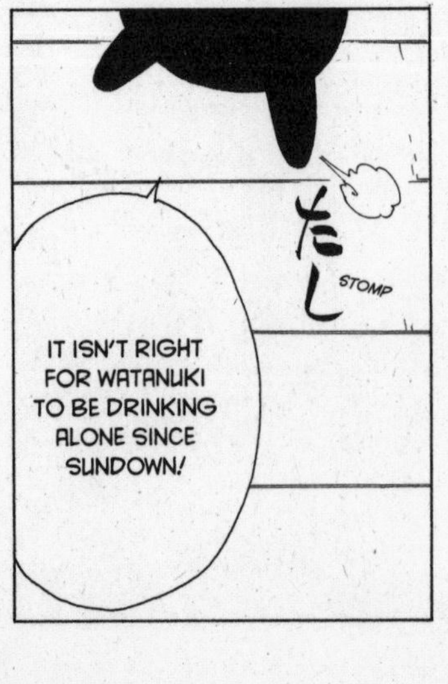
たし
STOMP
IT ISN'T RIGHT FOR WATANUKI TO BE DRINKING ALONE SINCE SUNDOWN!

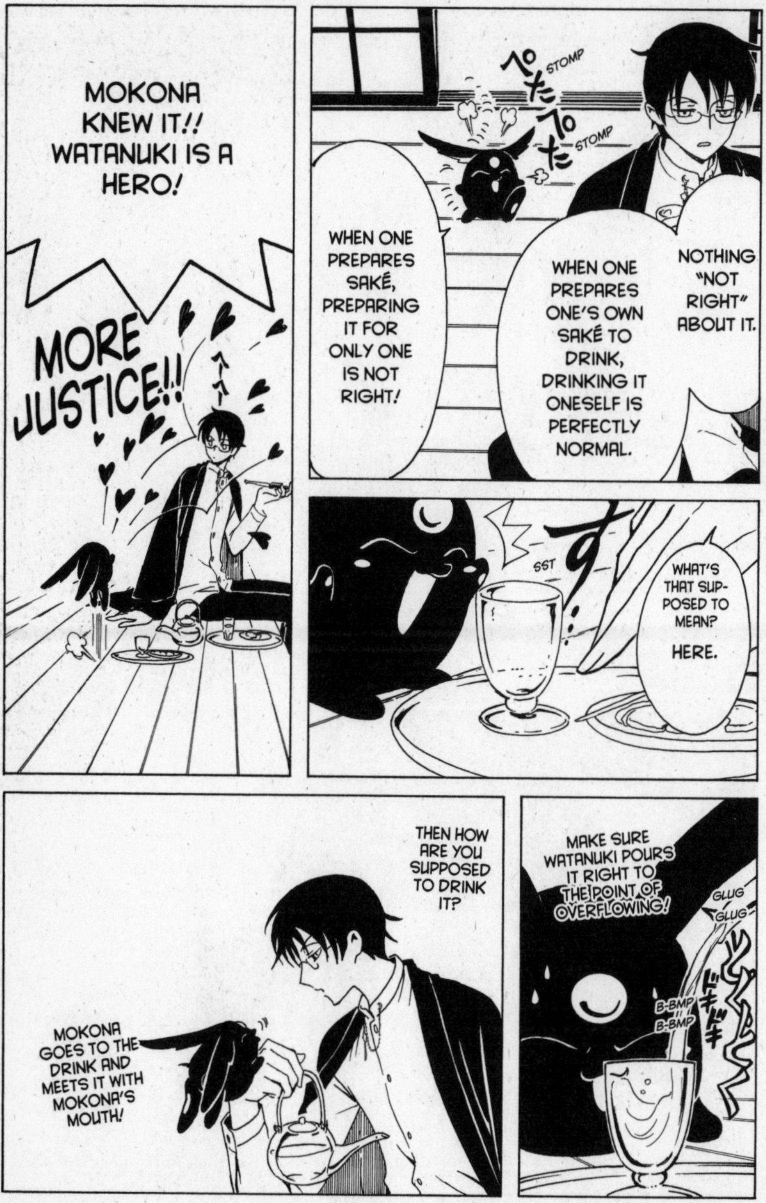

ぺた STOMP
ぺた STOMP
NOTHING "NOT RIGHT" ABOUT IT.
WHEN ONE PREPARES ONE'S OWN SAKÉ TO DRINK, DRINKING IT ONESELF IS PERFECTLY NORMAL.
WHEN ONE PREPARES SAKÉ, PREPARING IT FOR ONLY ONE IS NOT RIGHT!
WHAT'S THAT SUP-POSED TO MEAN?
HERE.
す SST
MOKONA KNEW IT!! WATANUKI IS A HERO!
MORE JUSTICE!!!
MAKE SURE WATANUKI POURS IT RIGHT TO THE POINT OF OVERFLOWING!
とくとく GLUG GLUG
ドキドキ B-BMP B-BMP
THEN HOW ARE YOU SUPPOSED TO DRINK IT?
MOKONA GOES TO THE DRINK AND MEETS IT WITH MOKONA'S MOUTH!

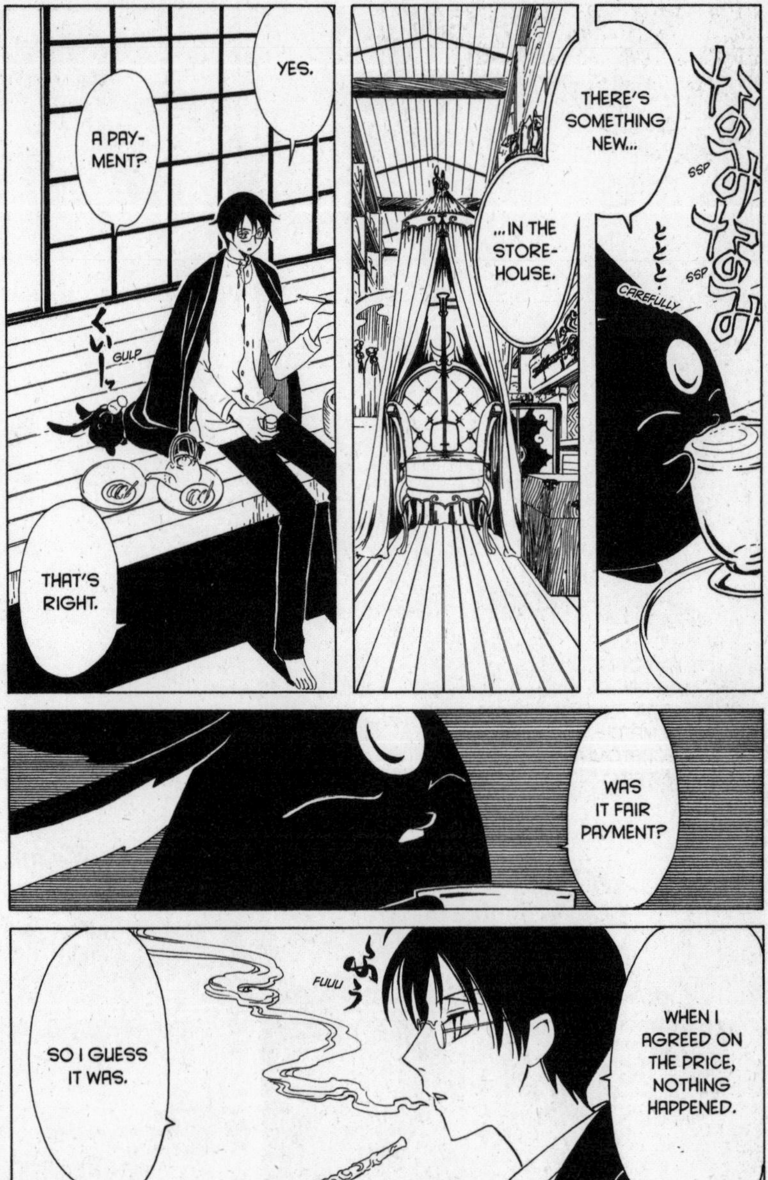
THERE'S SOMETHING NEW...
SSP
SSP
CAREFULLY
...IN THE STOREHOUSE.
YES.
A PAYMENT?
GULP
THAT'S RIGHT.
WAS IT FAIR PAYMENT?
WHEN I AGREED ON THE PRICE, NOTHING HAPPENED.
FUUU
SO I GUESS IT WAS.

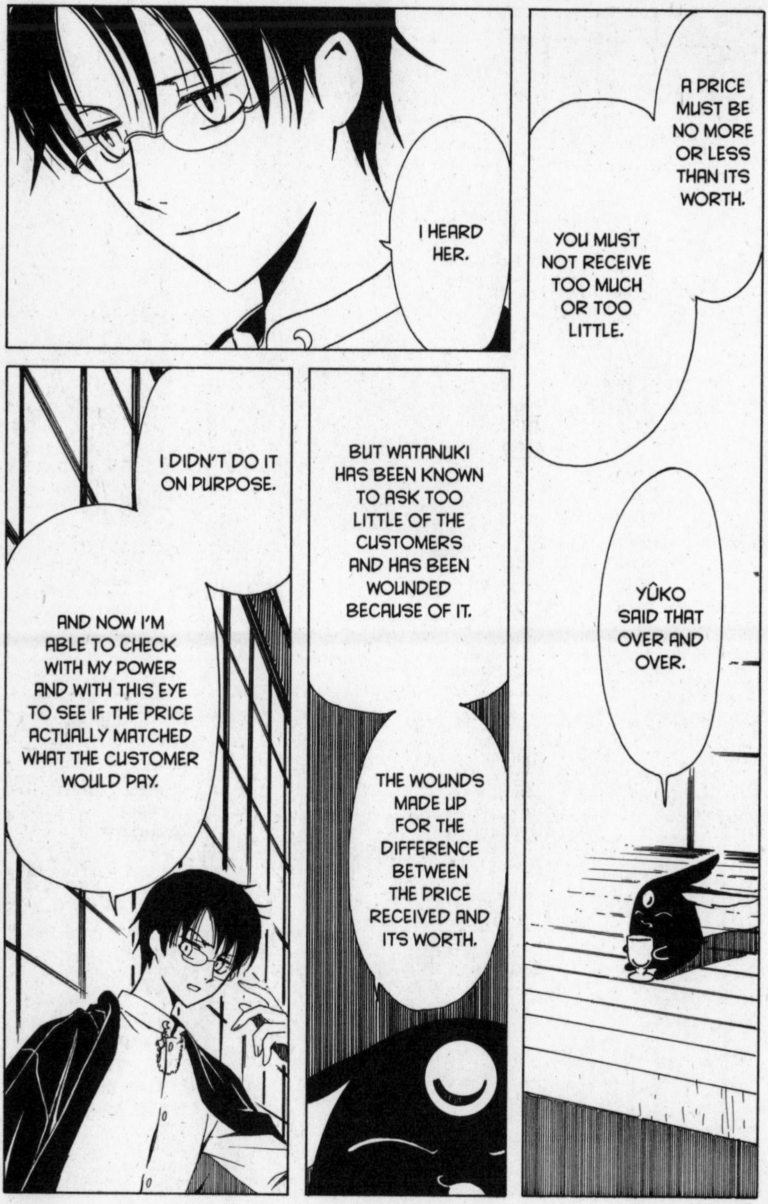
A PRICE MUST BE NO MORE OR LESS THAN ITS WORTH.
YOU MUST NOT RECEIVE TOO MUCH OR TOO LITTLE.
YÛKO SAID THAT OVER AND OVER.
I HEARD HER.
BUT WATANUKI HAS BEEN KNOWN TO ASK TOO LITTLE OF THE CUSTOMERS AND HAS BEEN WOUNDED BECAUSE OF IT.
THE WOUNDS MADE UP FOR THE DIFFERENCE BETWEEN THE PRICE RECEIVED AND ITS WORTH.
I DIDN'T DO IT ON PURPOSE.
AND NOW I'M ABLE TO CHECK WITH MY POWER AND WITH THIS EYE TO SEE IF THE PRICE ACTUALLY MATCHED WHAT THE CUSTOMER WOULD PAY.

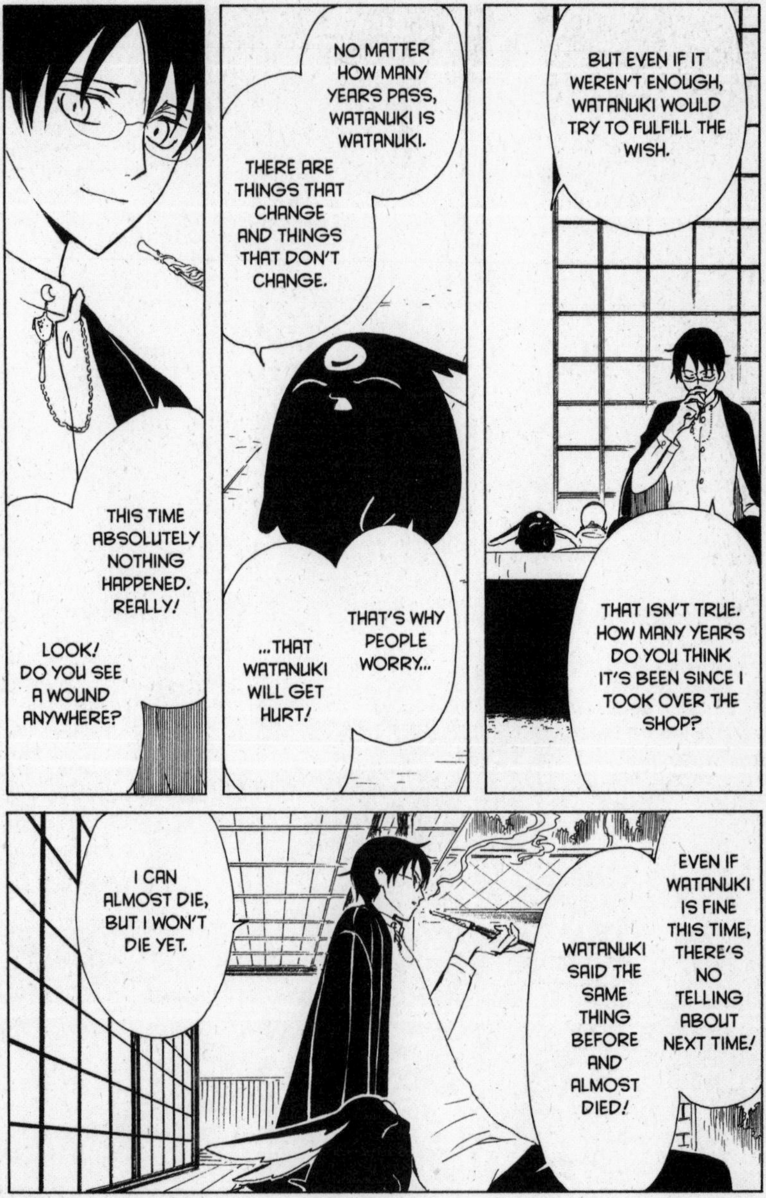
BUT EVEN IF IT WEREN'T ENOUGH, WATANUKI WOULD TRY TO FULFILL THE WISH.
THAT ISN'T TRUE. HOW MANY YEARS DO YOU THINK IT'S BEEN SINCE I TOOK OVER THE SHOP?
NO MATTER HOW MANY YEARS PASS, WATANUKI IS WATANUKI.
THERE ARE THINGS THAT CHANGE AND THINGS THAT DON'T CHANGE.
THAT'S WHY PEOPLE WORRY...
...THAT WATANUKI WILL GET HURT!
THIS TIME ABSOLUTELY NOTHING HAPPENED. REALLY!
LOOK! DO YOU SEE A WOUND ANYWHERE?
EVEN IF WATANUKI IS FINE THIS TIME, THERE'S NO TELLING ABOUT NEXT TIME!
WATANUKI SAID THE SAME THING BEFORE AND ALMOST DIED!
I CAN ALMOST DIE, BUT I WON'T DIE YET.

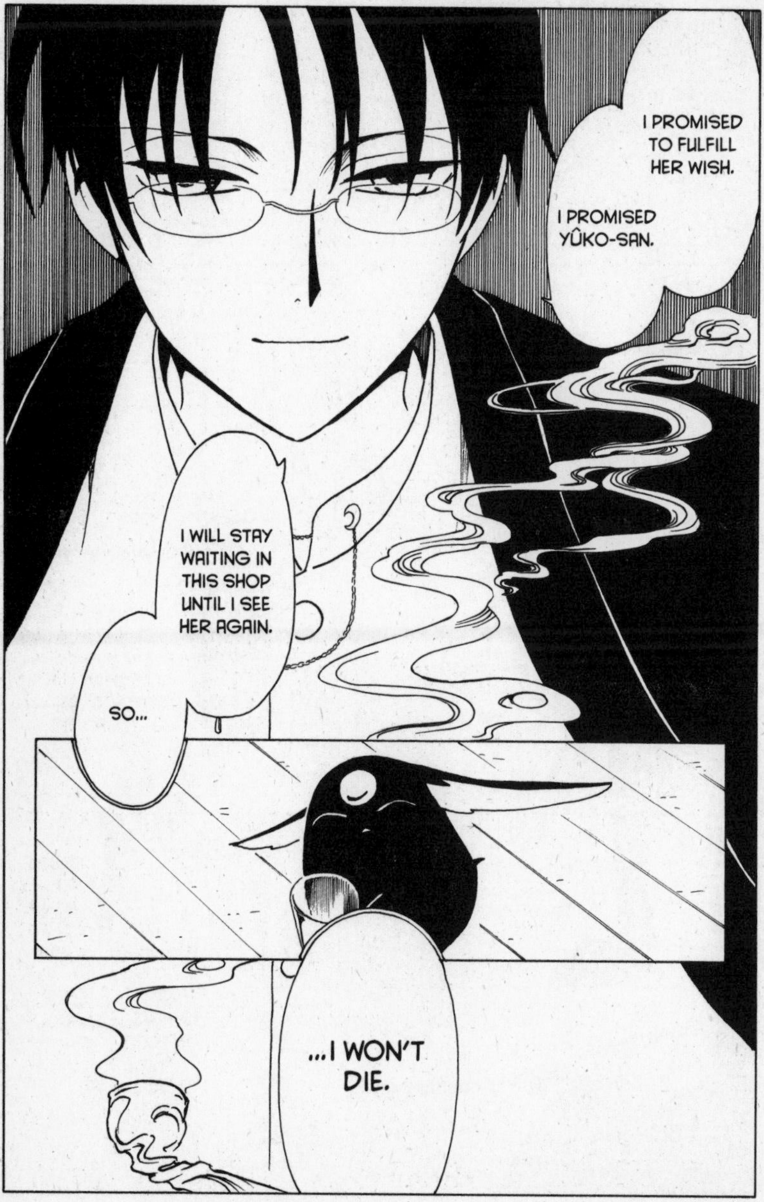
I PROMISED TO FULFILL HER WISH.
I PROMISED YÛKO-SAN.
I WILL STAY WAITING IN THIS SHOP UNTIL I SEE HER AGAIN.
SO...
...I WON'T DIE.

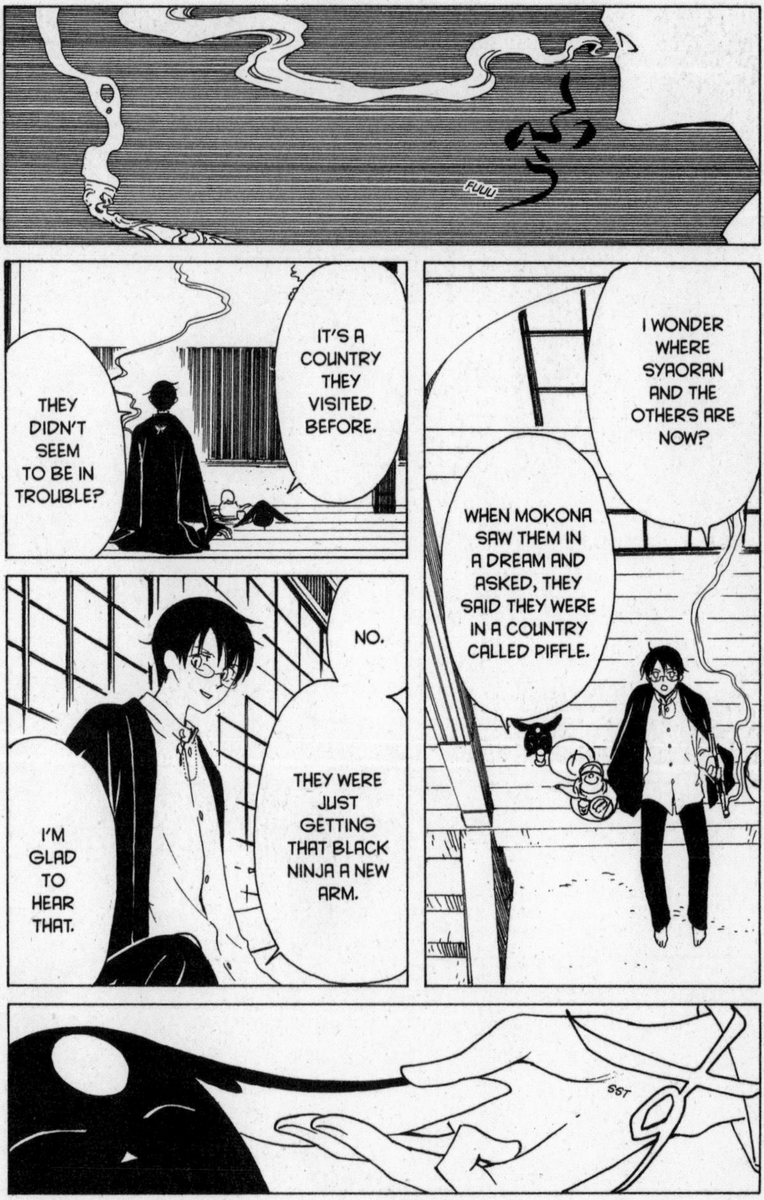
FUUU
I WONDER WHERE SYAORAN AND THE OTHERS ARE NOW?
WHEN MOKONA SAW THEM IN A DREAM AND ASKED, THEY SAID THEY WERE IN A COUNTRY CALLED PIFFLE.
IT'S A COUNTRY THEY VISITED BEFORE.
THEY DIDN'T SEEM TO BE IN TROUBLE?
NO.
THEY WERE JUST GETTING THAT BLACK NINJA A NEW ARM.
I'M GLAD TO HEAR THAT.
SST

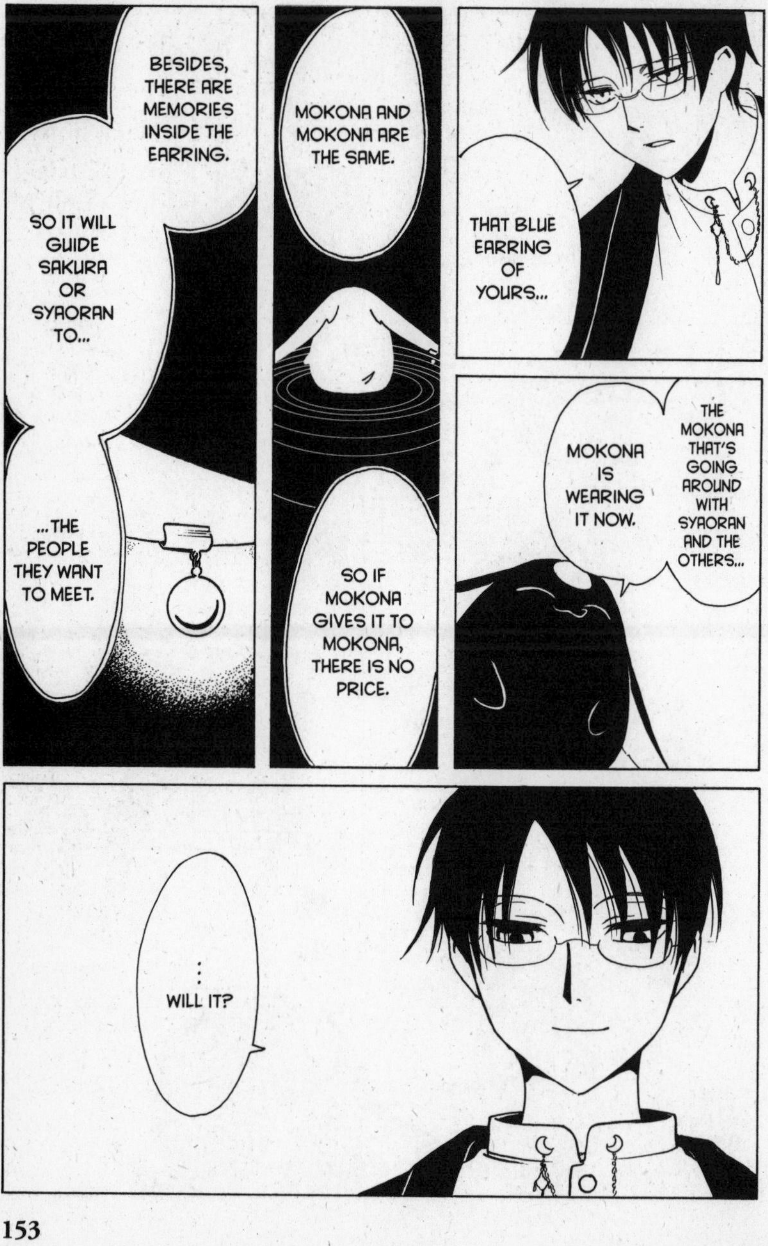
THAT BLUE EARRING OF YOURS...
THE MOKONA THAT'S GOING AROUND WITH SYAORAN AND THE OTHERS...
MOKONA IS WEARING IT NOW.
MOKONA AND MOKONA ARE THE SAME.
SO IF MOKONA GIVES IT TO MOKONA, THERE IS NO PRICE.
BESIDES, THERE ARE MEMORIES INSIDE THE EARRING.
SO IT WILL GUIDE SAKURA OR SYAORAN TO...
...THE PEOPLE THEY WANT TO MEET.
...
WILL IT?

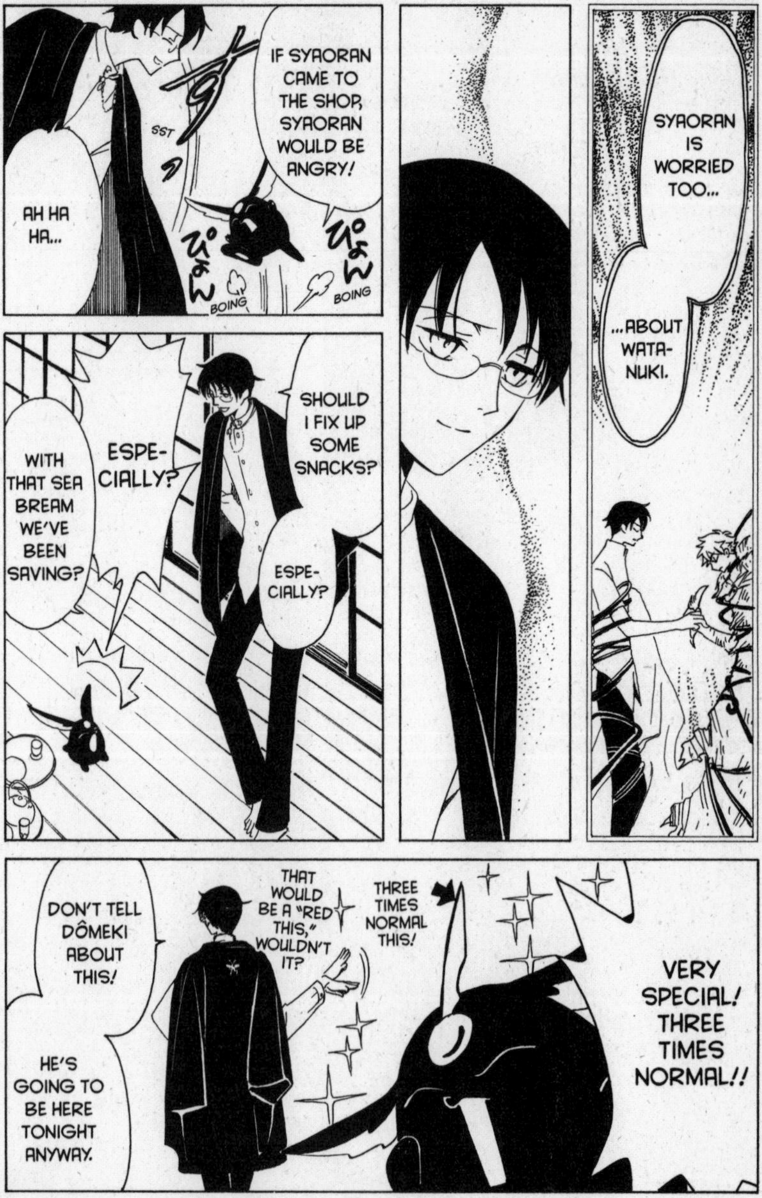
SYAORAN IS WORRIED TOO...
...ABOUT WATA-NUKI.
IF SYAORAN CAME TO THE SHOP, SYAORAN WOULD BE ANGRY!
SST
ぴょん
BOING
ぴょん
BOING
AH HA HA...
SHOULD I FIX UP SOME SNACKS?
ESPE-CIALLY?
ESPE-CIALLY?
WITH THAT SEA BREAM WE'VE BEEN SAVING?
VERY SPECIAL! THREE TIMES NORMAL!!
THREE TIMES NORMAL THIS!
THAT WOULD BE A "RED THIS," WOULDN'T IT?
DON'T TELL DÔMEKI ABOUT THIS!
HE'S GOING TO BE HERE TONIGHT ANYWAY.

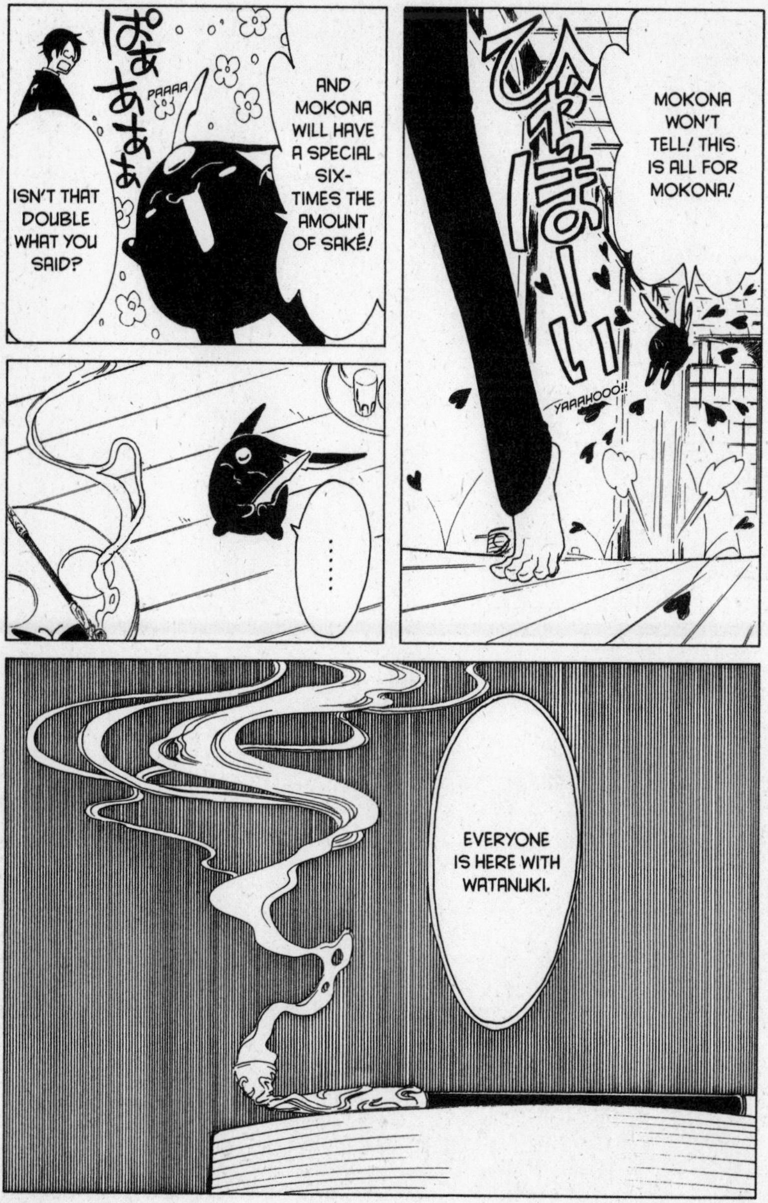
MOKONA WON'T TELL! THIS IS ALL FOR MOKONA!
YAAAHOOO!!
AND MOKONA WILL HAVE A SPECIAL SIX-TIMES THE AMOUNT OF SAKÉ!
PAAAA
ISN'T THAT DOUBLE WHAT YOU SAID?
......
EVERYONE IS HERE WITH WATANUKI.

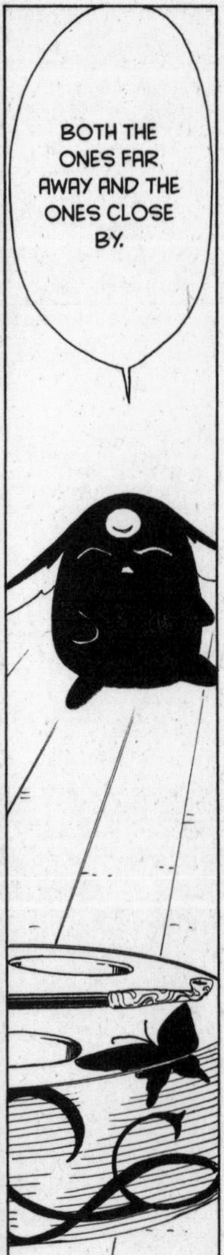
BOTH THE ONES FAR AWAY AND THE ONES CLOSE BY.

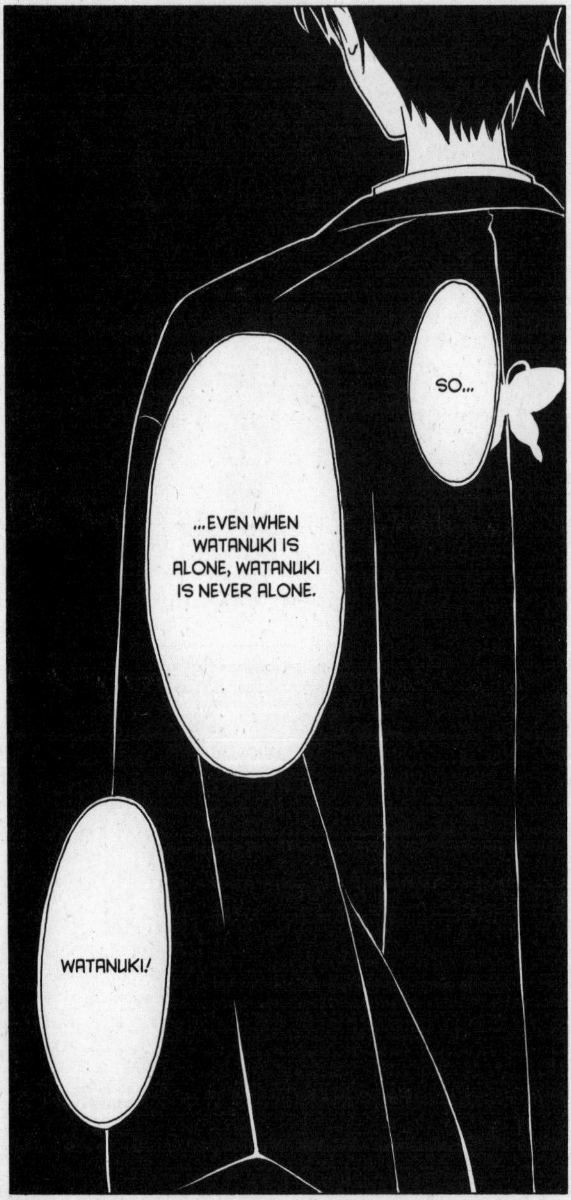
SO...
...EVEN WHEN WATANUKI IS ALONE, WATANUKI IS NEVER ALONE.
WATANUKI!

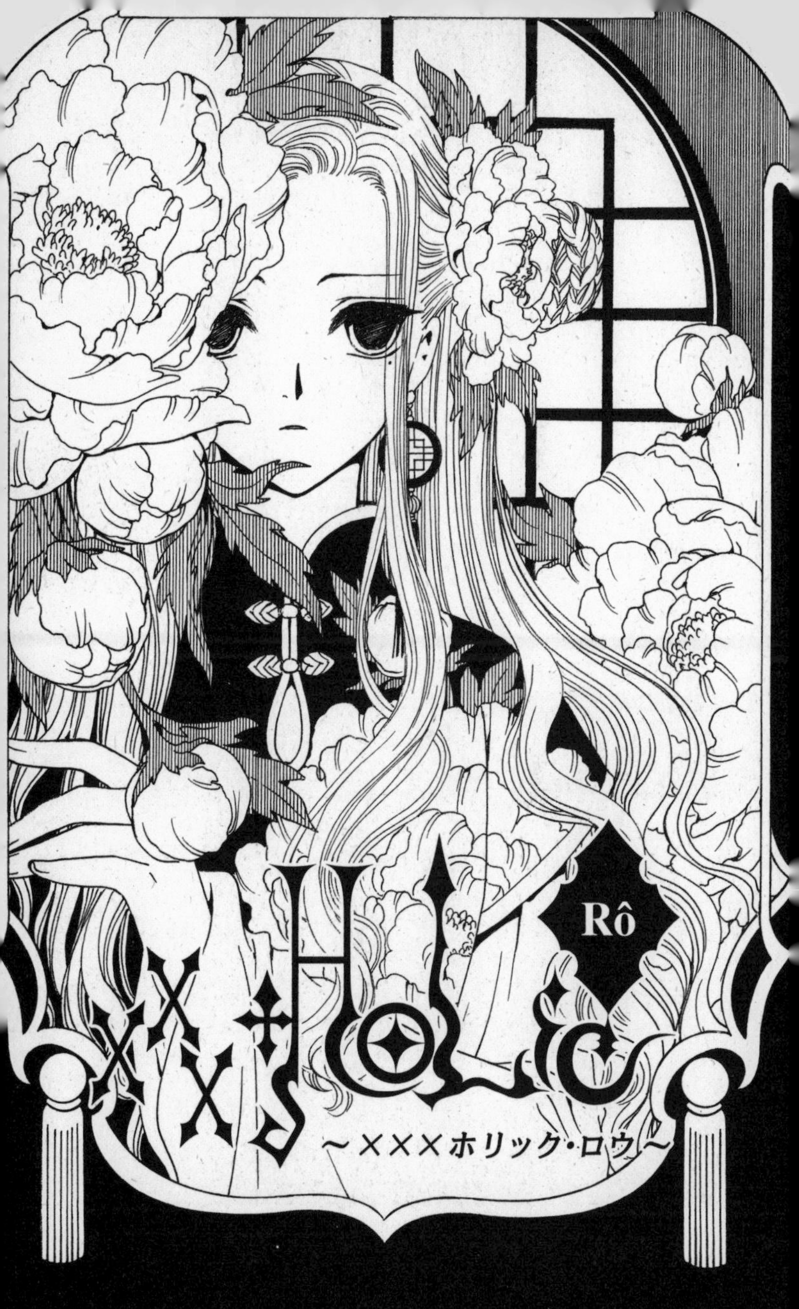
xxxHOLiC
Rô
～×××ホリック・ロウ～

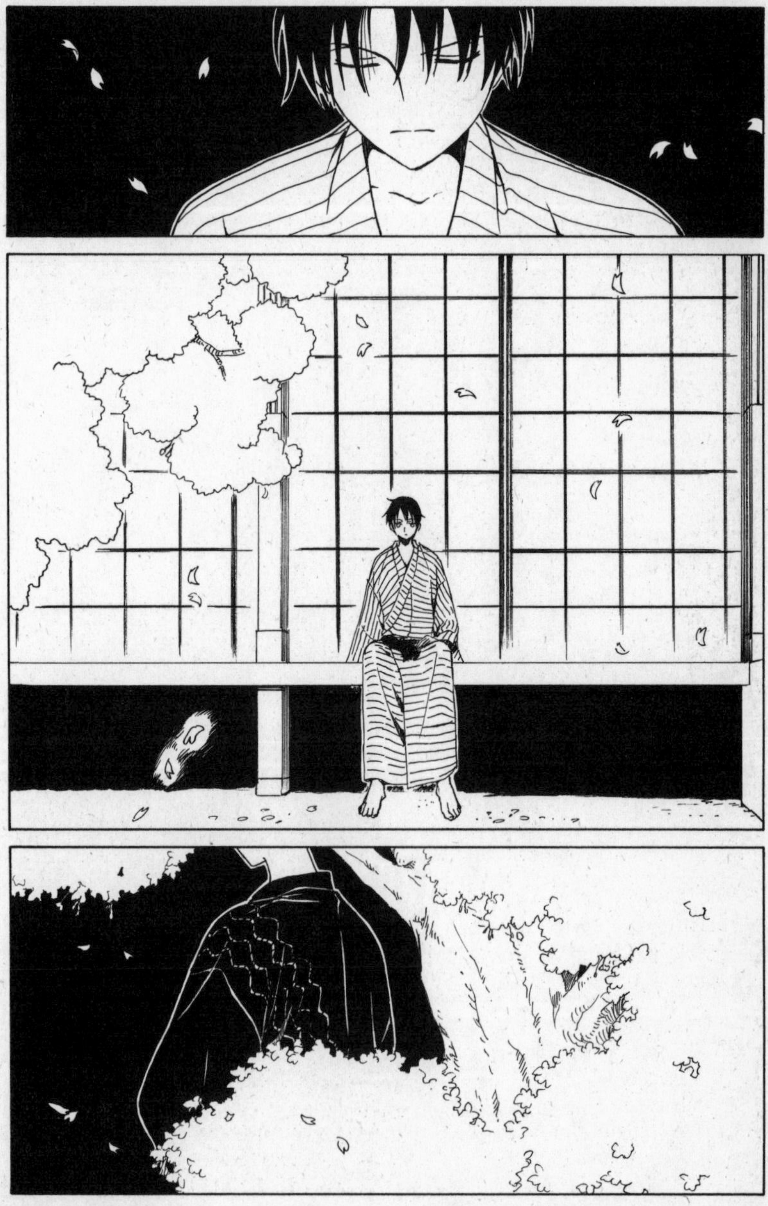

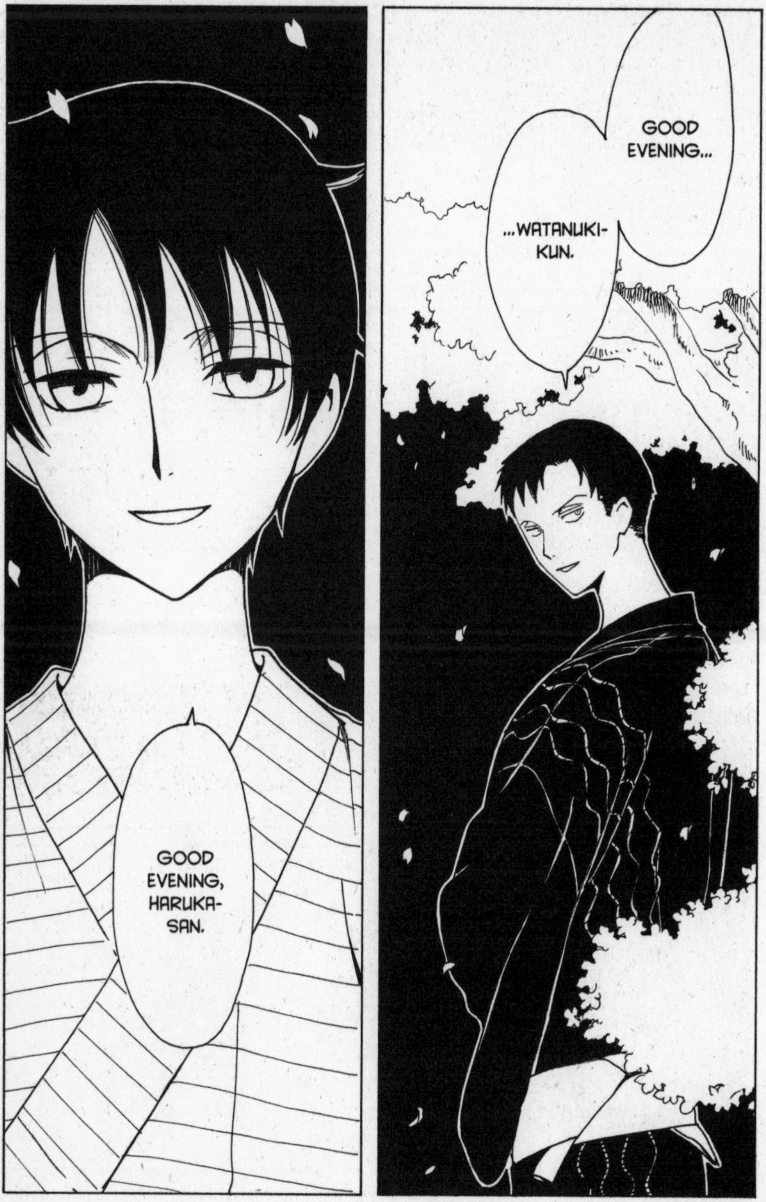
GOOD EVENING...
...WATANUKI-KUN.
GOOD EVENING, HARUKA-SAN.

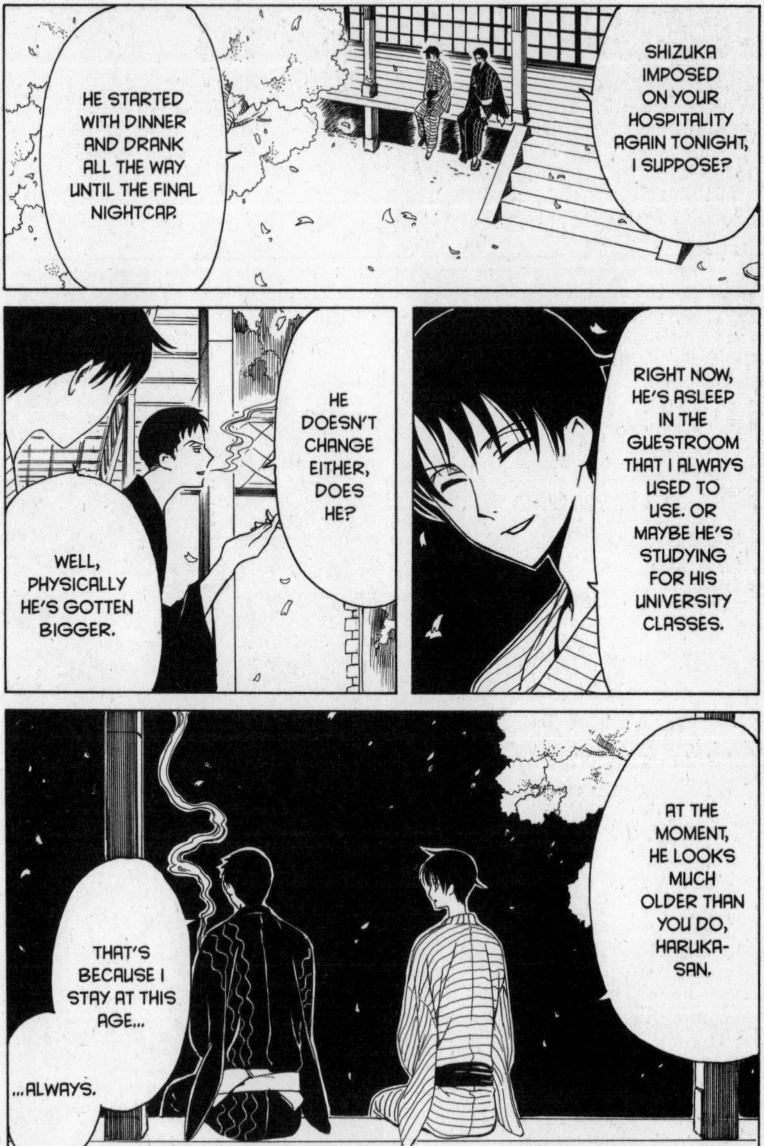
SHIZUKA IMPOSED ON YOUR HOSPITALITY AGAIN TONIGHT, I SUPPOSE?
HE STARTED WITH DINNER AND DRANK ALL THE WAY UNTIL THE FINAL NIGHTCAP.
RIGHT NOW, HE'S ASLEEP IN THE GUESTROOM THAT I ALWAYS USED TO USE. OR MAYBE HE'S STUDYING FOR HIS UNIVERSITY CLASSES.
HE DOESN'T CHANGE EITHER, DOES HE?
WELL, PHYSICALLY HE'S GOTTEN BIGGER.
AT THE MOMENT, HE LOOKS MUCH OLDER THAN YOU DO, HARUKA-SAN.
THAT'S BECAUSE I STAY AT THIS AGE...
...ALWAYS.

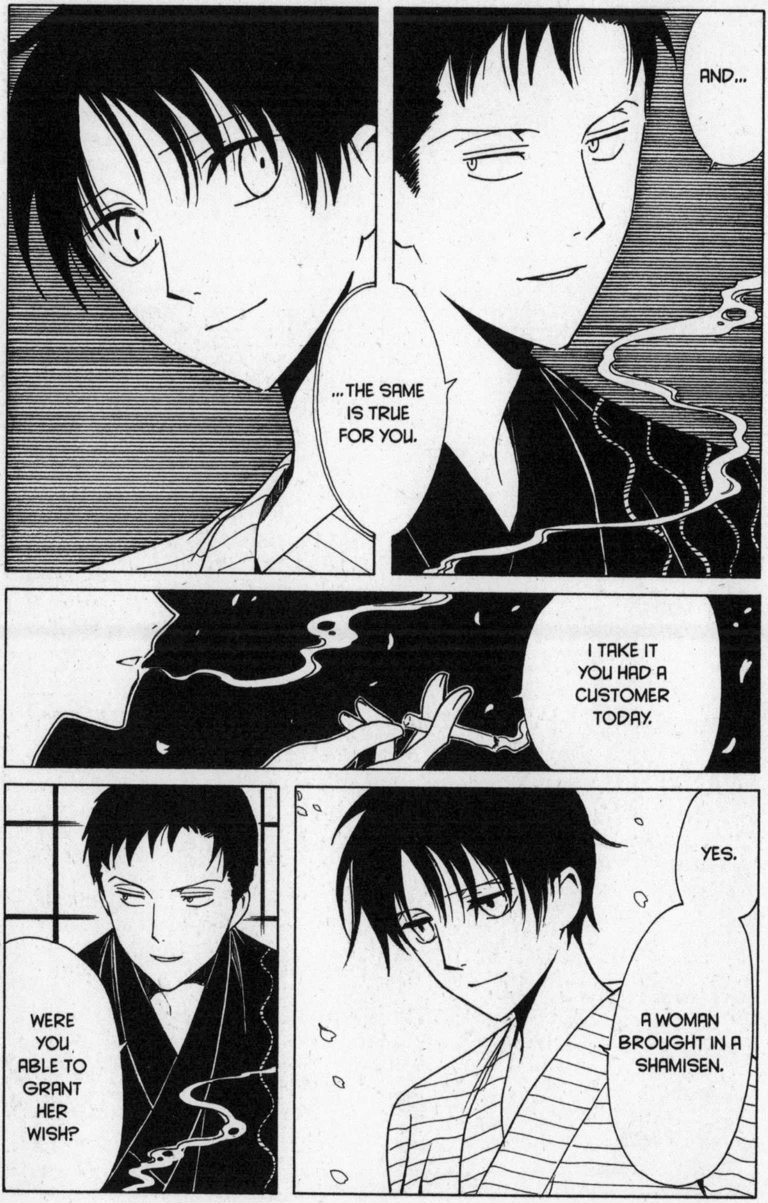
AND...
...THE SAME IS TRUE FOR YOU.
I TAKE IT YOU HAD A CUSTOMER TODAY.
YES.
A WOMAN BROUGHT IN A SHAMISEN.
WERE YOU ABLE TO GRANT HER WISH?

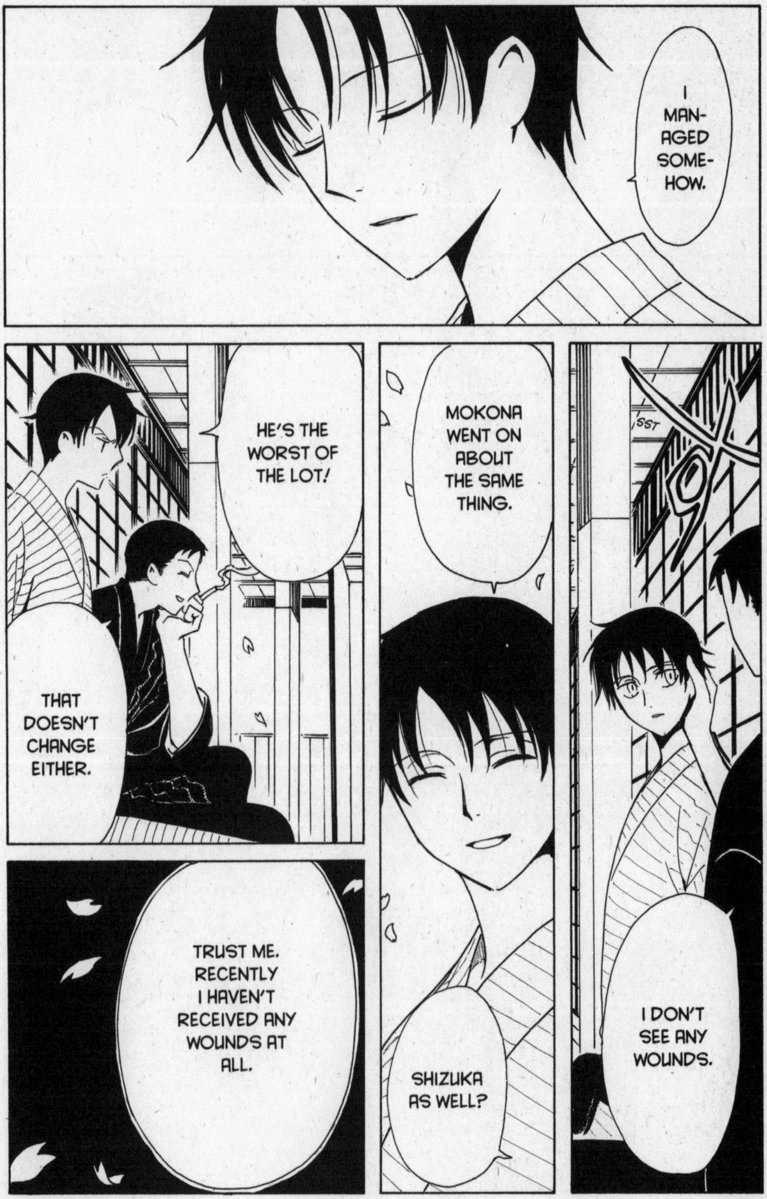

I MANAGED SOMEHOW.
SST
I DON'T SEE ANY WOUNDS.
MOKONA WENT ON ABOUT THE SAME THING.
SHIZUKA AS WELL?
HE'S THE WORST OF THE LOT!
THAT DOESN'T CHANGE EITHER.
TRUST ME. RECENTLY I HAVEN'T RECEIVED ANY WOUNDS AT ALL.

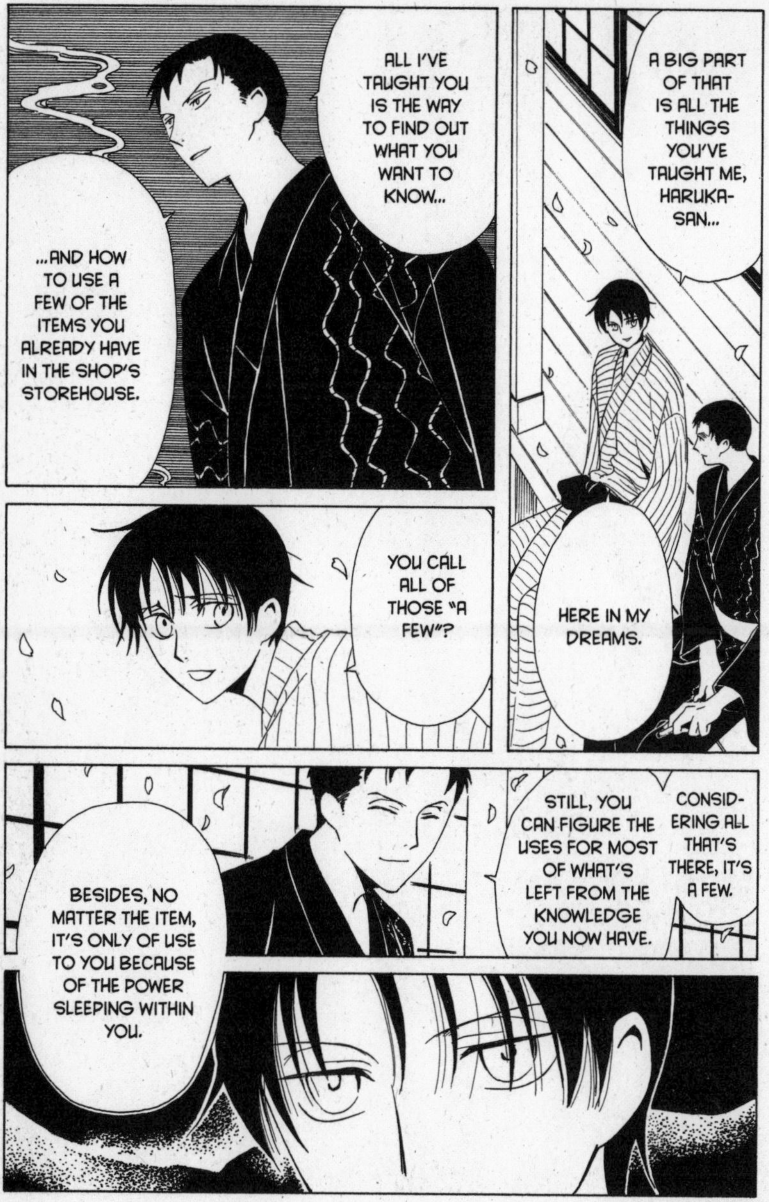
A BIG PART OF THAT IS ALL THE THINGS YOU'VE TAUGHT ME, HARUKA-SAN...
HERE IN MY DREAMS.
ALL I'VE TAUGHT YOU IS THE WAY TO FIND OUT WHAT YOU WANT TO KNOW...
...AND HOW TO USE A FEW OF THE ITEMS YOU ALREADY HAVE IN THE SHOP'S STOREHOUSE.
YOU CALL ALL OF THOSE "A FEW"?
CONSID-ERING ALL THAT'S THERE, IT'S A FEW.
STILL, YOU CAN FIGURE THE USES FOR MOST OF WHAT'S LEFT FROM THE KNOWLEDGE YOU NOW HAVE.
BESIDES, NO MATTER THE ITEM, IT'S ONLY OF USE TO YOU BECAUSE OF THE POWER SLEEPING WITHIN YOU.

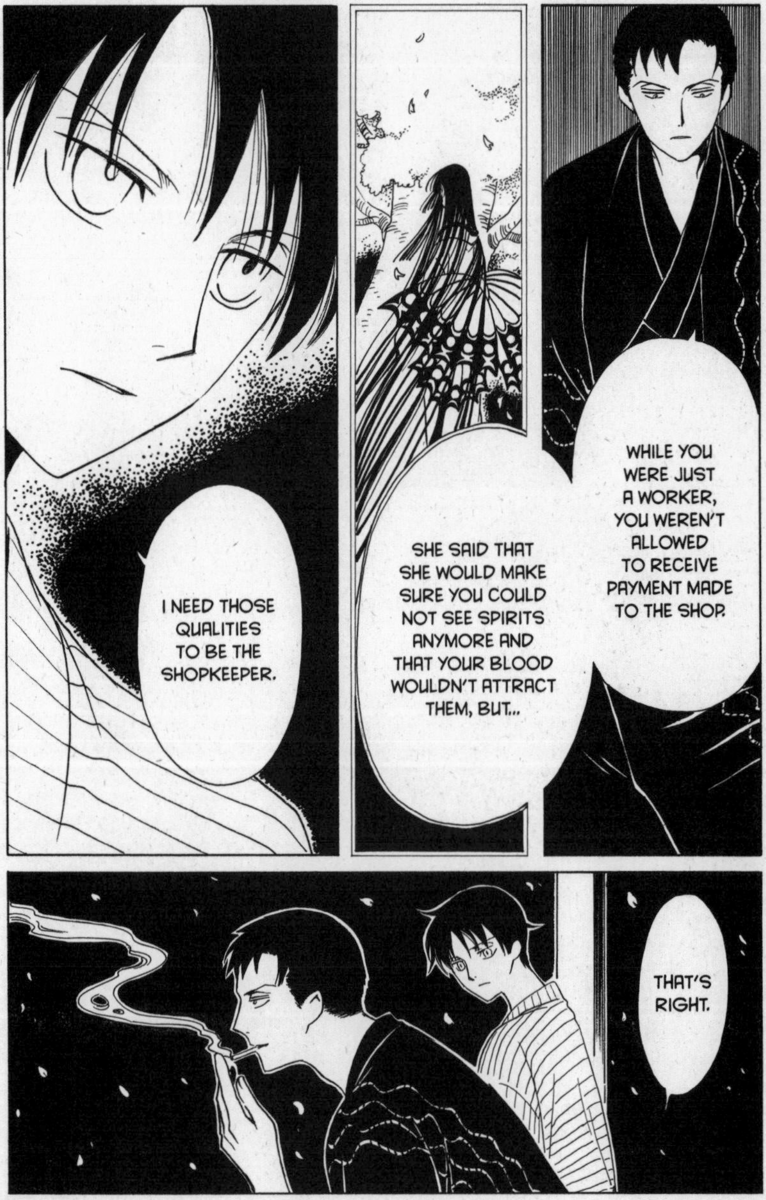
WHILE YOU WERE JUST A WORKER, YOU WEREN'T ALLOWED TO RECEIVE PAYMENT MADE TO THE SHOP.
SHE SAID THAT SHE WOULD MAKE SURE YOU COULD NOT SEE SPIRITS ANYMORE AND THAT YOUR BLOOD WOULDN'T ATTRACT THEM, BUT...
I NEED THOSE QUALITIES TO BE THE SHOPKEEPER.
THAT'S RIGHT.

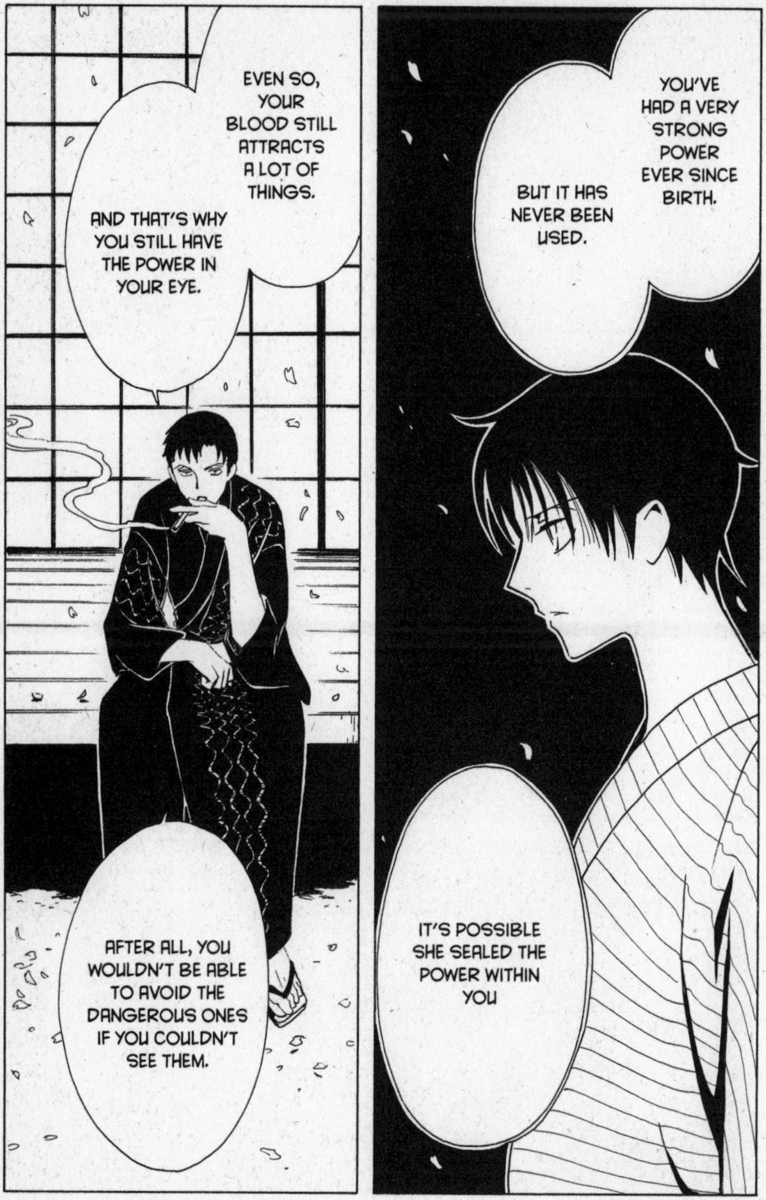
YOU'VE HAD A VERY STRONG POWER EVER SINCE BIRTH.
BUT IT HAS NEVER BEEN USED.
IT'S POSSIBLE SHE SEALED THE POWER WITHIN YOU
EVEN SO, YOUR BLOOD STILL ATTRACTS A LOT OF THINGS.
AND THAT'S WHY YOU STILL HAVE THE POWER IN YOUR EYE.
AFTER ALL, YOU WOULDN'T BE ABLE TO AVOID THE DANGEROUS ONES IF YOU COULDN'T SEE THEM.

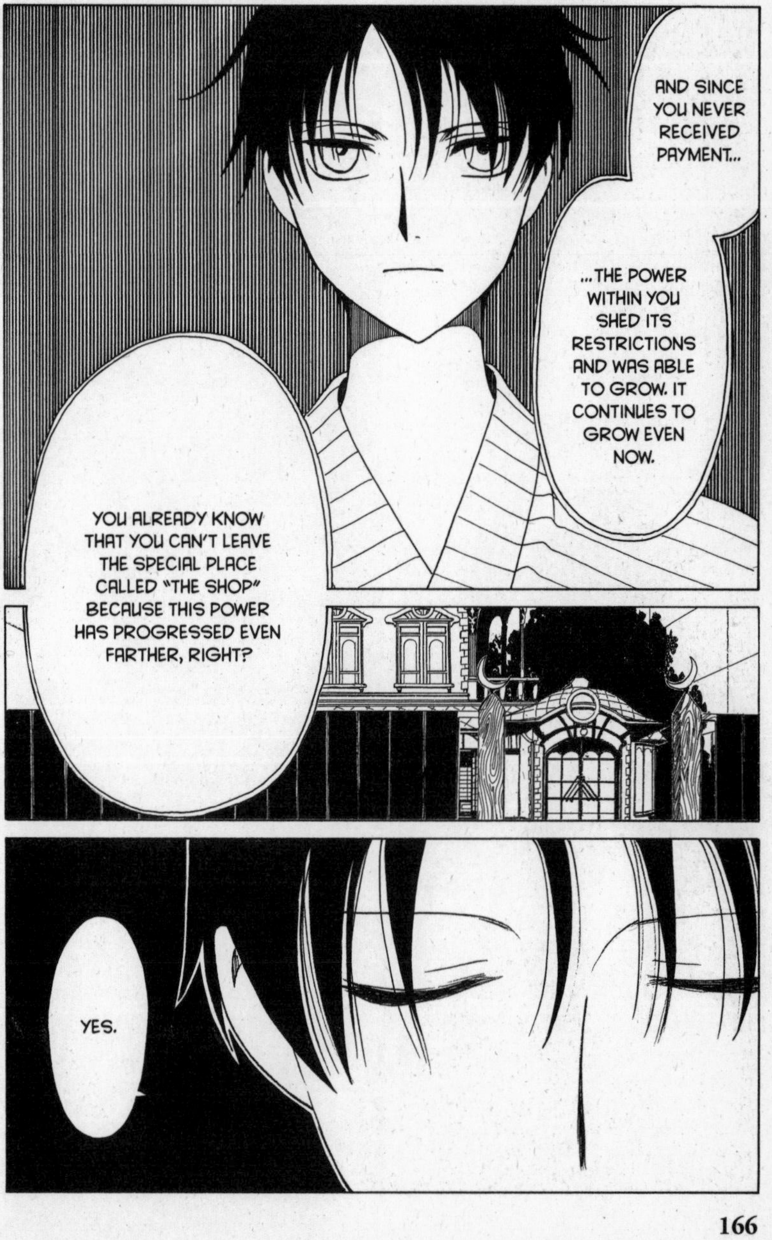
AND SINCE YOU NEVER RECEIVED PAYMENT...
...THE POWER WITHIN YOU SHED ITS RESTRICTIONS AND WAS ABLE TO GROW. IT CONTINUES TO GROW EVEN NOW.
YOU ALREADY KNOW THAT YOU CAN'T LEAVE THE SPECIAL PLACE CALLED "THE SHOP" BECAUSE THIS POWER HAS PROGRESSED EVEN FARTHER, RIGHT?
YES.

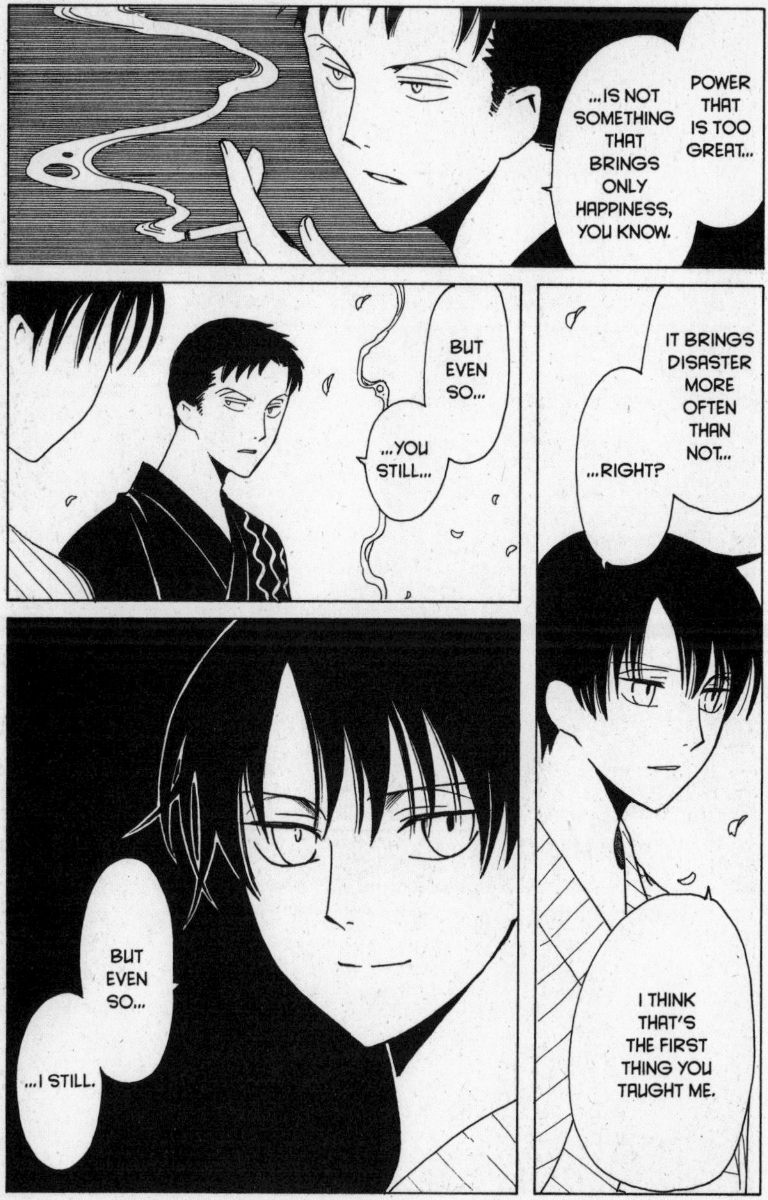
POWER THAT IS TOO GREAT...
...IS NOT SOMETHING THAT BRINGS ONLY HAPPINESS, YOU KNOW.
IT BRINGS DISASTER MORE OFTEN THAN NOT...
...RIGHT?
I THINK THAT'S THE FIRST THING YOU TAUGHT ME.
BUT EVEN SO...
...YOU STILL...
BUT EVEN SO...
...I STILL.

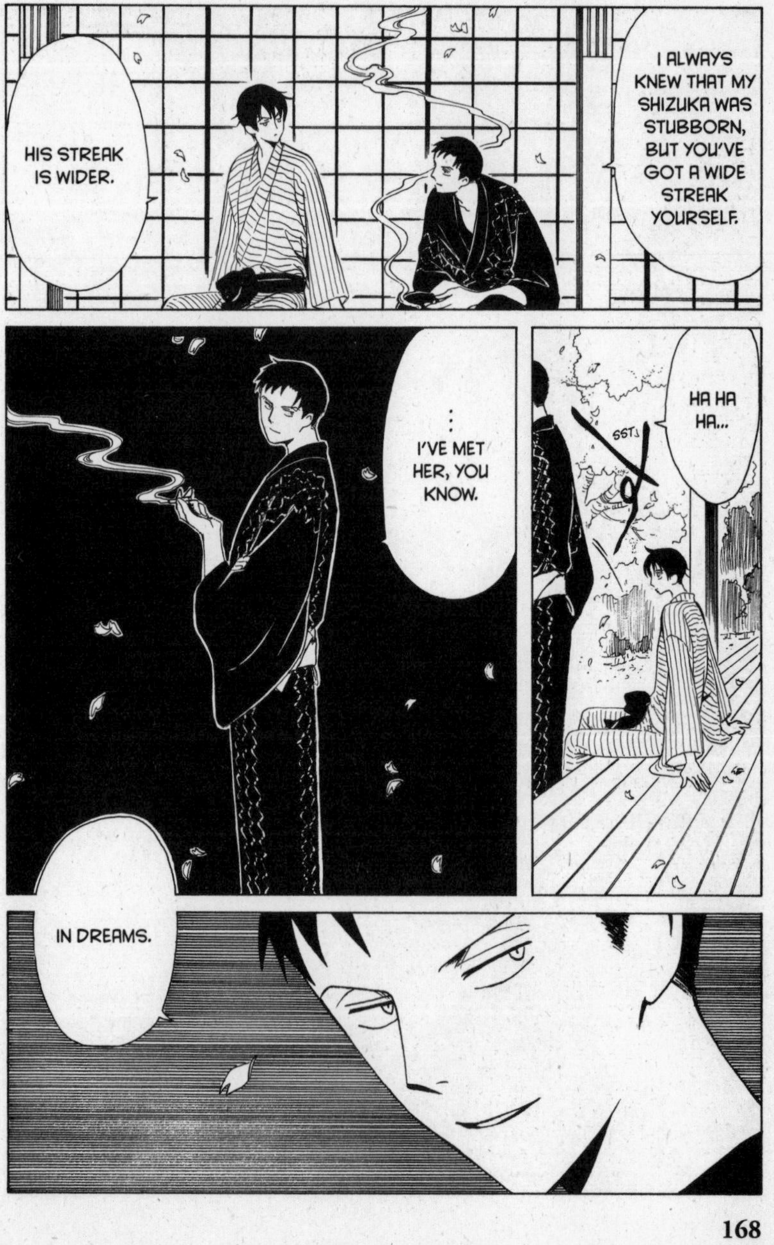
I ALWAYS KNEW THAT MY SHIZUKA WAS STUBBORN, BUT YOU'VE GOT A WIDE STREAK YOURSELF.
HIS STREAK IS WIDER.
HA HA HA...
SST
... I'VE MET HER, YOU KNOW.
IN DREAMS.

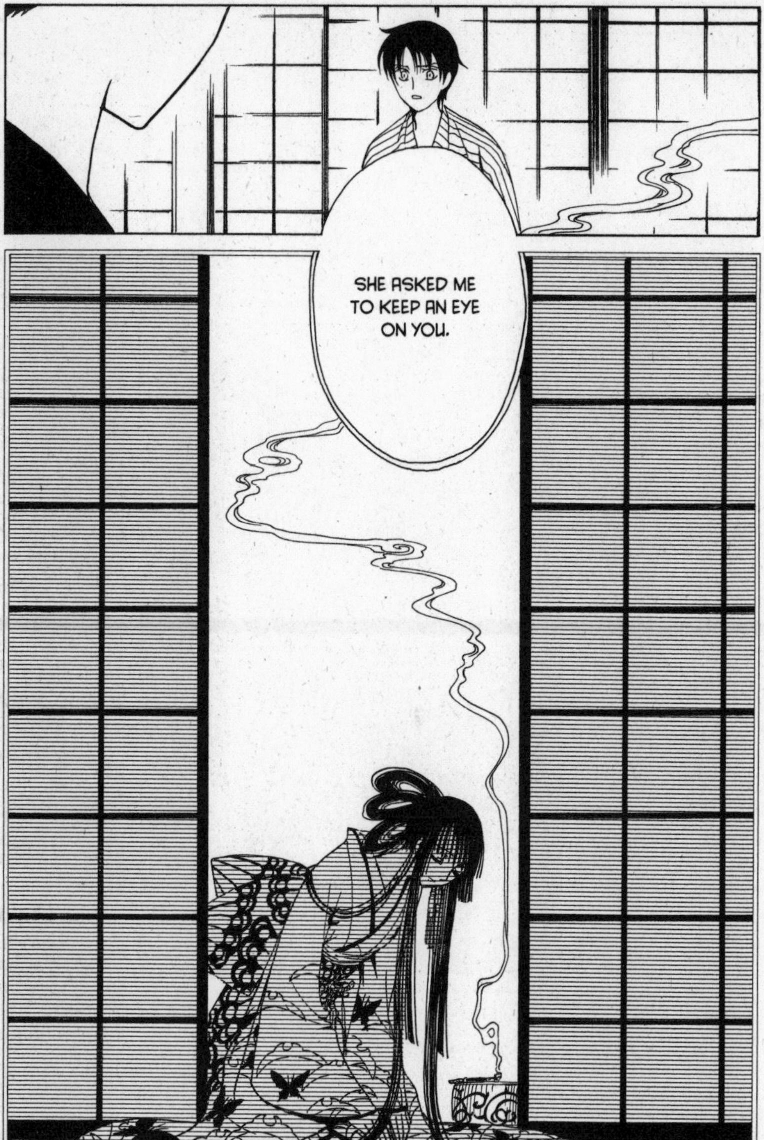
SHE ASKED ME TO KEEP AN EYE ON YOU.

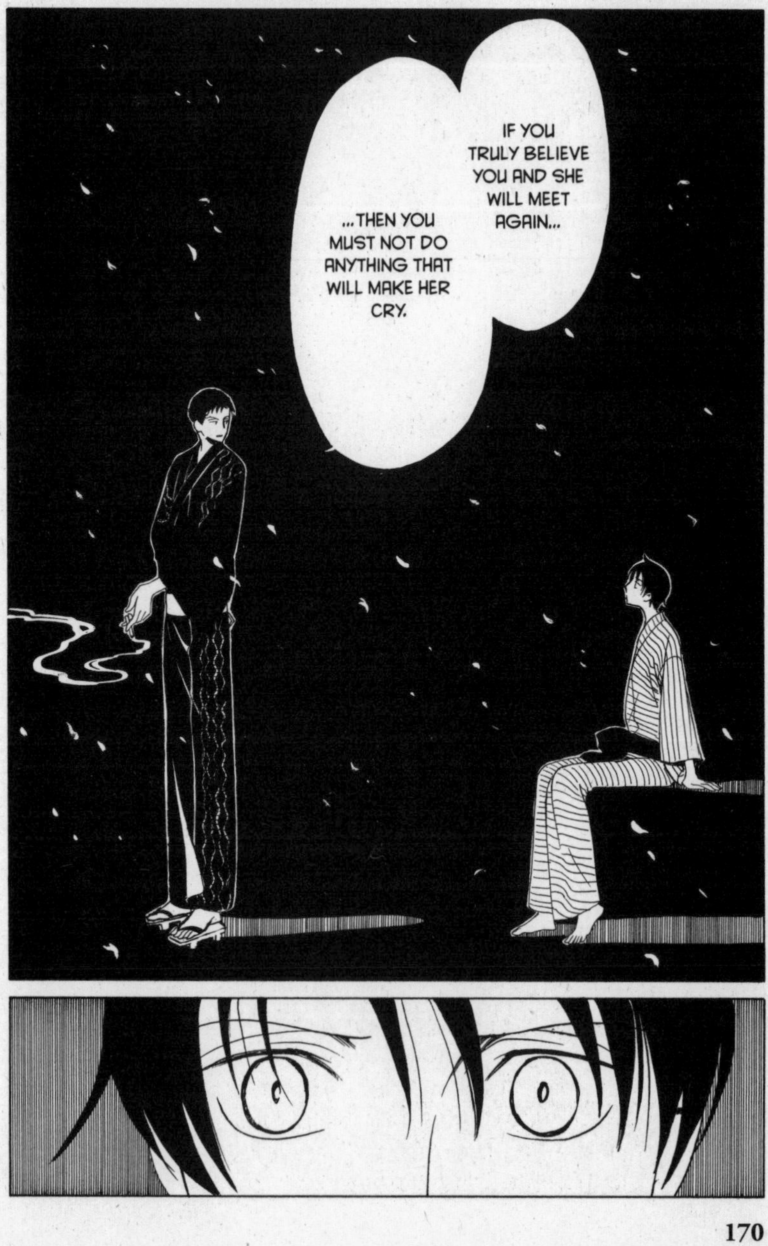
IF YOU TRULY BELIEVE YOU AND SHE WILL MEET AGAIN...
...THEN YOU MUST NOT DO ANYTHING THAT WILL MAKE HER CRY.

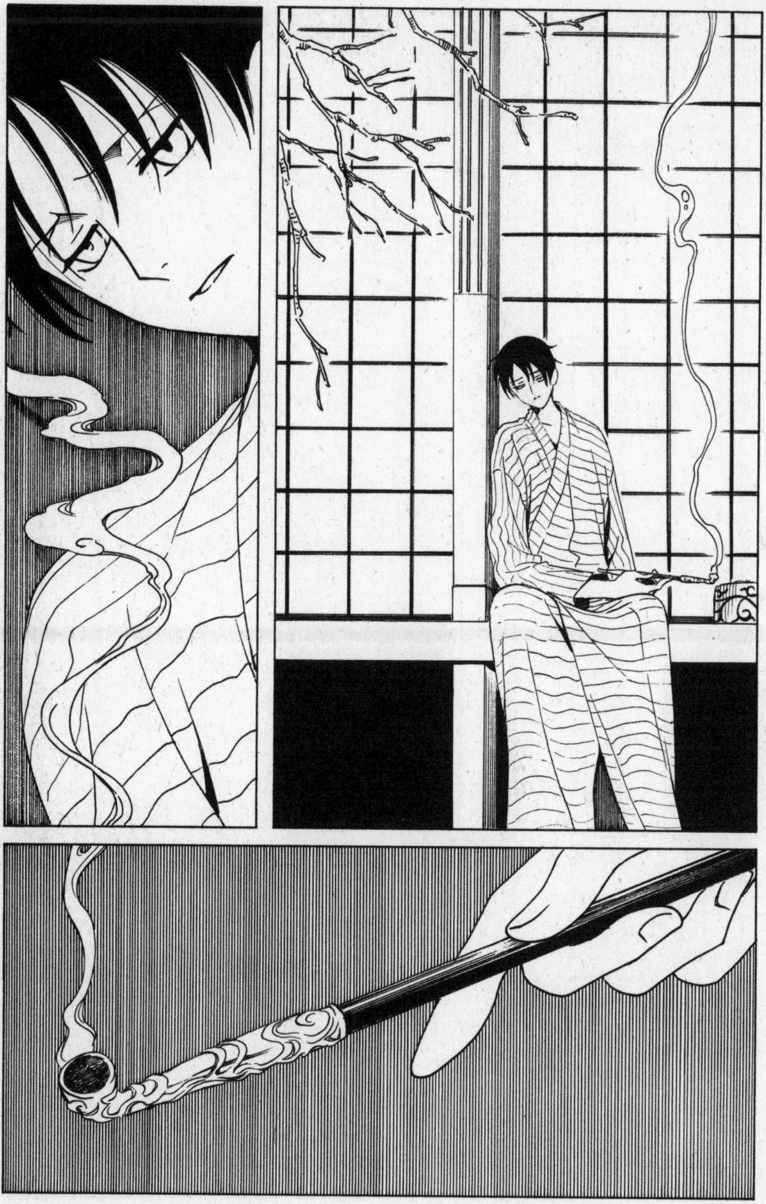

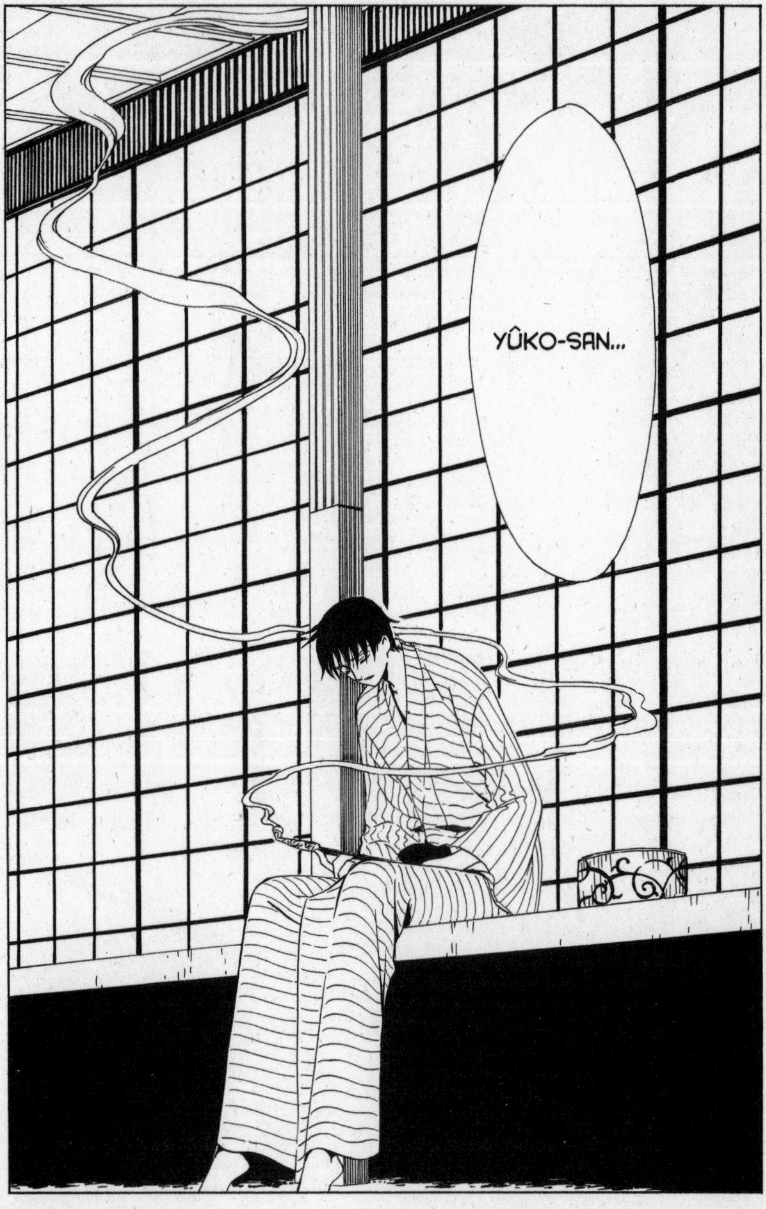
YÛKO-SAN...

⊰ Continued ⊱

in *xxxHOLiC*, volume 17

AND I WILL BE ALWAYS WAITING. ALWAYS.

About the Creators

CLAMP is a group of four women who have become the most popular manga artists in America—Nanase Ohkawa, Mokona, Satsuki Igarashi, and Tsubaki Nekoi. They started out as *doujinshi* (fan comics) creators, but their skill and craft brought them to the attention of publishers very quickly. Their first work from a major publisher was RG Veda, but their first mass success was with Magic Knight Rayearth. From there, they went on to write many series, including Cardcaptor Sakura and Chobits, two of the most popular manga in the United States. Like many Japanese manga artists, they prefer to avoid the spotlight, and little is known about them personally.

CLAMP is currently publishing three series in Japan: Tsubasa and xxxHOLiC with Kodansha, and Kobato with Kadokawa.

Translation Notes

Japanese is a tricky language for most Westerners, and translation is often more art than science. For your edification and reading pleasure, here are notes on some of the places where we could have gone in a different direction or where a Japanese cultural reference is used.

Page 55, The *kanji* for *Rô*

The *kanji, Rô,* in the title of this incarnation of xxxHOLiC has many meanings. It can be pronounced *komu,* meaning "crowded" or "requiring a lot of work"; *komeru,* as in "to concentrate" or be "devoted to"; *komoru,* as in "to seclude oneself" or "be stuffy"; or *kago,* as in "cage" or "basket." Any one of those, or a combination of them, could be implied by this character.

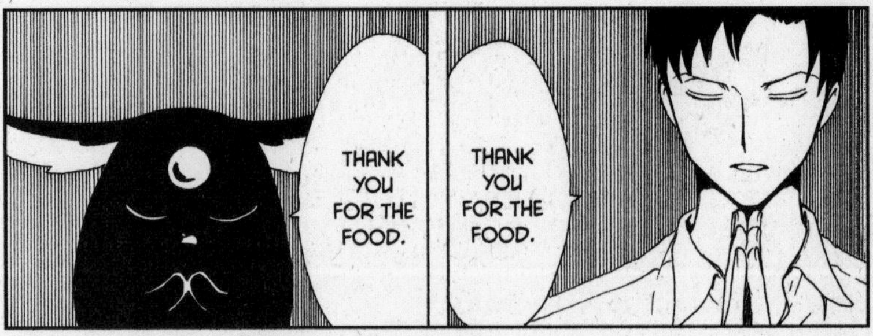
THANK YOU FOR THE FOOD.
THANK YOU FOR THE FOOD.

Page 59, Thank you for the food

As described in the notes of previous volumes, this is a standard Japanese phrase, *ittadakimasu,* which literally means, "I am about to receive," but is said in gratitude for having food to eat.

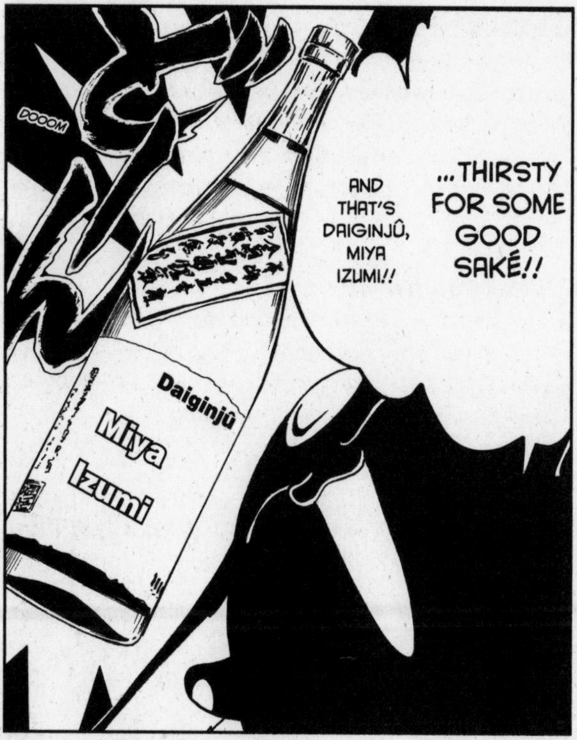
DOOOM
Daiginjû
Miya
Izumi
AND THAT'S DAIGINJÛ, MIYA IZUMI!!
...THIRSTY FOR SOME GOOD SAKÉ!!

Page 64, Daiginjû Miya Izumi

Daiginjû Miya Izumi is a saké from the Aizu-Wakamatsu region of Japan, a little more than two hours by train north of Tokyo in Fukushima prefecture. Miya Izumi saké is made in a 350-year-old brewery-cum-museum (the Aizu Saké History Museum), and the brand is famous all over Japan. Miya Izumi saké has won the top prize several times over from the Japanese National Institute of Brewing.

Page 66, Grandmother

Although the custom of assigning a familial name such as grandmother, grandfather, aunt, or uncle to an unrelated person who fills a similar role in one's life is pretty much a global custom, it is used more often in Japanese culture than in most. In this case, the elderly fortune-teller has taken on the role of "grandmother" in Kohane's life, and as such, Kohane refers to her using the same title she would for a blood relation.

Page 66, Beef *Shigure-ni*

As described in volume 15, *shigure-ni* is a cooking process in which one boils meat in a mixture of soy sauce, *mirin* (sweet saké), and ginger. In this case, the meat is beef.

Page 67, Thank you for the meal

Just as one says *ittadakimasu* (see the note on page 176) at the beginning of a meal, one says *gochisou-sama* (literally, "it was a feast") at the end of every meal.

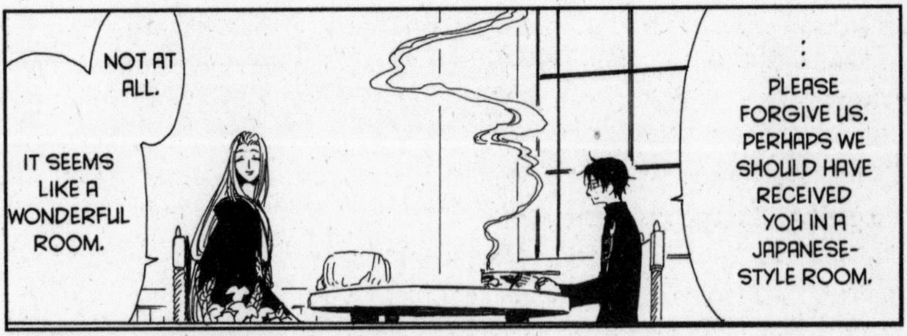

...
PLEASE FORGIVE US. PERHAPS WE SHOULD HAVE RECEIVED YOU IN A JAPANESE-STYLE ROOM.
NOT AT ALL.
IT SEEMS LIKE A WONDERFUL ROOM.

Page 87, Japanese-style room

Most Japanese houses and apartments built these days contain Western-style rooms that one furnishes with chairs, tables, and other normal Western pieces. But usually at least one room is done in Japanese style, floored with *tatami* rush mats and *zabuton* cushions to sit on, low tables, and other standards of traditional Japanese residences.

Page 91, *Shamisen*

The *shamisen* (also called *samisen*) is a remodeled version of an imported instrument called the *sanshin* that itself was an import from China. Around the mid-1500s, the instrument was imported from the Ryukyu islands to the Kansai region (the region including Osaka, Kobe, Kyoto, and Nara) and on the southern island of Kyushu. In Kyushu it was played by blind priests, but on the main Japanese island of Honshu, the *shamisen* was quickly adopted by Japan's entertainers. It became a main feature in the accompaniment to Kabuki theater in the Edo period. It is now considered to be essentially Japanese.

Page 93, *Tsugaru-jamisen*

The *Tsugaru-jamisen* that the *shamisen* player mentions is a product of what used to be the Tsugaru region of Edo-period Japan at the northernmost tip of the main island of Honshu. It is a hardier version of the instrument and is now almost as popular as the standard version, with nearly 50 percent of the *shamisen* made being qualifying as *Tsugaru-jamisen*. A few years ago, it was only 10 percent.

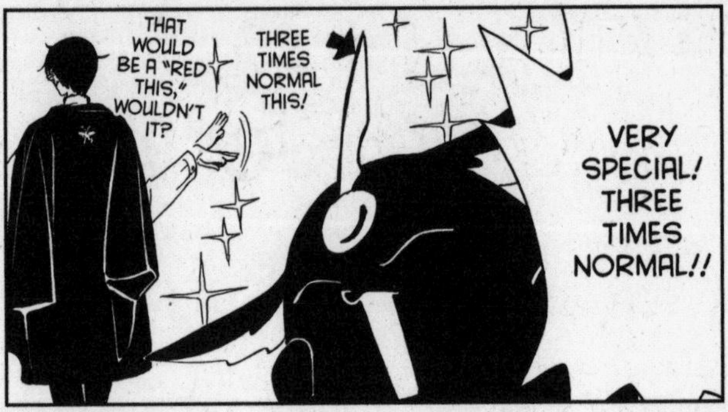
VERY SPECIAL! THREE TIMES NORMAL!!
THREE TIMES NORMAL THIS!
THAT WOULD BE A "RED THIS," WOULDN'T IT?

Page 154, Red This

This is a reference to the first anime version of *Mobile Suit Gundam*, in which Char Aznable's Zaku mobile suit (painted red after Char's nickname, the Red Comet) was able to fly at three times the speed of a normal Zaku. The ornament on Mokona resembles an antenna that sticks up from the head of the Zaku.

RESERVoir CHRoNiCLE

TSUBASA

BY CLAMP

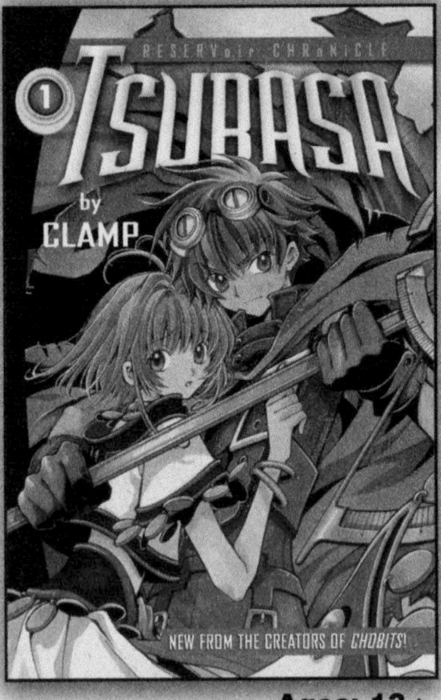
RESERVoir CHRoNiCLE
1
TSUBASA
by
CLAMP
NEW FROM THE CREATORS OF *CHOBITS*!

Ages: 13+

Sakura is the princess of Clow. Syaoran is her childhood friend, and leader of the archaeological dig that cost him his father. Fans of Cardcaptor Sakura will recognize the names and the faces, but these aren't the people you know. This is an alternate reality where everything is familiar and strange at the same time.

Sakura has a mysterious power, a power that no one understands, a power that can change the world. On the day she goes to the dig to declare her love for Syaoran, a mysterious symbol is uncovered that will have vast repercussions for Sakura and Syaoran. It marks the beginning of a quest that will take Syaoran and his friends through worlds that will be familiar to any CLAMP fan, as our heroes encounter places and characters from X, Chobits, Magic Knight Rayearth, xxxHOLiC, and many more! But all that matters to Syaoran is his goal: saving Sakura.

Special extras in each volume! Read them all!

DEL REY

VISIT WWW.DELREYMANGA.COM TO:
- View release date calendars for upcoming volumes
- Sign up for Del Rey's free manga e-newsletter
- Find out the latest about new Del Rey Manga series

MUSHISHI

YUKI URUSHIBARA

THEY HAVE EXISTED SINCE THE DAWN OF TIME.

Some live in the deep darkness behind your eyelids. Some eat silence. Some thoughtlessly kill. Some simply drive men mad. Shortly after life emerged from the primordial ooze, these deadly creatures, mushi, came into terrifying being. And they still exist and wreak havoc in the world today. Ginko, a young man with a sardonic smile, has the knowledge and skill to save those plagued by mushi . . . perhaps.

WINNER OF THE KODANSHA MANGA OF THE YEAR AWARD!

Now a live-action movie from legendary director Katsuhiro Otomo (*Akira, Steamboy*)!

Special extras in each volume! Read them all!

KITCHEN PRINCESS

STORY BY MIYUKI KOBAYASHI
MANGA BY NATSUMI ANDO
CREATOR OF ZODIAC P.I.

HUNGRY HEART

Najika is a great cook and likes to make meals for the people she loves. But something is missing from her life. When she was a child, she met a boy who touched her heart— and now Najika is determined to find him. The only clue she has is a silver spoon that leads her to the prestigious Seika Academy.

Attending Seika will be a challenge. Every kid at the school has a special talent, and the girls in Najika's class think she doesn't deserve to be there. But Sora and Daichi, two popular brothers who barely speak to each other, recognize Najika's cooking for what it is—magical. Could one of the boys be Najika's mysterious prince?

Special extras in each volume! Read them all!

SAYONARA, ZETSUBOU-SENSEI

BY KOJI KUMETA

THE POWER OF NEGATIVE THINKING
VOLUME 1

Nozomu Itoshiki is depressed. Very depressed. He's certifiably suicidal, but he's also the beloved schoolteacher of a class of unique students, each charming in her own way. For all of them, it's a special time, when the right teacher can have a lasting positive effect on their lives. But is that teacher Itoshiki, a.k.a. Zetsubou-sensei, who just wants to find the perfect place to die?

SAYONARA, ZETSUBOU-SENSEI
THE POWER OF NEGATIVE THINKING
VOLUME 1
KOJI KUMETA

Available anywhere books or comics are sold!

VISIT WWW.DELREYMANGA.COM TO:

- Read sample pages
- View release date calendars for upcoming volumes
- Sign up for Del Rey's free manga e-newsletter
- Find out the latest about new Del Rey Manga series

RATING OT AGES 16+

DEL REY DEL REY MANGA デルレイ

www.delreymanga.com

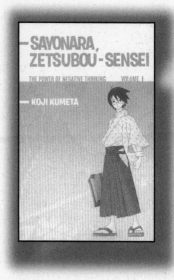

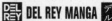

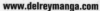

TOMARE!

[STOP!]

You're going the wrong way!

Manga is a completely
different type of reading
experience.

To start at the *beginning,*
go to the *end*!

That's right! Authentic manga is read the traditional Japanese way—from right to left. Exactly the *opposite* of how American books are read. It's easy to follow: Just go to the other end of the book, and read each page—and each panel—from right side to left side, starting at the top right. Now you're experiencing manga as it was meant to be!